NOV 7 - 2014

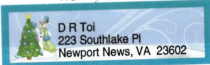

The
Law of Love
& Its
Fabulous
Frequency of
Freedom

with Jasmuheen

THE LAW OF LOVE

Produced by Jasmuheen &
The Self Empowerment Academy
PO Box 1975, Noosa Heads, QLD, 4567, Australia
Fax: +61 7 5447 2540

First released – January 2005
e-Book produced – January 2005
Second Edition Update – June 2007

ISBN: 978-1-84799-846-0

http://www.selfempowermentacademy.com.au &
http://www.jasmuheen.com/

Please respect the work of the author
& help S.E.A. promote planetary peace … for more copies go to
http://www.selfempowermentacademy.com.au/htm/cia-education.asp
or as a hardcover book http://stores.lulu.com/jas-1

Painting on cover "Tao Transmissions"– acrylic on canvas by Jasmuheen 2004
Painting 'cosmified' by Tommy at
http://www.lightandcolor.org/jasmuheen-art/

Sacred Agni Verse at the start of each chapter by Eltrayan.

Dedication

To the
miracle seekers
& the
miracle makers
of our world.

Up-date & Introduction

Your inner voice gives fair warning,
A quest for answers is dawning,
It's alchemy of mind's morning.

Stories abound throughout many cultures and religions of beings who are said to possess great wisdom, boundless love and miraculous power; from the eight immortals in the Taoist tradition, to the feats of Buddha and the insights of Mohammed and the Christ. These are but a few of the many wondrous ones whose stories are easily known.

Some may feel that the experience and possession of miraculous power is restricted to the chosen few, that only certain pre-selected individuals can rise above the status quo and demonstrate the freedom that comes from living the Law of Love. This in itself is a belief destined to maintain limitation, for the only thing we are limited by is our mind.

Some people may say that what I propose in this journal is something that is impossible or miraculous. Some may say that it all defies the laws of nature yet that is what miracles do, they are events that operate beyond our *known* laws of science. What we have forgotten is that the laws of nature and the laws of science are driven by the Law of Love.

For a long time I have found myself walking between the worlds, experiencing enough of the gifts of the more subtle realms, to know that Freedom is more than just a heart song and that like the river of Grace, Freedom pulses a certain beat, a rhythm in our blood, a beat that dances in our soul, a beat that when released brings us into a state of limitless BEing.

As a metaphysician I've long held to the theory that the elements of the fields can be woven together into a rhythm of such perfect harmony that time and age and death and limitation all suspend themselves and become replaced by the self rejuvenating river of the now. A space of being and a place of feeling, where the true Tantra of the Tao is witnessed, then experienced and enriched as it Itself enriches, a space where as the watcher we get to recognize, experience and even create miracles. I have also discovered in this journey that miracles belong to the realm of science and that our ability to recognize this is tied to our ability to understand the Law of Love.

To the Shaman of our world, the art of moving energy is the art of shape-shifting and we can apply this to ourselves personally and also to our communities. Shifting energy so that we co-exist in harmony as we fulfill our highest potential is the art of shaping a brighter now and a brighter future. It is the art of attaining freedom.

I had no idea when I was inspired to begin writing *The Law of Love* that it would also focus on the art of Shamanistic shape-shifting yet when I read John Perkins's book *Shapeshifting: Techniques for Global and Personal Transformation* I realized that many metaphysicians are now focused on just that – finding and personally applying and then sharing tools for both personal and global transformation. Of course we are all doing it in our own way, guided by pre-agreed codes that inspire us to fulfill certain things. My journey with shape-shifting has focused significantly on Divine Nutrition for as we shared in *The Food of Gods* manual, everyone is hungry for something – love, wealth, knowledge, peace, freedom or enlightenment, the list of human hungers is endless and thankfully there is a way of satiating them all.

Somehow I had hoped when I completed the third book in the Divine Nutrition Series *The Food of Gods* that since it provides simple methods of feeding all of our hungers, it would be the last I would choose to write on the subject. However it seems that there is always more and that I am to enter into another level of personal initiation that my inner one is now inviting me to record.

As I travel this world sharing our research in the Divine Nutrition fields I continually find people who have the desire to be free. Some desire Freedom from the need to age or die, or Freedom from the need to create disease or even to eat or drink or sleep. Others desire Freedom to control the molecules of our bodies so that the universe supports us in a limitless river of synchronicity and joy and Grace. To witness these freedoms come into being, is often called a miracle.

I wrote in *The Food of Gods* that this type of Freedom is what I have come to call Level 3 in the Divine Nutrition Program, a level where we know how to release enough Love through our systems so that everything comes into a miraculous state of perfect balance and harmony.

The dance of Freedom is a complex one until we understand not just the science of the fields but also how the universe is programmed to recognize and respond to us all. When we understand this, doors of limitless possibility reveal themselves to us and beckon us to enter and explore.

This journal thus becomes my journey through these doors, a journey to what the Buddha calls the Pure Land, to what others call Shamballa. Some people may feel inspired to join me on this journey for as you read through these pages something within you may respond in excitement, for perhaps this is part of your journey too. If that is so then please note that some aspects of this journey should not be attempted until you have understood and applied the principles and meditations in our other manuals and also confirmed that you are in the calibration range to do this safely *.

Some people may see this level of Freedom as a restrictive lifestyle choice, because there are certain lifestyle actions we need to implement and maintain in order to manifest these Freedoms; yet to others this level of Freedom opens within them hitherto unimagined doors that when accessed bring their own sublime rewards. I call these ones the seekers of miracles.

As this journey unfolded, I found myself downloading a constant stream of data from Universal Mind. Once I accepted the title of "The Law of Love" and the idea of Its freedoms, it was as if a gate opened and my dreams and meditations were suddenly flooded with data – data on destiny, data on how we can find it, embrace it, fulfill it or sideline ourselves, data and tools on how to achieve real freedom, data and visions on shape-shifting Shaman, data on how to create miracles and how to apply these to our world and even data on prophecy and the cross road of choice. I was also guided to summarize all of the freedom tools that we have provided in our various manuals at the Academy over the years and to offer these in Part 2, along with tools that were downloaded during a month long retreat that I attended with the Taoist Masters in Thailand.

Finally when this book was complete it was tour time again and yet my guidance was not to release it until after my tour was complete. Usually I will release a book before touring to teach its principles and yet an inner voice kept saying: "Wait, there is more." This more came as a wonderful confirmation tool in the form of David Hawkins's book *Power vs. Force*, to provide a powerful safety model to what we are proposing within the no food, no fluid aspect of the freedom agenda and we offer this testing mechanism as a post script at the end of the manual.

And so once again, this book, like all books that I download, has developed a life and a flavor unique unto itself. All I can do upon its release is trust that it will find its place of relevance within our constantly shape-shifting world. – Namaste Jasmuheen

* These manuals are provided at
http://www.selfempowermentacademy.com.au/htm/cia-education.asp

Contents

Dedication		5
Introduction		7

PART 1
THE LAW OF LOVE

1.	The Law of Love & The Lives of Miracles	15
2.	Devotees of the DOW & Synchrodestiny	20
3.	Shape-shifting Shaman: The Dance of Freedom	29
4.	The Seekers of Miracles	36
5.	The Makers of Miracles – Attributes & Action	44
6.	Goals & Status	47
7.	Synchronicity & Sacred Support Systems	54
8.	The Lure of Love	63
9.	The Harmonious Heart	71
	Meditation 1: Heart Lock-In	77
10.	Being – The Freedom of Now	80
11.	Fiddling the Fields – Resurrection & Redemption; Regeneration & Reclamation	85
12.	Sensing	92

PART 2
THE WIZARD'S TOOL BOX
The Alchemy of Doing & BEing

13.	Shape-shifting Space – New Field Designs & Activation	100
	Meditation 2: Perfect Bio-Body Part 1	101
14.	Mathematics, Molecules & Movement	108
	Meditation 3: Perfect Bio-Body Part 2	109

15.	Dark Room Downloads	113
16.	Tao, Tools & Talisman – Doing It	126
	Meditation 4: Accessing our Pre-agreements.	130
	Meditation 5: The Balance of Yin/Yang: Exercising the Pineal gland, feeding the brain, having heart orgasms and using self intercourse to nourish us.	131
	Meditation 6: System Flush and Hydration with breath rhythm.	131
	Meditation 7: Additional Inner Plane Feeding Codes.	133
	Meditation 8: Healing Sounds.	135
	Meditation 9: The GSC formula – the magic mix of Glucosamine, Saliva & Chi.	136
	Meditation 10: The 'Perfect Life, Perfect Love, Perfect Paradise' Programming Code.	142
	Meditation 11: 11 Strand Healing System	142
17.	Inter-Dimensional Matrix Mechanics Synopsis of Freedom Tools & Meditations	150
18.	The Immortal Body & the Tao of the DOW	162
19.	Coming In To The Light	167
20.	The Pure Land	170
	Meditation 12: The Harmony Code	173
21.	Arrangements of Grace	176
22.	Journey Through the Field of Love	180

Post Tour Postscript – Additional Testing Mechanisms	186
The Law of Love – Epilogue & Update June 2007	192
Further Data	195
Bibliography	198
Jasmuheen's Background	199
Educational e-books	201
Educational Audio	203

Part 1

THE LAW OF LOVE

Chapter 1

The Law of Love & the Lives of Miracles

All miracles are born from love,
Refinement beaming from above,
The messenger's a snow-white dove.

In the 7th century A.D. a girl called Ho Hsien–Ku was born in China. It is said that at age 14 she became an immortal after meeting Lu Tung-Pin a Taoist Immortal who taught her the secrets of inner alchemy. After spending time with the great Chinese Goddess Hsi Wang Mu, she gained the ability to be able to nourish herself by feeding only on heavenly dew and the omnipresent chi force. Able to de and rematerialize at will, and often seen by the pure-hearted to be floating on rainbows, Ho Hsien-Ku still appears to the virtuous and the innocent, or to the oppressed people who are in need of divine intervention. She is now over 1,400 years old.

Is Ho Hsien-Ku's story fact or fiction; is it a miracle or a metaphor?
Perhaps it is just a legend that like many is designed to stretch our imagination and open us up to greater fields of possibility. Perhaps these are the types of attributes that we receive when we fully understand the Law of Love.

At the end of 2002, I found myself at the cross roads of choice, a place where you intuitively know that you are about to shift gears and go in another direction.
For some this is a scary place to be.
To others it is exciting.
For me it was intriguing.
I knew that I had finally completed an intense decade of a time where all the astrological forces working with me had supported me to launch the Divine Nutrition Program onto the global stage. I also knew that a new chapter in my journey was soon to begin.
On one level, my personal journey in expanding my own boundaries has been limited as it has taken me nearly 11 years to explore and adjust to the "no food, no sleep" Freedom game and to also take all our personal experiential research to the global stage and to try to present it in a way where others may grasp the miracle of it all. Here we have

gathered thousands of like minded people, Freedom seekers like me who are active in the game of either seeking or making miracles.

Sometimes I have taken three steps forward then two backwards as I've learnt the operation of the fields and how to utilize their inner and outer energy flows to my maximum potential and enjoy the state of Shamanic Ecstasy. All of it has been invaluable. Still, 11 years is a long time to explore something fully – to live it, to deal with the repercussions of the choice and to also provide enough educational data to be free from ignorance and its fears.

It hasn't been an easy path, for there have been no manuals to read, no set guidelines to follow and no obvious rules, until at last we came to understand the science of the fields which means understanding how the energy flow within and around us can be altered by our will and thought and action. It is said that science comes when a model can be duplicated and repeated so if miracles can be found to be based on a model then they too can be repeated and be known as science.

In the metaphysical sense what we will discuss in this manual is a form of Shamanic shape-shifting that is based on the reality that every human biosystem is driven by Divine DNA codes that support us into Freedom. These codes form a part of our nature that our culture and our cyclical human experience seem to have overridden and hidden, veiling the Freedom codes deep within us, where they lie dormant until we ask for more. And in the asking something shifts to give birth to miracle seekers, the ones that are driven to remember these codes.

There are things that some people accept as normal – like war and dis-ease – while others see these as unnecessary, as anomalies in the field, things that can be retuned via the shifting of energy into a more harmonious beat.

Yet in order to have external harmony we need to have internal and so at the end of 2002, I was called to rearrange my external life so that my internal life could come into another level of harmony that would bring a new level of freedom to my world.

All I could feel, as I set about rearranging my life, was this over powering need for freedom particularly to explore more of the inner planes and the limitless realm of the One that breathes and gives me life, the One I call my DOW. All I kept hearing was an inner voice guiding me to explore more of the Law of Love and so I listened and began a new chapter as the watcher of, and the dancer with, the law of Love.

A decade or so ago when I was writing the book *In Resonance*, I was guided to research and add a chapter on Universal Laws of which I found around twenty eight. What I also found is that all of these Laws were subtle or refined expressions of the Law of Oneness – which states that everything is interconnected and hence all parts inter-relate and what affects one part, affects the whole.

What drives or feeds the Law of One, is the Law of Love.

The Law of Love states that all life, all atoms, all molecules, all energy fields have come into existence due to the Love of the original force of creation. It also states that when we treat all life with love, honor and respect as if It is part of us, then the

Law of Love will magnetize us to Its river of Grace and embrace us back into Itself as one of Its own.

The Law of Love finds the seekers of miracles and Its Grace teaches us how to recognize, enjoy and also how to create them. And in the experiencing of these miracles we find ourselves already made perfect and also free.

According to the Catholic Encyclopedia, miracles are said to be wonders performed by supernatural powers, a sign or an expression of a special gift and explicitly assigned to God. Coming from the Latin word 'miracula' the witnessing of miracles usually promotes awe or excitement as the act is seen to come from Divine Grace.

Some say that the wonder of a miracle is in the fact that its cause is hidden and its effect is unexpected, hence it is something extraordinary. To me there are expressions all around us of both minor and major miracles. Both types can place the watcher into a state of "wow this is incredible!" a state of appreciation and awe where our heart is touched and opened. Watching the birth of a child is like watching a miracle be born, watching the sun rise and set each day and the colors that are magically beamed across the sky, these to me are minor miracles, explained by science, yes, part of nature yes, and worthy of our praise and appreciation.

Life to me is a miracle, even just the science of it – our blueprint of genetics and our potential for higher expression; the way that atoms and molecules move through space and time to provide matter for this blueprint. The depth and range of emotions that we can access; the limitless thinking capabilities that we possess along with the tools to manifest whatever is our hearts desire – the whole human mechanism to me is a miracle of divine expression, especially more so when we begin our journey of discovering what else is locked away within us.

The path of freedom and the gifts that adherence to the Law of Love reveals, can often be seen as miraculous.

- ॐ   Is a major miracle just something that as yet is unexplained, seeming to express a higher, more divine connection?
- ॐ   If so then each human being contains within them, major miracles just waiting for expression.
- ॐ   Yet what if each major miracle can be explained?
- ॐ   Then it becomes simply the science of life, a process that is perhaps governed by something as basic as the Law of Love.

In the time of the Christ it is said that water was turned into wine, that loaves of bread multiplied themselves so that one loaf could feed the many, that the sick were healed and the believer's were risen from the dead. All of these were classified as major miracles and it was not until Jesus began to perform these miracles that his ministry was noticed. It was not just his words that touched the hearts of his people but also his 'miraculous' deeds yet were they really miracles or were they just examples of how the universal forces respond to someone who has anchored themselves in the heart of compassion and love?

In the metaphysical world the molecules of matter exist because of the Law of Love and they are programmed to respond to this law and can thus be commanded or invited into rearranging themselves in a myriad of ways. Water can gather the elements from the atmosphere around it and by changing the energy mix of these elements, be transformed into wine. A loaf of bread can duplicate itself by using those same elements. Both acts need to be directed by a power that has great belief in its own command and mastery to create such things, a power aware of and living by the Law of Love.

The question is also not so much "how can these miracles happen?" but why have we forgotten how to work in this way? Remember how Jesus said in the Gospel of Mathew: "The things I do, You shall do and even greater".

Is the skill of doing this just restricted to those who possess ancient secret knowledge or the shape-shifting Shaman of our world?

What does it take for the molecules and atoms in a human biological system, to rearrange themselves, or release within themselves, a different mix of elements? A mix of air, earth, fire, water, astral light, akasa and cosmic fire – a mix of seven elements that govern our existence, a mix that can be rearranged within us to produce what appear to be miracles. All life is made of these elements and all elements contain consciousness and all are birthed because of, and respond to, the Law of Love. The how and why of it all we will look at more deeply throughout this journal as we shape-shift ourselves into a freer level of being.

Miracles have a life that can be activated, they have a purpose and they have a time. They have a path of unfoldment and the way they trigger this path is embedded in every atom in the core of the consciousness that allows it its existence, a consciousness that is a Divine DNA code that is driven by the mathematics of the Law of Love.

And so it was that I began the year of 2003 living in a wonderful beachside apartment that I had turned into my own personal ashram, a sacred space that reverberated with such amazing levels of harmony and that demonstrated the power of love in action. Self love means listening to the voice of our DOW, applying its guidance and trusting that any transformation we are inspired to enter into is perfect for us, and so began a new time in my life.

THE LAW OF LOVE

The Law of Love states that all life, all atoms, all molecules, all energy fields have come into existence due to the Love of the original force of creation. It also states that when we treat all life with love, honor and respect as if it is part of us, then the Law of Love will magnetize you to Its river of Grace and embrace you back into itself as one of Its own.

The Law of Love finds the seekers of miracles and Its Grace teaches us how to recognize, enjoy and also how to create them. And in the experiencing of these miracles we find ourselves already made perfect and also free.

According to the Catholic Encyclopedia, Miracles are said to be wonders performed by supernatural powers, a sign or an expression of a special gift and explicitly assigned to God. Coming from the Latin word 'miracula' the witnessing of miracles usually promotes awe or excitement as the act is seen to come from Divine Grace.

GRACE IS A SIGN THAT WE ARE ALIGNED TO THE LAW OF LOVE.

Chapter 2

Devotees of the DOW
& Synchro Destiny

Taste the tasteless, enhance the small,
To see over the garden wall,
You have to stretch and stand up tall.

In the 11th century AD there was a Sung Empress who had two brothers. One was a hedonist and a murderer and the other became a seeker of the Tao. His name is Tsao Kuo-Chiu. One day as he roamed the mountains Tsao met two of the eight immortals – Chung-Li and Lu Tung-Pin – who asked him what he was doing. He told them that he was nurturing the Tao and studying the way. When one of them asked him where the Tao was Tsao pointed to heaven and when they asked him further as to where heaven was, Tsao Ku-Chiu pointed to his heart.

To this Chung-Li beamed and said:

"The heart is heaven and heaven is the Tao. You have indeed found the truth and the way. You understand the origin of things."

And so they invited Tsao Ku-Chiu to travel among the immortals and journey throughout the universe with them. It is said that Tsao Ku-Chiu is still alive today.

Was it coincidence that brought the trio together?
Destiny?
Or was it a simple universal response to the life Tsao was choosing to live, a life that tuned him to the immortals' realm enough for him to catch their eye?

As I began my ashram life at the beach, I felt like a celibate nun as my only desire was to explore the fields of inner silence. After years on the road constantly mingling with a multitude of curious, supportive and skeptical, solitude became my friend and my food. It was as if everything was perfect, complete, had been attended to and now I was on vacation and in this space nothing was real anymore. As I slowly unhooked from my worldly game, my global persona and my workaholic self, I found myself in a void of my own creation. Instead of working 22 hours a day consciously tuning myself and downloading data from Universal mind, I let it all go, all the habits, all the programs, all the focus and began to dwell in a self created void.

As if sensing I needed to unhook from my busy service agenda, all my telepathic connections also closed, as if a "Gone on holidays" sign had been hung on the inner plane doors that I normally have open to my cosmic colleagues.

The silence and solitude were liberating and I began to come into a space of such stillness that all I could feel was appreciation for the beauty of my natural beach surroundings.

After 30 years of living in, and traveling to, polluted cities where regular field transformation becomes habitual, I found living at the beach a blessing. Daily walks at sunrise or sunset, upon a stretch of pure white sand, with warm waters lapping at my feet, was one of the greatest gifts I could give myself and as time went by I began to see nourishment in a totally different way and so the book *The Food of Gods* was born.

In the stillness of my new life, nature was effortlessly explored on a much deeper level and I felt and saw the evidence of prana in motion. The deeper I dove into the natural world of my DOW, the more I felt and saw the Law of Love in motion.

Appreciation gave birth to gratitude which deepened my devotion. Before long the only thing that felt real to me was my DOWs' smile.

To the devotee of the Divine One Within – our DOW – DOW smiles are one of the most solid physical representations of our perfect alignment with the force that breathes us. A DOW smile always begins in the heart. It begins as a tingling feeling of joy or deep contentment, of 'just rightness'. Having flooded through our heart, this feeling then creeps up our chest and our throat and then it commandeers our mouth twisting it into the largest smile we can imagine, it is a smile that seems to spread across our face making our mouth appear wider and wider and stretching the muscles until we feel we could smile no more. This heart smile of our DOW then stays anchored across our face for what feels sometimes like an eternity and no amount of 'trying not to smile' works. It's as if another force has joyously taken control over the muscles of our face.

And in these moments all we feel is that everything is perfect within our world.

DOW smiles are my barometer for when they come I know that I am exactly where I need to be and that the one who is breathing me is happy and when my DOW has so much control over my being that it can express itself like this, then all of me is joyous.

Devotees of the DOW are devotees of the Tao and both are often seeking some level of fulfillment of the freedom agenda. The Tao in Chinese philosophy is a way of being, of living in a harmonious flow with all of the elements of life and the flow of the Tao is the Law of Love in motion.

Devotees of the DOW are individuals who have recognized the loving nature and supreme intelligence of the Divine One Within us all which is also the Divine One Without – or around – us all.

Being devoted to something means giving it enough time and attention to keep it alive and healthy. Devotion has an aspect of reverence, or at least recognition and respect in the knowing that the animal, hobby or person that we may be devoted to is worthy of our focus.

The Law of Love & Its Fabulous Frequency of Freedom
with Jasmuheen

Many metaphysicians have realized that in order to maximize the Grace of the flow of the Tao we need to be completely aligned to the power of our DOW, for this inner being when it receives our focus and attention thrives and ignites itself within us in such an amazing way that our life on all levels becomes enhanced for it is our DOW that loves us, breathes us and gives us life. The realm of our DOW is our heaven and as the Taoist immortalist Chung-Li said, the entry to this heaven is through our heart.

I became a devotee of my DOW as soon as I began to meditate. It was at this same time that I had one of my first experiences of what Dr Deepak Chopra calls synchrodestiny, as the events surrounding my introduction into meditation appeared to be perfectly orchestrated, and even divinely supported, so that I could partake of this ancient initiation with my DOW.

Fully booked planes suddenly had a seat, money came for the ticket, accommodation suddenly appeared and total support flowed as I traveled the thousand kilometers to meet with the meditation instructor whose tools I knew would align me to my DOW. Because this was my hearts' desire, it was all synchronistically staged to come into being.

I have since found that if our desires are connected with the discovery and experience of our DOW then all the universal forces support this coming together with such harmony that all we can do is smile.

Although I have spent more than three decades now fully focused on my DOW and enjoying many of its gifts, there is only one thing that totally captivates my attention and that is DOW smiles and everything in that instant feels right within my world.

Another time that we feel that all is right with our world and that we are magically aligned with the Tao, is when we witness and experience Grace for this is to witness the force of synchrodestiny at work.

The story of how I was introduced to the phrase 'synchrodestiny' is in itself an example of how the Law of Love – via synchronicity – delivers its fabulous frequency of freedom, the freedom to create in a way that is full of Grace and struggle free, the freedom to witness both minor and major miracles.

In early 2004 I was at my favorite beachside coffee shop editing some of the downloads that I'd begun to receive for this book when a woman smiled and said:

"Hi remember me?"

Her face was familiar so I responded: "Sure how are you?"

After some basic polite chat she said: "I hope you don't mind but I am seated with an English woman who would love to meet you."

When the woman and her husband came to join me at my table, she was all smiles and said as she sat down:

"Wow this is a perfect example of what Deepak Chopra talks about in his latest book "Synchro Destiny"! I have your book "Living on Light" and I've wanted to meet you for ages!"

It turns out that she had recently met and clicked with Kim, the woman who approached me, and they'd agreed to socialize further over coffee. They were discussing Deepak's book when Anita, the English woman, mentioned my work with DOW power. To this Kim said: "Oh I think I know her, she comes into my shop now and then." Just as Anita asked her if she could arrange a meeting, Kim looked up, saw me a few tables away and said: "Actually I think that's Jasmuheen seated over there!"

At Anita's mentioning of Deepak's new book, my inner voice said: "Read it and refer to it in 'The Law of Love'."

While I highly recommend the reading of Deepak's book on this subject, I would like to take a few moments here to clarify how it connects with the Law of Love and Its fabulous frequency of freedom and how synchrodestiny works with the miracle seekers and the miracle makers of our world. Synchrodestiny is also a gift of being aligned with our DOW.

After this little chance meeting I of course bought Deepak's book and found that it held information required for me to explain more of the Law of Love. In this book Deepak classifies life into three levels of existence of three domains – the physical, the quantum and the virtual and all are levels of expression in the field of universal intelligence, the realm of our boundless DOW.

The physical domain is "the world we know best, what we call the real world. It contains matter and objects with firm boundaries, everything that is three-dimensional, and it includes everything we can experience with our five senses – all that we can see, hear, feel, taste or smell … The physical world as we experience it is governed by immutable laws of cause and effect, so that everything is predictable."

In this domain, the type of freedoms that we will discuss in this manual seem improbable.

Dr Chopra then continues: "At the second level of existence everything consists of information and energy. This is called the ***quantum domain***. Everything at this level is insubstantial, meaning that it cannot be touched or perceived by any of the five senses. Your mind, your thoughts, your ego, the part of you that you typically think of as your 'self' are all part of the quantum domain. These things have no solidity, and yet you know your self and your thoughts to be real."…

Discussing this concept further, on page 38, Dr Chopra goes on to say: "events in the quantum domain occur at the speed of light, and at that speed our senses simply cannot process everything that contributes to our perceptual experience." And that "Energy is coded for different information depending on how it vibrates. So the physical world, the world of objects and matter, is made up of nothing but information contained in energy vibrating at different frequencies."

"The third level of existence consists of intelligence, or consciousness. This can be called the ***virtual domain***, the spiritual domain, the field of potential, the universal being, or nonlocal intelligence. This is where information and energy emerge from a sea of possibilities. The most fundamental, basic level of nature is not material, it is not even energy and information soup; it is pure potential. This level of nonlocal reality operates beyond the reach of space and time, which simply does not exist at this level. We call it nonlocal because it cannot be confined by a location … it simply is."

"This intelligence of the spiritual domain is what organizes "energy soup" into knowable entities. It is what binds quantum particles into atoms, atoms into molecules, molecules into structures. It is the organizing force behind all things."

These three fields exist due to the Law of Love and each field bequeaths gifts to its inhabitants. Restricting our awareness levels to the physical field allows us to experience the gift of life through our five senses. Exploring the quantum and the virtual domains by activating two more senses, beyond the five that allow us to experience the physical realms, requires a conscious act of expansion of our awareness so that we can receive more freedoms via the Law of Love. The gift of experiencing a constant, Graceful flow of synchronicity can be addictive and also a strong motivation for tuning ourselves further to our DOW.

In the book *The Food of Gods* I spoke about the musical beat of the cells, how the cells gather data and store emotional imprints through the journey of life and if not dealt with these imprints can become discordant noises, even if dealt with, understood and the learning gained and the bio-system emotionally moving on; imprints are still stored in these cells taking up space overlaying a certain frequency that I call 'heavy metal music'. Underlying every atom and every cell is a classical music beat of the Divine spirit that breathes us and gives the essence of life to each atom, an essence which then feeds the cellular structure of the body.

Due to the high levels of chaos and lack of order of command in our world, that classical music beat becomes so weak and ineffectual that eventually the whole system breaks down and dies.

I have often spoken of the chain of command within a human system, how the physical body is like a foot soldier, the emotional body is like the Colonel and the mental body is like the General, how each one can ignore the other to do whatever it is they are motivated to do, and how they are always triggered by something the General does as the Commander. For example the mind has a perception which forms an attitude which releases an emotional response both of which filter down into the physical system – toxic thinking promoting toxic feeling promoting toxicity in the body. Add toxicity of feeding mechanisms often driven by emotionally toxic reasons and you have a system that is laboring to express any level of its divinity at all and gets caught in the vicious cycle of dis-ease and death.

From our earlier experiential research, we know that the DOW is anchored through the doorway in the heart and that it spreads beautiful fine filaments of light like a matrix through all our atoms and cells – a classical music pulse. We know that this divine Being has constructed for itself, as a way of attracting molecules in the first place, a beautiful body of light which pulses through our chakra system and through our meridian system. These are basic truths within certain metaphysical traditions.

We know also that our western biological system understanding generally ignores the DOW and also ignores its etheric body – unaware of the existence of such things. We also know that due to the type of pulsing and music that is constantly bombarding it and filling its cells, the average bio-system must then wind itself down into the normal cycles of death for it does not have enough energy or radiance to sustain itself into the reality of physical immortality and the freedoms discussed in this manual.

We know too that in many religious teachings, there is the idea that this Divine essence, our DOW is immortal already. It is perfect, it is pure, it is enlightened, it is all powerful, all knowing, everywhere, within us, around us, existing through the light-body matrix, speaking to us through the meridian system, through the chakra system and through our very atomic structure. How loud it speaks to us is totally dependant on our thoughts words and actions and on what our drives are – how much 'heavy metal' music we are allowing through the system or whether we are living a lifestyle that allows the divine and natural 'DOW beat' to become louder and stronger.

In the teachings of the Tao masters they say that most bio systems are in chaos with no clear chain of command, randomly sparking off each other with organs filled with energy that does not nourish us and that the divine spirit within us is totally ignored and hence cannot reside as fully as it has the potential to within our physical system.

They say that it is not until we begin to acknowledge it, pay attention to it, awaken it, work with it, invite it to make its presence more known within us and also support all this by cleansing and preparing the system through meditation etc, that it has room to grow and so they call this initial process, the beginning of the immortal body.

They visualize and imagine the fetus or baby immortal body awakening by being fed by the Lesser and Greater and Greatest Kan and Li practices and by our lifestyle and by the processes that we discuss in the 'Tao and Tools' chapter.

Located between the first and second chakras, parallel to our own womb, the Taoists say that in time, with due care and practice, that this immortal fetus – our DOW – will grow. What they mean by this is that the more we align with the DOW, the more we indulge in thoughts, words and actions that feed it and give it a space to grow more powerfully within us, then the more it can work through us and make its presence felt.

We know that the DOW works through our 6th and 7th senses of intuition and knowing, which are its higher voice, and we can assume that it resides fully in a finer energy band within us on the inner cosmos, deep within another layer of our being, a layer that is not normally manifested into this physical realm. We know then that it bridges through space and time and the dimensions into our physical system – sometimes just as a feeling of intuition, sometimes as a clear telepathic impulse. This manifestation works in many ways particularly when a human being asks questions like who am I, what am I doing here, is there more to life, can we live in harmony and peace etc. These, as I have often shared, are the core questions that awaken our immortal nature within and bring us into such a perfect rhythm and flow with life that everything unfolds with Grace.

Deepak Chopra says in his book *Synchrodestiny* that: "Coincidences are messages. They are clues from God or spirit or nonlocal reality urging you to break out of your karmic conditioning, your familiar patterns of thinking. They are offering you an opportunity to enter a domain of awareness where you feel loved and cared for by the infinite intelligence that is your source. Spiritual traditions call this a state of Grace."

As more and more individuals desire to discover and experience their highest potential – as both human and spiritual beings – the more information they attract into their personal field via the DOW mind. As Deepak shares: "Coincidences are messages from the nonlocal realm, guiding us in the ways to act in order to make our dreams, our intentions manifest."

At the end of his book on *Synchrodestiny* – page 254 – Deepak looks at the seven levels of consciousness that we can experience as we align ourselves more consciously to our DOW. These are also connected to the brainwave patterns we discuss in detail in *The Food of Gods* manual.

Briefly, the **first level** of consciousness a human enjoys is deep sleep, the **second level** is dreaming, the **third** is when we are awake, the **fourth** is when we enter the Alpha brain wave state and begin, via meditation, to be tuned to our soul. It is in this level that we can begin to glimpse synchronicity in action.

The **fifth level** Deepak calls cosmic consciousness and as our brain wave patterns have moved through the Alpha and entered the Theta fields we find our intuition increases, we are aware of both our local and non-local fields of intelligence and we become more creative and insightful.

The **sixth** state is called Divine consciousness and it is a level where we move in and out of the Theta to Delta brain wave patterns, it is a level of natural telepathy, where we feel interconnected and 'at one' with all.

The **seventh level** of consciousness is unity consciousness or 'enlightenment', where as Deepak shares the perceived and the perceiver become one and the world becomes an extension of our whole being. In this state we transcend life and death and find that miracles are commonplace as our pituitary and pineal glands now operate at their full potential.

Humanity is currently being driven by a mass dream for a better world, a world where we are free to live in harmony while we express our highest nature. For this reason alone, the DOW mind of the virtual domain is supporting our desire for true freedom and will deliver all that we need to support this. The sooner we understand the Law of Love, the sooner this will occur.

Given all of the above, it is obvious then that what we hold to be real or truth depends entirely on an individual's state of consciousness. For someone operating out of levels 1 to 3, the type of freedoms we are about to discuss may seem incomprehensible but for those who are exploring and experiencing levels 4 to 7 it is a different matter entirely. In these levels, the idea of the shape-shifting Shaman begins to hold intrigue as a new field of study called the **anthropology of consciousness** begins to embrace the power of some of the ancient ways.

THE LAW OF LOVE
CELLULAR FIELD PULSES

• Cells filled with HEAVY METAL type music of the BETA FIELD WORLD BEAT of ME, ME, MINE – feeling separate

• VIRTUES – LACK OF – imbalance - disharmony

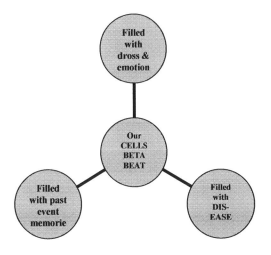

• Cells filled with the CLASSICAL type BEAT of our DOW

• Awareness of US & a feeling that ALL IS ONE & INTERCONNECTED

• VIRTUES – ABUNDANCE OF

• – harmonized – attitude of Gratitude & Appreciation

• WHICH FIELD PULSE DOMINATES???

TOOLS TO RETUNE CELLULAR PULSE

• HEALING SOUNDS for cleansing – ch. 16

• FORGIVENESS – learning & letting go & moving on plus BODY LOVE & LOVE BREATH RETUNING (as in The Food of Gods)

• VIOLET LIGHT FLOODING

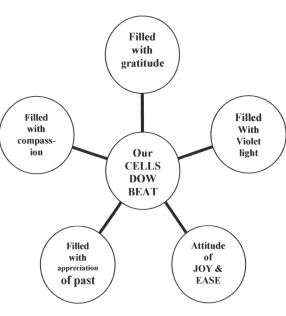

SEVEN LEVELS OF CONSCIOUSNESS
THE LAW OF LOVE

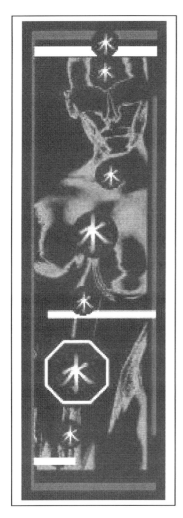

SUMMARY: According to Dr Deepak Chopra we can operate via 7 levels of consciousness. Briefly, the first level of consciousness a human enjoys is deep sleep and the second level is dreaming, the third is when we are awake and the fourth is when we enter the Alpha brain wave state and begin, via meditation, to be tuned to our soul. It is in this level that we can begin to glimpse synchronicity in action.

The fifth level Deepak calls cosmic consciousness and as our brain wave patterns have moved through the Alpha and entered the Theta fields we find our intuition increases, we are aware of both our local and non-local fields of intelligence and we become more creative and insightful.

The sixth state is called Divine consciousness and it is a level where we move in and out of the Theta to Delta brain wave patterns, it is a level of natural telepathy, where we feel interconnected and 'at one' with all.

The seventh level of consciousness is unity consciousness or 'enlightenment', where the perceived and the perceiver become one and the world becomes an extension of our whole being. In this state we transcend life and death and find that miracles are commonplace as our pituitary and pineal glands now operate at their full potential.

Chapter 3

Shape-shifting Shaman
The Dance of Freedom

To meditate and look beyond,
Is in the realm of hat and wand,
The biggest fish, stay deep in the pond.

In the Han dynasty, 2nd century AD, a man called Li Tieh-Kuai was introduced to Taoist practices by the sage Lao Tsu. It is said that over the 40 years that Li lived in the mountains, he was often so involved with his meditations that he forgot to eat or sleep and that eventually Li was taught the internal alchemy practices for immortality by the Goddess Hsi Wang Mu.

One day when Li decided to visit Lao Tsu in the etheric realms using the practice of bi-location, he asked one of his students to keep an eye on his body and to protect it from wild animals. Apparently the student received a message that his mother was dying and so he burned Li's body so that he could leave and attend to her. When Li returned 7 days later and found his body uninhabitable he moved his consciousness into the corpse of a lame beggar who had just died and was thus transformed from being a handsome and healthy man into one who was lame and no longer physically attractive.

At the same time Li transformed the beggar's old bamboo staff into an iron crutch and a magic staff that was able to transmute matter and create magical potions. A sage well known for his benevolence, Li Tieh-Kuai tended the poor and the sick and was able to make himself so tiny that he could live inside a gourd that he carried. It's said that although he ascended into heaven in the form of a dragon, he returns to earth frequently to be of aid to those in need.

Li Tieh-Kuai is the perfect example of a being who knew freedom from human limitation for he knew enough of internal alchemy to be free from the need to eat or sleep or stay confined to his physical form.

The freedom journey calls us all in such different ways. For me it was a call to relocate into a more natural beachside environment, to unhook from the busy-ness of my service life – the later being a situation that I would finally achieve at the end of another year but before I did I was given another assignment.

On a wintry day in December 2003 I was walking down the Avenue Place de Gracia in Barcelona, thinking "what a wonderful name for a street", when I found myself called to look in a jewelry shop and drawn to a perfect heart shaped amethyst ring that stood perched upon a golden band. Embedded with pink tourmaline crystals, the amethyst heart and its' setting was exquisite and the ring drew me into itself as a potential talisman will often do. A talisman is an attractor, director and amplifier of energy that is often symbolically shaped. Within no time the ring had seated itself snuggly on the middle finger of my right hand – the one that rules the wizard heart and as I continued my journey in the dusk light down the avenue of Grace, an inner plane voice began to make itself known.

"The amethyst is for Freedom which comes in the shape of the heart for it is only when Love flows that you can begin to feel free. The more Love that flows, the more Freedom and miracles you will experience." And so the discourse continued between myself, the student of the elements, and the universe that surrounded me and somewhere deep in this dialogue I found myself forming new agreements.

"3 years. A commitment of the next 3 years."
"To?"
"Freedom of course, fun and Freedom."
"Freedom?"
"From all human limitation."
"Sleep?"
"Yes."
"Food and fluid?"
"Yes."
"Aging?"
"Yes."
"Time?"
"Yes."
"Freedom to create miracles?"
"Yes."
"Freedom from basic human limitation?"
"Yes."
"Why?"
"Because you can and because you pre-agreed and because it is time."

I can't say that I'd become bored with my personal journey as I had spent the past decade on an intense roller coaster ride where I had seen so many miracles, yet I had come to realize that it was time to move on and that I wanted to go even deeper into my own field of faith. Taking leaps into, or through, the field of faith was not something I had been active in for a while although that is not to say that my journey had not required great leaps of faith and trust from time to time. Yet it is different to have an experience that is so real and so true and to stand tall in faith in that experience and to share it with those with more skeptical eyes, compared to bounding off into the unknown on a path that we have previously not trod.

Exploring the unknown always requires a leap of faith and so I decided to take up my new Freedom challenge and at least do what I could to be prepared. Part of this journal covers some of the journey of this preparation as rather than record it retrospectively like I did with the *Living on Light* manual, I was guided to record this journey as I underwent each step – regardless of the outcome which at this time is still uncertain.

It is possible for me to attain this type of Freedom?

Yes, I believe it is. How? That is yet to be determined for there are many paths to explore.

More over can a way be found that can be duplicated safely and successfully by others who are also pre-programmed to achieve these types of freedom?

This also is yet to be determined.

Are these types of freedoms miraculous?

To some perhaps they are, but to others, who are choosing to expand their own consciousness, they are just natural states of being and a benefit of embracing a life governed consciously by the Law of Love. To the Shaman of this world, it is just a matter of some internal shape-shifting.

I can't remember when I first began to discover and live in more of the Shaman's world. For some of us, Shamanism is something that we carry within us from other times, an imprinting that serves us and so we retain it deep within, allowing it to guide us via our higher senses. Traditionally a Shaman is known among the indigenous as a healer, a visionary who can inspire or guide the tribe through the Shaman's ability to tune to the unseen realms or via their connectedness with the Universal Voice that guides all life. In some traditions a Shaman is a magician or metaphysician but in all traditions what determines the status of a Shaman is their personal experience which gifts them with an expansion of consciousness and knowledge of the way through the seven levels of consciousness discussed in chapter 2.

Among the Shaman there is a term called Shamanic ecstasy which is an experience that comes to an initiate when they align themselves with the Law of Love. Ecstasy for the Shaman is about achieving a state of exaltation where a person literally transcends their limited self and bathing in the sixth and seventh levels of conscious, becomes truly free. This state of exaltation comes after great training and various initiations that are designed to merge the Shaman's baser nature with his/her DOW. When this merging occurs joy and ecstasy flood the being and another way of BEing is revealed.

There is also a term in Shamanic traditions called shape-shifting which is about rearranging energy fields into different patterns. Shape-shifting is a skill that can be applied to human systems or to community or global fields using the type of techniques that we discuss in the Biofields & Bliss Trilogy. Shape-shifting requires faith and a lack of fear and the belief that it is possible, particularly when applied to the Shaman's skill of changing their bodies into the form of a bird or animal.

The secret of the success of the shape-shifting Shaman is tied directly to their understanding of the Law of Love. Successful shape-shifting – whether it be into another form or whether it be the skill of redirecting energy to create a different internal or external world – is also determined by a shape-shifters understanding of unity and which level of consciousness they are predominantly operating from.

Accepting the reality that all life is
a) interconnected,
b) part of the whole, and
c) forms cells in the greater body of the quantum and virtual field;
   is just the beginning point for a Shaman and shape-shifter and something that allows them to achieve the things they do.

Successful Shaman believe in the power of the dream, they know that
a) to create change we need to first change our dreams and that
b) happiness is dependant on our feelings of connectedness with our DOW as the force that gives life. They also know that
c) successful shape-shifting can only occur through the direct utilization of this force, through knowledge of, alignment with and experience of It.

To the Shaman of our world, working via the Law of Love is the pathway of the creation of a dis-ease free life and a sustainable future. Air, water, earth and fire are known to the Shaman of South America as the four Sacred Sisters and to them only the honoring of these elements and the respect for and preservation of life – including the plants and waters of earth – only via this honoring can freedom come, but this freedom is limited until we also honor and work with the higher elements of the more subtle realms.

Working with Astral Light, Akasha and Cosmic Fire brings another level of success to the shape-shifting Shaman. We can work with these elements through
a) a process of conscious alchemy,
b) via adjustments with the percentages of time and how we spend it,
c) where we place our attention in every moment and
d) via our dreaming.

All of this determines which elements we will magnetize to our field and how they then flow through us and around us and hence which realm we will shape-shift into – as individuals and as a species.

Whether a Shaman's role is to support the transformation of their own being or to support the transformation of a global species and their planet, success can only come with the intention of harmony and the acceptance of the unified force that drives all worlds. It is this unified force that allows us to draw to ourselves the wisdom of the Buddha, the compassion of the Christ, the insight of Mohammed and the strength and the vision to change the dream – the dreams we have for our selves, our children and our future.

Not everyone desires the freedom to shape-shift into the spaces we will discuss in this manual, not everyone seeks a euphoric state of being, not everyone seeks to see the Divinity in all life and not everyone desires to create a healthy sustainable world, however for those who do then living by the Law of Love is step one, but first we must **dream the change then act to make it a reality.**

First I dreamt of changing the way I was living my life until the end of 2002. Taking a sabbatical of what I originally thought would be a few months of beachside living, I continued with a deeper more honest journey of introspection, a journey of assessment of all that I had created. When we find ourselves in a space of less Grace then it is time for an honest assessment for we do create it all.

I realized during this time that my work as I knew it in the world, with the Divine Nutrition Program, was not only complete but the Grace had repositioned Itself and was calling me to follow It and to make an inner shift to keep in Its glorious flow. Once I understood this, I listened to my inner voice and took the necessary steps to create the shift back into Its field. Although none of this sounds challenging, personally for me it meant a huge reorganization of both my physical and emotional life, a reorganization that involved people I loved and one that needed to be done with sensitivity and dignity and support for all.

My inner Self had called me to:
a) relocate to a beachside ashram of my own creation where I could increase my solitude and silence time to prepare the energetics for the next step, without any unnecessary disruptions and
b) decrease my travel commitments by 50% and open up a void of time for more in depth personal training where I could also explore the formula for the making of miracles while I fulfilled more of my own personal freedom agenda and
c) to bring myself back into a state of daily DOW smiles.

When we live in a physical world, physical world laws and actions must be adhered to. When we live between the worlds as many metaphysicians now do, universal laws can be worked with and applied, so we literally can work on all levels. For the creation of change and of miracles, first we need to have a clear vision of what we wish to achieve, then we need to create the space and put the energy grids in place, then call in and apply any necessary support structures and then we need to open ourselves to a state of allowance. Sometimes even just getting a clear picture of what we wish to create can be difficult as often all is revealed one step at a time, a step that we must trust to take and then take it and once taken, trust again that a new step will be revealed.

Relocating from a busy city to a high prana beach environment was physically easy as it entailed having my accommodation angel team scout ahead and find the perfect apartment, then lead me to it and then move myself in. The angels are often the first sacred support system that a devotee of the DOW has access to. Emotionally, leaving my husband and our family home was another matter for all I knew was that the lifestyle we had created together was not the right frequency to support my next step. I also knew that I did not have the right to ask him to create the changes in his life to the degree that would support my next level coming to fruitition. Why? Because it is simply not part of his destiny and nor is he interested in living so extremely.

As we all know things are so easy in hindsight where clarity and understanding often abound and I would have loved to have had the insight then that I do now. Yet taking the next step sometimes is a test in itself – a test of our faith, a test of our desire, a test of where we place our loyalty and to who and what. I have always known that I did not come into this embodiment to find my 'soul mate', get married and just do the 'family/career' game. Yet I know that if I can also have these things in a way that supports what I have come to do, then that is a wonderful bonus. I acknowledge that all of these things have given me great gifts of insight and understanding into the Law of Love and that for many there is no greater spiritual initiation than learning the dance of harmonizing human relationships, a dance that I am still learning.

The choice for us is to be awake or to be asleep. For some this means to be awake in the dream of a mass reality of human limitation and to influence the awakening of the dream, to inspire the birth of another dream where the mass reality of humanity is one of a life without struggle. For me the freedom from struggle came when I awoke to the love and power of my DOW.

In his book *The Mastery of Love* Don Miguel Ruiz talks about the 'dream' as an illusionary state where people are asleep to their own true nature and how we can awaken to our DOW and break free from limiting illusions. Based on the teachings of the Toltec's he shares in his book how when we are asleep to the glory of our Divine nature, how we are influenced by fear based realities and how in our quest for love and acceptance we may place ourselves in disempowering situations. These situations in life always gift us with learning and wisdom as we eventually discover the endless source of love within.

I think my favorite story in the book *The Mastery of Love* is about the magic kitchen where Don Miguel sets the scene about a person who has an abundant magical kitchen, a kitchen that has the ability to manifest instantly any food you think about, in an endless supply. One day a person arrives and offers to supply you with an endless supply of pizza if you'll surrender control of your life to him and do everything he says. Now because you have this magical kitchen that creates the best pizza in the world you decline the offer and invite him in instead to eat with you.

Don Miguel goes on to say that if however you were starving with no food and the man came with his endless supply of pizza and his request to control your life, then you may acquiesce. The point to the story is that we have forgotten the magical kitchen of our heart and how we have access to limitless food – love – and hence we do not need to place ourselves in disempowering or dishonoring situations to receive love as we all have a never ending source within. Tuning ourselves so that this never ending love can flow freely occurs naturally as we seek to know our DOW, for our DOW is the creator of our magical kitchen and its food is love.

The path of the Shaman and the DOW devotee is a path of self mastery and as we begin shape-shifting into this state, we become the seeker of miracles.

THE LAW OF LOVE
SHAPE-SHIFTING SHAMAN – synopsis

Shamanic ecstasy: Ecstasy for the Shaman is about achieving a state of exaltation where a person literally transcends their limited self and bathing in the sixth and seventh levels of conscious, becomes truly free. This state of exaltation comes after great training and various initiations that are designed to merge the Shaman's baser nature with his/her DOW. When this merging occurs joy and ecstasy flood the being and another way of BEing is revealed. There is also a term in Shamanic traditions called shape-shifting which is about rearranging energy fields into different patterns. Shape-shifting is a skill that can be applied to human systems or to community or global fields and requires faith and a lack of fear and the belief that it is possible, particularly when applied to the Shaman's skill of changing their bodies into the form of a bird or animal.

The secret of the success of the shape-shifting Shaman is tied directly to their understanding of the Law of Love. Accepting the reality that all life is a) interconnected, b) part of the whole, and c) forms cells in the greater body of the quantum and virtual field; is just the beginning point for a Shaman and shape-shifter and something that allows them to achieve the things they do. Successful Shaman believe in the power of the dream, they know that a) to create change we need to first change our dreams and that b) happiness is dependant on our feelings of connectedness with our DOW as the force that gives life. They also know that c) successful shape-shifting can only occur through the direct utilization of this force, through knowledge of, alignment with and experience of It.

To the Shaman of our world, working via the Law of Love is the pathway of the creation of a dis-ease free life and a sustainable future. Air, water, earth and fire are known to the Shaman of South America as the four Sacred Sisters and to them only the honoring of these elements and the respect for and preservation of life – including the plants and waters of earth – only via this honoring can freedom come, but this freedom is limited until we also honor and work with the higher elements of the more subtle realms.

Working with Astral Light, Akasha and Cosmic Fire brings another level of success to the shape-shifting Shaman. We can work with these elements through a) a process of conscious alchemy, b) via adjustments with the percentages of time and how we spend it, c) where we place our attention in every moment and d) via our dreaming.
All of this determines which elements we will magnetize to our field and how they then flow through us and around us and hence which realm we will shape-shift into – as individuals and as a species.

Chapter 4

The Seekers of Miracles

Being creates everything here,
Non-being provides its career,
Moving between them, the seer.

There once was a sage who knew the miracle of how to turn his horse into a collapsible paper-like form so that the man could fold up and store his horse in his pocket. When ready to travel again the man would moisten the paper-like horse with water which would transform it back to its usual size and horse form, except that this horse was also magical in that it could travel for thousands of miles in just moments.

Born in the 8th century AD the sage who was called Chung Kuo-Lao was destined to become one of the Taoist immortals whose job, apart from fortune telling, was to help souls to reincarnate.

As with the previous three immortals whose lives we have briefly touched on, there are many other stories of the skills of Chung Kuo-Lao and the miracles he performed but what of people born this century, people who exist here and now? People who we can meet who predominantly reside in this plane rather than beings who reside in the etheric realms in higher dimensions who visit us from time to time?

For a long time I was a seeker of miracles until I witnessed enough so that with my faith confirmed, I began to become a miracle maker. At this now point in time, the greatest miracle that I could support in the making would be to inspire humanity to remember their DOW.

Personally I have seen so much that all my dreams have been fulfilled and there is nothing to seek any more and yet this is a state of being that can also have its limitations.

While I have met so many amazing people in my travels, people preprogrammed to expand the boundaries of the status quo, rarely have I met someone who has really inspired me to personally go to another level in my own freedom journey, that is until I met Zinaida.

Zinaida and her story first came to my attention, in Warsaw Poland in the summer of 2002. As I sat meditating in the back of the hall waiting for my event to start, a strange little man with a scruffy beard and beady but laughing blue eyes, suddenly appeared and sat close to me and began to speak with me, via a translator, in a mixture of Russian, German and broken English. It was as if he was trying to find the right way to communicate his words and I sensed he had something important to say.

Apparently he had walked for hundreds of miles traveling from the southern states of Russia to Poland, to tell me of his news and, arriving road weary and scruffy from his travels, managed to by pass the security of my organizer and present himself into my field. I found the chaos that surrounded his entry quite amusing and subdued those around me enough so they were comfortable to let him stay, for I know that the only reason the universe would support such an entry was because I needed to hear what he had to say. I had long ago learned to pay attention to those who could find their way into my field and also how to screen myself from unnecessary field intrusions. I would like to say that I remember his name especially since I met with him some 18 months later when I finally made it to St. Petersburg and found myself in the regal presence of Zinaida, and yet it was his message and his face that remain with me instead.

Part of our conversation went something like this:
"You know you are the fifth?"
"Fifth?"
"Yes, the fifth system I have found."
"Fifth system?"
"Yes of Divine Nourishment."
"Ahh…" I acknowledged.

And with this he proceeded to tell me of Zinaida Baranova. Much of what he said, due to the language barrier between us, just skimmed the surface of my brain and yet I understood that Russia was receiving some interesting downloads as its pioneers explored Divine Doors. Our exchange over the weekend that followed allowed another of my own inner doors to open, although I was used to hearing stories of many miraculous things. Seekers of miracles are often known to find them.

I have long held the practice of two realities, the first being to:
- ॐ Pay attention to who comes into my field. No matter what they look like, if the universe supports them enough to get so close to me, then there must be a valuable message so it's advisable to pay attention and listen.
- ॐ The second reality I accept is the knowledge that magic and the miracles of life will reveal themselves in their own time and that if things are destined to be, they will be. So all I need to do is to acknowledge this via a prayer of intention and open the door of possibility and allow.

This second reality has helped many of my important relationships to blossom. Sometimes we might meet someone and feel as though we may have something to do with them in the future, or sometimes we can be unsure as to where a dance with them may fit in as not all the pieces of our puzzle may have been presented clearly to us in the initial meeting. Hence the following prayer.

Generally when I feel like this – or they do – we hold hands and say:
- ॐ *"Dear Mother/Father God, if it is in our Divine Blueprint to serve together then we now call on the support of all universal forces to bring this into being with joy and ease and Grace. We ask for the perfect connection Divine Self to Divine Self and that*

all the resources we need – time, money, wisdom, people, inspiration – come to us in perfect time. So it is. So it is. So it is."

This program of intention is enough to bring that which is predestined, into a smooth state of being, beyond constraints and limitations of our mind.

So I paid attention to this quaint little man who had traveled so far to see me, guided by the joy within his heart and happy to be part of the coming time of change for he was a seeker of miracles who had witnessed a miracle in the making.

Eighteen months later I find myself in the old Hare Krishna temple in St. Petersburg holding yet another press conference which appears to be dotted with more curious ones than reporters. Nonetheless the show goes on and at some point a space is opened for a very regal woman to not only approach me but to also enfold me in a very warm and tender embrace. The crowd in the room claps and tears glisten in their eyes. Her name is Zinaida and over the course of the coming days I manage to hear more of her story.

Apparently when she was in her mid forties her son was killed and the loss and grief she experienced was so intense it virtually broke her heart. All she could do at this time, and for a long time after, was pray. Over the next 20 years, her prayer became her soul's nourishment and her sanctuary against the harsher realities of life and during this time her devotion to the Christ steadily grew until one day an inner voice said that it was time to let the Christ's Love nourish her physical body. Unaware of my journey and research with the Divine Nutrition program, Zinaida listened to this voice and stopped taking physical food. A month later, this same inner voice told her to stop drinking fluids as well.

"So what did you do?" I asked.

"Why I stopped of course." She beamed like someone who always unquestionably trusted their inner voice. I found myself amazed for I too, had long ago received the same instructions, yet clinging to my old ways of being, refused to go the extra mile and to take another leap of faith. Only now, nearly 11 years later can I consider that original request.

We chatted for some time about her physical and social adjustments before she revealed to me the answer to a personal puzzle. When I asked her if there had been any physical discomfort from no longer taking fluid, she replied:

"Only the itching."

"The itching?" I asked suddenly intrigued for itching had plagued me on and off for years.

"Yes," she responded, "but thankfully it finally stopped. Every day for 3 years I itched continually but I've been free of this now for 6 months."

"What do you think it was? The burning of the dross?" I ventured and she said: "Just a frequency adjustment to a finer vibration in the body's cells."

As she continued to share our time was interrupted by the arrival of my favorite on road beverage – the cappuccino – a treat that to me represents a 3 course meal. Out of habit I asked her if she would like a drink and she just sat there in her contented regal cloud and softly said:

"No thank you, I take all that I need from the air." And she waved her hands around to indicate the atmosphere around us.

Zinaida's journey with this may seem like a miracle and it is also something that is not easily replicable. A middle aged mother who experiences such a shock and grief that she retreats into prayer, which in turn releases such Love and devotion through her system that she becomes free from some of her more human limitations, is not a model to repeat. On one level what occurred to Zinaida is easy to understand for as we discussed in the book *The Food of Gods* the more Divine Love we allow to flood through our system, the more Grace and miracles we perceive and experience in life.

I have long learned to trust and work with the reality that "everything is always perfect" while acknowledging that as beings with free will we all always have choice. A decade ago I chose to ignore the urgings of my inner voice which – like Zinaida's own intuitive advice – came exactly a month after I had also freed myself from the need to take nourishment from physical food. It was a voice that said: "You know you don't need to drink either," a voice that offered an invitation to be even more extreme in my lifestyle choice and yet as I was not personally ready, this voice lay ignored yet it was a voice that could bring miracles. Nearly a decade later Zinaida did listen to her inner voice, she didn't question or deny it and so she made her transition stoically with the pure heart of one with great faith and so the seeker of miracles became the miracle maker.

Over these few days I enjoyed the pleasure of being in the presence of this woman who tests now say has a biological age of 30 even though her outward physical appearance looks like the 68 year old woman she was when we met. Yes its true her skin looked a little dehydrated and that she lost 20 kilograms before her body weight stabilized but at an original weight of over 90 kilograms, losing 20 was beneficial. She says that she has never been healthier and happier and that all those around her fully respect and support her life style choice although many marvel at the miracle. I too have often looked a little less sparkly than I could have over the years as constant travel and a 20 hour work day have taken their toll even though my internal pranic flow has kept me well nourished.

I know now that if I had listened to my inner voice so long ago, to move myself beyond the need for fluid, that my life now would be quite different, yet I also know that we must make all leaps of faith when we are ready and that we cannot be pushed or cajoled or coerced especially if we want change like this to last. I know also that it has taken me a decade to share what I have come to know, after living it and learning to find a space to live the miracle of a Freedom life, for some types of Freedoms can paradoxically create restriction especially in a world where this type of Freedom challenges old beliefs.

I remember the third time my DOW invited me to go to the next level in the Divine Nutrition Program and free myself from the need of fluid, for I responded with:

"When the world becomes vegetarian, then I'll take this next step." It was a convenient answer that was destined to buy me some time. Somehow it has been important for me to integrate these changes slowly and I have also been distracted with the global service of being a public spokesperson for the Divine Nutrition Program and dealing with the responses that this type of research provokes.

Freedom from the need to take food, fluid, to age, to sleep or create disease was never a huge fascination for me. Developing enough control over my body's molecular structure to be able to dematerialize and rematerialize at will has always held far greater appeal, however my research within the field of becoming free from human limitation has given me far greater insight into the benefits of such levels of molecular command and even greater insights into the gifts of the Law of Love and the miracles It brings when we allow It to be fully operational in our life.

Nonetheless, every human being is driven by something deep within to fulfill what I call their Divine Blueprint. This is like a pre-agreed cosmic manifesto that will come to pass with our participation and where each step of the journey of fulfillment brings us the reward of virtues, which is perhaps a greater gift than the joy of a journey's completion. Freedom, like enlightenment, is a never ending journey as our capacity to expand and accept more light is always growing.

As I have shared in my other books, when something is part of human evolution, the potentiality of it is released into the etheric channels that surround the earth where individuals, whose personal fields are open to such miraculous possibilities, can tune in and download the data necessary to bring it into more of a global reality.

Surfing the inner net during our times of contemplation, introspection and meditation provides the surfer with an amazing array of insights and choices and reminders and possibilities, many of which carry great support energetically for manifestation. Hence exploring Freedom from perceived limitations via utilizing the Law of Love, is something that will always be cosmically supported. Similarly the seekers of miracles are always given the tools to recognize and experience them.

Prahlad

I had heard of another woman in Paris who had neither eaten nor drank anything for over 20 years and as I made my way down to Romania after my visit to Russia and meeting Zinaida, I was given news of the 76 year old Indian man, Prahlad Jani, who had taken nothing for some 68 years.

Apparently when he was 8 years old, an Indian Goddess appeared before him and freed his system from the need to take food or fluid. Unaware of how he could do this all he said was that he had a hole in the roof of his mouth through which the Divine food could flow. He called this food 'the elixir of life'.

He was of course talking about Amrita, the nectar produced by the pituitary gland, what the Yogi's call the fountain of youth. When stimulated the pituitary gland produces more nectar which is the body's own source of Divine food and in Prahlad's case his body releases enough nectar to provide him with these Freedoms. Prahlad's journey was investigated and reported on by the same team of medical researchers I have been liaising with, Dr Sudhir Shah and his team and we will share a new Taoist Tool, to stimulate and create this nectar flow, in Part 2 of this manual.

Hira

As a new millennium dawned an Indian yogi found himself working intensely with a group of medical researchers in Ahmedabad in India where he stayed for a period of 411 days under 24 hour constant observation while they monitored his system which he fed with solar energy and a small amount of water. "A miracle!" the doctors involved concluded. Somehow the results of this work synchronistically found their way to me and were hence opportunely included in my book *Ambassadors of Light*. His name was Hira Ratan Manek.

A year or so later I found myself standing outside a hotel in Ahmedabad beside this very tall yogi, with both of us staring intently into the blazing midday sun while photographers of the local newspapers snapped away. Unable to hold my gaze for more than a few seconds, I watched in amazement as Hira fed himself indulgently in this way, his eyes never blinking he stared and stared as if he would be able to do it all day. His capacity to absorb prana directly via solar energy is now both well documented and demonstrated.

He once told me that any person can do this regardless of their lifestyle and that the sun was so pure and so powerful that its rays were absorbed directly into the brain through the eyes, where they flooded the inner system of a body and burnt up all that was not of this pure light – hence the transformation. Nine months of solar gazing, slowly building up your capacity by seconds each day – doing it only at dawn and dusk – was enough to feed a physical system in another way. Provided this was also maintained by direct contact of our feet to the earth for some 45 minutes per day afterwards. I will not elaborate further on Hira's methodology as it is covered in his website www.solarhealing.com (and the medical research has been shared in my previous work). Suffice to say that feeding our physical systems purely by solar energy alone seems miraculous, even though in metaphysical circles we know that the sun is a cosmic generator for Christ light and that the Christ light is so pure and so loving that when it is stimulated to increase its flow through us, miracles happen on both a personal and a global level.

In an interview that I did with Hira in 2003 for our free online magazine, The ELRAANIS Voice*, Hira or HRM as he is more commonly known, said of solar gazing: "It enables one to harmonize and recharge the body with life energy and also awaken the unlimited powers of the mind very easily. It easily enables one to attain liberation from the threefold sufferings in life i.e. mental, physical illness and spiritual ignorance."
* http://www.selfempowermentacademy.com.au/htm/files/pdfs/TEV1-Vol6.pdf

Regarding the global benefits of solar nourishment on our world and our future, Hira's response was: "Global healing in all directions is the global benefit. There will be peace, peace and peace everywhere. No energy crisis because sun energy will never end. No pollution because sun energy never produces pollutants. No obesity and no hunger. No AIDS and no cancer. All will be mentally, physically and spiritually fit. Total Health will rule the world. I see a world with human welfare and world peace."

If as Hira has proven, a human bio-system can take its nourishment directly from the sun and hence experience such health that the body is free from the need to take food, can we also do this without utilizing the sun? Can we all open up the atoms within our cellular structure to draw the energy of prana in from the inner universes and experience freedom from dependence on the sun? These were the type of questions that Hira's research initially raised within me.

In a quest to answer these questions, 3 years after meeting Hira, I would find myself exploring and experiencing the teachings of the ancient immortal Tao masters as I spent 3 weeks in complete darkness fine tuning my body to feed itself without sunlight or physical food and in Part 2 of this manual we share more of this in detail.

It is true that a miracle is something that seems to defy rational explanation as in the case of Zinaida. Yet Hira and his medical team have made great headway in the study of the human mechanism, particularly in the role of the pituitary and the pineal glands and we covered this is detail in *The Food of Gods* manual. In this journal we take this further and add ancient techniques of the Taoist masters to ensure our freedom journey.

As I have often shared, one of the fantastic rewards of DOW devotion and alignment is the magical or constant flow of Grace in life. Grace is an energy that seems to carry us on its wave so that we can be not just the miracles seekers but also the ones who find. At this same time that I met with Zinaida I was synchronistically given a wonderful book by Michael Newton called *Destiny of Souls* and then later I discovered his first book *Journey of Souls*. I mention these here as the research covered in both books provides a great service to our world.

One of the most debilitating energies in our world and lives is fear and it is also one of the greatest control mechanisms to keep people and societies in a state of limitation, a state where true freedom is impossible. For many in life one of the greatest fears is death, the idea that we will no longer have consciousness and form. Imagine what a miracle it would be to some people if they were given the freedom of instant immortality?

What I loved about Michael's books is that this is exactly the sort of freedom his research delivers. After interviewing hundreds of people while under deep hypnosis, Michael provides fascinating insights into what happens when we physically die, about where our consciousness moves to, beings we are met by and guided by, soul groups, karmic agreements, planning for new incarnations and so much more until the immortal nature of our being becomes self evident.

In my field discussing reincarnation and the indestructibility of energy and life between lives is preaching to the converted as all of this is a commonly accepted reality by those who gravitate to my research. What I loved about these two books is that they confirmed so much of what I have received directly from universal mind in my own meditations as I have sought answers to the mathematical operation of the fields of life.

Newton's subjects while under hypnosis provide great insights into the reality of light lines and grids and dimensional doors and our keynote and so much more that all adds a wonderful base for Part 2 of this journal. Hence I cannot recommend highly enough that these books be read as they offer insights that will provide the reader with freedom from many fears and limitations. And when we are free of these things we become open to experience more miracles.

There are many wonderful stories of miracle seekers and miracle makers in our world today and also in our history. I have chosen Zinaida, Hira and Prahlad only as their stories support some of the agendas in this journal.

THE LAW OF LOVE – summary

- **LOTUS CHILDREN**
- **INDIGO CHILDREN**
- **CRYSTAL CHILDREN**

**MIRACLE SEEKERS & MIRACLE MAKERS
CO-CREATING A HEALTHY - HAPPY FUTURE**

➢ Lotus Children – children of the maya or the mud.
Challenge – to be radiant masters in a world of illusion.

➢ Indigo Children – bringers of chaos & change.
Challenge – to be understood & sensitively supported.

➢ The Crystal Children – healing & smoothing the way.
Challenge – to be recognized, listened to and appreciated.

➢ Throughout this century, different models of humanity have been born and each model has had a specific purpose. The LOTUS children are the wave of the baby boomers who came with a huge desire for inner and outer peace which they recognized could only come through self knowledge and so they embraced free love and /or eastern mysticism with its yoga and meditation principles and later self-help therapy. Their mission was to be the miracle seekers and to lay the foundation for a new millennium of a peaceful, sensitive co-existence and to be a radiant example of masters who can harmoniously and happily exist in a world of illusion. The LOTUS children come to bridge the worlds.

➢ When the baby boomers grew older, perhaps tired and more complacent, the INDIGO children came to shake up our systems further and say *"Hey, things could run a little better here for the whole. My standards are higher than this and my needs aren't being met."* Highly creative and sensitive they are demanding to be listened to and ask for a refinement of our educational and social systems for they come as the bringers of change. Misunderstood, the Indigos often end up ignored, seen as 'too difficult' or sedated; yet they too are just the seekers of miracles.

➢ Next came the Miracle Makers, the CRYSTAL children, children awake to their DOW nature, who bring many gifts. Often free of karmic imbalances, they come to inspire, to heal, to bridge the animal and human worlds by honoring and loving all life and the environment of earth. Choosing light diets, many are telepathic, all are empathetic and many are examples of the power of unconditional love. Their role is to smooth the way after the discordian baby boomers and Indigos have shaken up the systems and reset standards. The Crystal children come to be inspirational examples of love in action and they need little from us except our love and appreciation.

Chapter 5

The Makers of Miracles
Attributes & Actions

*Without looking the sage sees all,
The wholeness of the Tao enthralls,
No thought of self-creating walls.*

Another being born in the 8th century AD who is said to be still alive is the Taoist master Lu Tung-Pin. Often seen mounted on a tiger he was initiated into the secrets of internal alchemy by fellow immortal Chung-Li Chun. Able to fly through the air and walk on clouds he carries a supernatural sword that was given to him by a dragon so that he can become invisible to evil spirits.

Roaming China and seeking the pure hearted, Lu Tung-Pin would find those who risked their own comfort and often safety for others, and use his powers to help transform them into fellow immortals. Conversely he would punish any who oppressed the powerless or the poor. Loved and respected by the masses Lu spent 400 years on earth and periodically still appears.

Using practices like the Taoist Masters internal alchemy is a form of shape-shifting our bio-system into one that is no longer subject to disease or time and the lives of the Shaman shape-shifters and the seekers of miracles are often quite different to those lived in our more 'normal' western world.

Miracle seekers come in all sorts of packages but generally they are just open. They are open to witness, open to receive, open to know, open to enjoy, open to allow and open to grow. These attributes of openness walk hand in hand with other attributes and actions required by the seekers of miracles to access and operate the Law of Love so that they can go to another level and become shape-shifters or miracle makers. A miracle maker's life is filled with examples of synchrodestiny, examples which occur more regularly as we utilize the Law of Love.

Seeking, discovering, experiencing, enjoying and creating miracles are all dependant on the attributes we possess and develop and the actions we take in life. I'd like to mention some of the things which form part of the miracle maker's life and then elaborate on them in more detail.

These are:

- ❖ Allowance
- ❖ Alignment and Action
- ❖ Acceptance via Recognition and Experience
- ❖ Appreciation and Biofeedback
- ❖ Demonstration
- ❖ Downloads
- ❖ Direction and Field Enhancement
- ❖ Dreaming the Outcome

Allowance
Miracle makers allow the fields of possibility to present themselves for exploration and acknowledgement. Allowance is about being open, enquiring and inviting enough to witness how the universe can and does reveal its magic and miracles to all. Allowance is about creating a space for such things to enter into our field by keeping an open yet discerning heart and mind.

Alignment and Action
Alignment is about getting tuned to the channel where miracles happen regularly enough for us to enjoy them. So alignment comes via an action program such as the Luscious Lifestyles Program that forms part of Recipe 2000> with it specific program codes. This is a program discussed in detail in our *Four Body Fitness: Biofields & Bliss* manual, it is a program that is designed to tune our energy fields to the channel of Grace and allow us to operate via the Law of Love in a more conscious way. Miracle Makers take the time to get and stay tuned to the Channel of Divine Love and hence this puts us in the path of Its Grace which is where all miracles naturally happen.

Acceptance from Recognition and Experience
For many, being able to give is easy, being able to receive perhaps not so. The ability to be open to and accepting of miracles is imperative if we are to recognize them and experience them in life. Paradoxically our experience of miracles opens us up to accepting that they exist and that perhaps we can have more of them. The recognition and acceptance that we live within a loving and intelligent quantum field, is a basic step in the freedom game.

Appreciation and Biofeedback
Miracle Makers have an attitude of gratitude as we know that gratitude opens our fields up to receive more miracles. We also know that being appreciative of the flow of Grace, of the miracles we witness and enjoy, does the same. Appreciation also gifts us with the ability to be fully present in the now moment and to engage in active biofeedback with a conscious universal field. Learning to listen to and to read energy fields is a skill developed by the Miracle Maker and the appreciation of such interchanges adds another, deeper layer.

Demonstration
Miracle makers can demonstrate miracles in their lives, however, what they perceive, and others perceive, as miraculous, will vary for each one. Some may say a disease free life is a

miracle particularly if they have transformed their own life from one of great dis-ease to one of ease. Others may feel that the fact that they are appearing to get younger or to have stopped the aging process is a miracle, especially when this is confirmed via biological age tests.

Downloads

Miracle Makers have the ability to download all the data they need to create miracles. They download this data via their direct contact with Universal Mind and the blueprints it holds there for such things. These downloads are done via our 6th and 7th senses of intuition and knowing and by our ability to listen to the response of such a field to the answers of specific questions that we have learnt to formulate and ask. Learning the subtlety of correct question asking is a highly skilled art.

Direction and Enhancement

Miracle Makers learn the art of directing energy via thought, will and intention and how to use the energy grids to change, enhance and/or strengthen certain fields to then guarantee certain outcomes. Fields are the realities we attract and immerse ourselves in as a result of how we choose to tune our personal keynote or frequency. In Dimensional Biofield Science every living thing emits a frequency which can be adjusted.

Dreaming the Outcome

The art of visualization and of dreaming new realities into being are part of a shape-shifter's and Miracle Maker's tool kit of life. Miracles Makers, like Shaman, know the power of having a clear vision, focusing upon it, supporting it energetically and then how to let it go so that it can come into being aligned with the bigger picture that supports all the blueprints of life.

Miracle Makers work with all the Universal Laws, and understand from experience the alchemy behind the Law of Love. A Miracle Maker's life is an example of the Law of Love in action, they achieve what they set out to with joy and ease and Grace, free from the suffering of struggle.

All of the above is part of what I call Matrix Mechanics, a science which operates under the principles discussed in the Biofields & Bliss Series, and in Part 2 of this journal we will summarize all the matrix mechanisms required for the freedom agenda.

Chapter 6

Goals & Status

Laws of nature are thoughts of God,
The universe formed with a nod,
And ruled with a flexible rod.

The nephew of the great Tang poet and scholar Han Vu, Han Hsien-Ku was known as a wild child who also disdained the superficial nature of the world and so even though he was expelled from the Buddhist monastery for mischief, as a pure hearted teenager Han was still initiated into the internal alchemy practices by Lu Tung-Pin. Probing the mysteries of heaven and the Five Phases or elements of Energy, Han was intoxicated with the love of the Tao, a word that means the way or the path. Often seen mounted on a buffalo, carrying a flute that plays healing sounds, Han also performed wonderful feats such as creating a flower with verses written in gold on its petals, verses that fore-told the future of his uncle.

Futures are based on the dreams that we have in the now.

During my first year of beachside living I downloaded *The Food of Gods* and finally felt that everything I had to say re our DOWs ability to feed us had been said. Receiving my new assignment in Barcelona meant opening up to another level again and yet sometimes in order to move into a new future we need to first acknowledge and let go of the past and so I found myself looking in depth at what I had already achieved in my own Freedom agenda.

I realized that I was no longer interested in providing proof for my journey or theories as I felt that I had provided enough for the world in my last 18 manuals. I also felt that it is now up to our scientists to provide the bridge into this metaphysical reality and knew that time would bring this. I realized as my life unfolded at the beach that all I wished was to be a story teller, guinea pig and model maker and that in this I was content.

In late November 2003 in Basel Switzerland, I was excited as I was soon to begin a ten month sojourn of no travel and also happy to fulfill my usual lecture/research sharing contract with PSI whose conference theme that year was on Spiritual Healing. Each year thousands gather to listen to cutting edge doctors, scientists and metaphysical researchers who share their research into human potential as we all seek to bridge the worlds and create a more honoring human world on earth. It's a good place to meet both the seekers and the makers of miracles.

At this event my first lecture followed on from the presentation of the Russian Doctor Konstantin Korotkov who gave a dissertation on the power of Love radiation and how it operates in energy fields and how this Love works with the electrons and photons in the body to provide enough prana to feed it. As images of this radiation using Kirlian photography were displayed on the screen, the audience could see how far the research had already come to prove my 'prana is Love and Love as prana can nourish a human bio-system enough to free it from the need to take food' theory that I have been living and sharing for this past decade. The fact that this information was shared before my presentation obviously opened the audience further to accept some of my propositions regarding what happens to the human body when we increase our Love radiation. So I know from this recent experience that there are doctors, scientists and researchers whose job it is to shed another light on our experiential journeys and that in time the things that I am suggesting here will become common to all, no longer seen as miracles.

As I have shared in previous books, my primary role with the 'Law of Love' field is to understand and research its gifts of Freedoms, apply them personally, live healthily through the changes, create and then refine the models so that they can safely be applied by others and then gift these models to the world. On another level it has been about seeking, finding and creating miracles so that our world can be a little more inspired to shape-shift itself into true civility, a planet where all are healthy and happy.

So let's clarify simply our goals for this new journey and also summarize what we have achieved so far this past decade:

Goal: **The fine tuning of a human bio-system into the below 7 levels of Freedom and the creation in doing so, of a safe proto-type model that can be applied by others who are pre-programmed for this path.**

Test subject – **me**.

Freedoms that come to devotees of their DOW:
1. Freedom from the creation of dis-ease.
2. Freedom from aging of the physical system.
3. Freedom from the 'normal requirements' of sleep.
4. Freedom from time constraints.
5. Freedom from the need for physical food.
6. Freedom from the need for liquid.
7. Freedom from the physical world laws that restrict a physical systems movement through time and space i.e. bi-location, dematerialization.

Time objective from date of conscious commencement:
Minimum: 3 months; Maximum: 3 years

Purpose: Personal Freedom and expansion (and amusement).
Global Benefit: Demonstration of the miracle of Divine Power and its gifts. (Hopefully also to provide inspiration for those who are interested to move beyond personal limitations.)

Tools: Personal will, discipline, mind power, time, DOW power and via lifestyle choice and matrix mechanics.

Help: **Inner Plane** – those guides, angels and Holy Ones predestined to support me.
External Plane – Talented energy workers destined to be part of this journey.

PERSONAL FREEDOMS
Current Official & Unofficial Research Status.

Freedoms attained so far as at January 2004:

1. Freedom from the creation of dis-ease.

Comment & Status: After years of research I am confident that the lifestyle I recommend in the *Four Body Fitness – Biofields & Bliss* book, has freed me – and can free others – from the creation of dis-ease. I now know how to maintain perfect physical, emotional, mental and spiritual health. No further research is required here. The attainment of such health has been evidenced by the continual flow of Grace in my life as Grace is a sign of a human bio-system demonstrating the Law of Love. Health to me is also about being in harmony on all levels which is reflected by how the world responds to us and us to it.

2. Freedom from aging of the physical system.

Comment & Status: Bio-resonance and kinesiology checks now reveal that while my chronological age is in my 48th year, my biological age is 31. No further research is required by me as all my re-programming tools and lifestyles actions are obviously working. My body desires to have a biological age of 25 and will eventually support itself into expressing this. This age has also been confirmed by my body via kinesiology. The use of rejuvenating matrix mechanisms such as the 11 Strand Healing System – in the Tao & Tools Chapter – helps to support this further.

3. Freedom from the need to sleep.

Comment & Status: After experiencing a reduction of 50% - 90% of 'my pre-prana only' lifestyle sleep requirements, and the time management benefits that this can bring, at this point I have chosen to do no further research into this field as after years of one to four hours sleep per night, I found I missed my dream time and also my out of body training time that I regularly enjoyed when my body was sleeping more. I also trust that as I eliminate fluid, my body will adjust itself to these new energy patterns regarding sleep. I am prepared to accept the no sleep consequence of this as a natural by-product which it seems to be and have learnt how to amuse myself 24/7 so as to avoid potential boredom. Freedom from the need to sleep, like living purely on prana, has its benefits and its challenges.

4. **Freedom from time constraints.**

Comment & Status: Have learnt how to exist and operate multi-dimensionally and cross the lines of time to access what I need from the past and the future energy lines. I have now taught this successfully to others as well as having personally tested and successfully used time expansion techniques. Have also understood the importance of being in the 'now' moment and the miracles and power that this focus and alignment brings. I share a few of my time management tools in the *Four Body Fitness: Biofields & Bliss* manual.

5. **Freedom from food.**

Comment & Status: After 11 years of personal experimentation with all aspects of this, I can now categorically state with confidence that if my physical body had no access to the nourishment of food, I would not die – provided I can maintain certain inner prana flow levels. Details of this research are provided in the Divine Nutrition Trilogy: *Pranic Nourishment – Nutrition for the New Millennium* and *Ambassadors of Light – World Health, World Hunger Project* and *The Food of Gods*.

6. **Freedom from liquid.**

Comment & Status: One of the initial focuses of this journal will be my journey into releasing my self from my emotional and mental dependency on fluid. My personal research and long term experimentation with this is now just beginning after having experienced various short term insights into this freedom. Have researched enough to understand the theory, now need to prove it to myself experientially while maintaining perfect health on all levels. I will begin to apply these principles, programming codes and body work during the 21 day dark room retreat in Thailand while working with Taoist energy Master Mantak Chia. I will apply what ever else is required to track, support and evidence this change and I will expand on this throughout this journal.

7. **Freedom from the physical world laws that restrict a physical systems movement through time and space.**

Comment & Status: Have experienced enough spontaneous 'out of body' time over the last few decades to confirm the existence of other realms, other beings and intelligences in other planes of consciousness.* Have no desire to explore further as no longer have any questions unanswered and still need to fully integrate some of the experiences I have outlined in the *Divine Radiance – On the Road with the Masters of Magic* book. My only desire now is to be able to control my molecular structure enough for conscious dematerialization and rematerialization at will. It is not my intention to achieve this during the course of writing this journal. I currently trust this gift will come after I have mastered the harmonious flow of the elements within my own system, however I suspect that as with all else, because I am creating mass models, I will need to understand the field mechanics of it all and find an easy formula or path for duplication by others. (Bi-location tools and some basic dematerialization techniques were touched on in the *In Resonance* manual. Bi-location is the ability to be in two places at once.)

* Also confirmed in Michael Newton's books.

Changing our frequency and aligning more to our DOW and its flow of Grace – via our lifestyle – is a simple safe way to establish how well we are working with the Law of Love. It is also a safe way to test and promote our trust levels prior to undertaking something as drastic as the 'no food, no fluid' game.

While I have outlined my personal status with the above freedoms, what I intend to do in this journal is to also summarize and elaborate on – where required – the various techniques that we can all safely apply to achieve these freedoms.

THE LAW OF LOVE
DEVOTEES OF OUR DOW FREEDOM –
summary

➤ Freedom from the creation of dis-ease.

➤ Freedom from aging of the physical system.

➤ Freedom from the need to sleep.

➤ Freedom from time constraints.

➤ Freedom from the need for physical food.

➤ Freedom from the need for liquid.

➤ Freedom from the physical world laws that restrict a physical systems movement through time and space i.e. bi-location, dematerialization.

The miracle of these Freedoms are attained by:

- ☺ Allowance
- ☺ Alignment and Action
- ☺ Acceptance via Recognition and Experience
- ☺ Appreciation and Biofeedback
- ☺ Demonstration
- ☺ Downloads
- ☺ Direction and Field Enhancement
- ☺ Dreaming the Outcome

THE LAW OF LOVE

LIVING ON LIGHT
synopsis

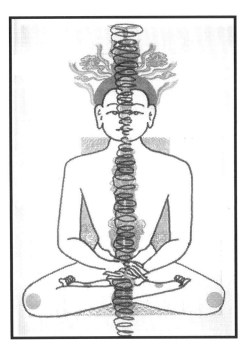

PRANA = CHI = UNIVERSAL LIFE FORCE

Summary – covered in the manual
The Food of Gods:

- PRE-PROGRAMMING & THE PIONEER
- FREQUENCY & KEYNOTE – LIFESTYLE – detoxified internal & external space
- BRAIN WAVES – ALPHA-THETA-DELTA
- 7 SENSES & THE 7 ELEMENTS
- IMMORTALITY & YOUTHING
- BODY LOVE – LOVE BREATH & DOW NAME POWER
- HEART MATH – Appreciation, gratitude, entrainment
- RADIATION vs. ABSORPTION

- THE PAST, PRESENT & FUTURE – PERSONAL & GLOBAL reality
- REPROGRAMMING & FREEDOM OF CHOICE
- EAT LESS, LIVE LONGER
- WATER & BODY CONSCIOUSNESS
- HEALTH – PREVENTATIVE MEDICINE
- RESOURCE SUSTAINABILITY

MATRIX MECHANICS:
- ☺ SPINNING CHAKRA COLUMN & INNER PLANE FEEDING
- ☺ PERSONAL BIO-SHIELD
- ☺ SELF-SUSTAINING TEMPLATES – Creation & Activation
- ☺ DIGESTIVE GRID
- ☺ 11 STRAND HEALING FEEDING HYDRATING SYSTEM
- ☺ PRANA FLOW PROGRAMMING

Chapter 7

Synchronicity & Sacred Support Systems

Guiding without interfering,
Listening that goes beyond hearing,
Helping with undergrowth clearing.

In the 3rd century of the Han dynasty there was an army general, or Marshall of the Empire, named Chaun Chung-Li who was pure hearted enough to be taught of the Tao by an old man. Leaving government service Chaun wandered the mountains and eventually while meditating found an old jade box that held secret instructions on how to become immortal. It was told that he followed the instructions religiously until one day his chamber was filled with rainbow clouds and celestial music and that a crane arrived and carried Chaun on its back into the realms of immortality.

Able to later wander the heavens alone he was still drawn to serve on earth and helped thousands to be released from their suffering often changing copper and pewter into gold and silver to give to the poor. It was Chaun who taught Lu Tung-Pin the secrets of immortality after persuading Lu of the emptiness of life and of the blissful nature of the higher realms. At over 1800 years old Chaun is often seen on earth as a messenger of heaven, carrying a fan and mounted on a chimera – a mythical animal that is sacred to Hsi Wang Mu, the Goddess of Immortality.

Having helpful friends and connections in life is valuable to us all for sometimes our journey here requires support systems that can recharge or redirect us.

At the end of 2002, just prior to my move to the beach, I found myself in the unenviable state of having literally lost my joy and my ability to witness miracles. Worse than this I had somehow also managed to remove myself from the glorious flow of the channel of Grace.

To an alchemist who is used to both being filled with the radiance of joy and supported by Divine Grace, these occurrences were daunting. For whatever reason, I had created a reality that screamed 'potential victim' for in the journey of my global service and nurturing others, I had forgotten to also create time to nurture myself. I had also stopped seeking miracles and had lost the art of creating new ones in my own life.

It was also more than this for the flow of Grace naturally surrounds a project that is destined to be, especially when the project is a necessary part of human evolution and so the

Divine Nutrition Program had been divinely supported with Grace from its inception. Similarly the Grace also decreases its focus when each part of the project is complete and repositions itself to feed and support the next step's evolution. This energy of Grace is like a drawing board that we, the artists, can utilize to bring a new creation into being. How powerfully it supports us depends on:
   a) how important this new creation is in the bigger scheme of things and
   b) how consciously and clearly we can align ourselves to it.

Our role as masters or Miracle Makers working with this stream of Grace is to be in the right place at the right time, to be in harmony with the Law of Love and with our Creator, and we do this via our frequency which we control via our lifestyle, perceptions and attitudes and the things we discussed in the previous chapter.

Freedom comes from letting go and Freedom comes from detachment and emotionally I have learnt some amazing things regarding my physical relocation. Sometimes being prepared to let everything go allows us to keep it and so it was with my move to the beach; for now a year later my relationship with my family is better than ever particularly with my husband who remained in the city to run his business. Both of us are now enjoying a semi celibate, yogic lifestyle living in our own ashrams. By shifting the mathematics of percentages and applying priority, I have repositioned myself back into the river of Grace. The benefits and 'how to's' of applying the mathematics of percentages will be covered in a later chapter.

I could digress at this point to go into the whole reality of having enough Love in a relationship – for ourselves and others – to allow us to have the Freedom to explore our higher urges as the first sacred support system we have is with our DOW and love of self and desire to know Self is the beginning of this relationship. However there are also support systems available to us that can help to facilitate our role as miracle seekers and miracle makers.

Apart from our DOW and our inner plane team of Holy Ones and angels we also have our external plane team.

One of my synchronistic support systems in this part of my journey is Lucinda. Lucinda was, I found to be, a hidden jewel in a health spa/beauty salon, who spirit led me to, to help me further as I transitioned through this new phase of Freedom. Aware of the type of stress that both a 'food and fluid free' choice could have on my bio-system, I wanted to be well prepared although at the time of meeting with Lucinda originally, I was still needing to prepare my external physical environment to support this next phase.

I could not even begin to describe the value of having someone like Lucinda enter into my life. To work with someone on the bigger picture, who understands the greater games of destiny and human evolution is a blessing. The fact that she also has her cosmic team and is a talented energy worker is another gift. And so for a year I worked intensely realigning basic neurons and electrons and rebalancing my auric field and all levels of my being to support this coming transition for unlike Zinaida with her leap of faith, one of my jobs with this is to create a safe, duplicable model.

The reason for mentioning meeting Lucinda at this juncture is that:
a) There is a lot we can do, and need to do, to prepare our systems for the levels of Freedom I am suggesting here and much of this preparation is already detailed in my book *The Food of Gods* and
b) Using systems like kinesiology provide confirmation as to our readiness to fulfill the freedom agenda plus
c) There is also a lot of help available to us in the physical and non physical worlds; help that will arrive when acknowledged and invited, help that is happy to support our bid for Freedom. I call this help a synchronistic sacred support system.

Synchronistic support systems are those that seem to materialize before us or around us without any effort on our behalf. They arrive because they are needed as if they are somehow predestined to come into play. Sacred Support Systems come as confirmation from the Universal Field of Infinite Intelligence and they are systems that also come into play with synchronicity as they are a system of support that will ensure that we fulfill something that we have agreed to do, something that is not just beneficial for us personally but also globally. We will go into more detail regarding all of this in the "Sensing" chapter.

There are so many modalities for freedom preparation, and for confirmation that we are either ready to begin or are already on the way to achieving these freedoms. These range from Bio-resonance machines that can detect any energy imbalances in any level of our system and then rebalance them vibrationally; to blood analysis systems such as haemaview, to kinesiology and iridology and more. All of these will provide data as to our personal state of readiness to move into such Freedoms and it is important to be well prepared and act responsibly enough so as to avoid potential bio-system damage as we defy the so called "normal" boundaries of human limitation.

I assumed when I wrote my first book in this Freedom series *Living on Light* that anyone drawn to undertaking the journey for such Freedoms would have automatically prepared themselves sensibly and responsibly. Unfortunately I have found that this is not the case and that people often take great risks in their bid for freedom.

The human bio-system is a complex and precious instrument. It is a temple designed to radiate the Divine nature of the One that breathes us, the One who pulses Its Love through our cells and nourishes us enough to gift us life. It is in essence immortal and self sustaining although we no longer give It the recognition It needs to display and reveal these gifts. When we do create a space for our DOW to express Its gifts fully in our life, this is also when we find ourselves experiencing miracles and the type of freedoms already discussed.

One of the gifts that I received from Lucinda was to do with the reality of priority for as she often expressed to me, when she first begins to work with an individual she tunes in and asks their Divine being, what priority is required to first address regarding their current process of healing or growth and change. Priority is about being in alignment with the now moment and also in alignment with where our DOW requires us to be.

How a therapist or support system facilitator works with us is crucial. When I asked Lucinda about this she said: "With sensitivity and with all those energies working with me I'm able to connect with someone who chooses to ask for assistance and together as client and therapist – if we can call it that – we share our potentials for change. With faith I ask my clients and my inner plane associates in life, how can we assist that persons own innate healing mechanism to make positive change so that healing or wisdom technology that that person carries with them forever is triggered and so that they can then take on board what they need, what they desire, and what they can deal with at the time."

Lucinda began our work by explaining also a little more about her methodology. "Basic kinesiology to me means biofeedback which can identify where there may be energetic imbalances creating symptoms physically, emotionally or spiritually. We can then work with the system on all levels and dimensions to identify these challenges that the body is actually containing.

"My system has become an antenna, a bio-electric antennae, when I work with others which in itself is a potentiality for all of us. It's a sensitivity to 'all that is'. It's a connection with 'all that is'. And so working as antennae with someone else I respond to their bio-electric responses and in so doing I'm able to share with them their own expansion and understanding of themselves."

For the last decade or so I have consciously lived by the universal Law of Resonance, the understanding and dynamics of which I have elaborated on in my book *In Resonance*. Hence it makes sense that over this past decade I have attracted to me and have been attracted to people of a like minded frequency – miracle seekers and miracle makers.

It's been fascinating to spend 9 years on the road sharing my research and to also interview every audience to find out what drives and motivates them. While those who are drawn or inspired to spend time with me came from a good cross section of society regarding their professions – from artists and musicians to doctors, lawyers and scientists – they do not represent the typical status quo society regarding their personal interests which are certainly not the 'norm' and even within these groups there is an amazingly diverse spread of interests. Again most of these can be classified as the seekers of miracles or those seeking the tools of the shape-shifting Shaman.

Generally 95% of those who see me are vegetarian, 98% meditate, 60% have committed their lives to service to create a better world, 40% are committed to acting impeccably, 95% intellectually understand they create their own reality. 100% want to exist in a world of peace and prosperity, health and happiness for all and most of these are willing to self responsibly work on their own lives in order to attain it and do so in a way that is good for all – including our planet – Gaia.

While all are interested in health and happiness and feeling fulfilled esoterically, in the realm of Freedom from human limitation, these groups naturally classify themselves further.

    a) Some have always felt that existing purely on prana, or chi, was not only possible for them but a natural state of existence. The personal and global benefits are both obvious and desirable to them. Within this group some feel the desire to not just be free of the need to take food but also of the need to take fluid.

b) Another group – that may also include some from group a), have always been fascinated by physical immortality and love the idea of creating and maintaining a self regenerating system that is free of the need to age or die. Many among this group still love the pleasure of food and fluid and have no interest in no longer taking these things.
c) Then we have the 'Star Trek' dematerialize and rematerialize interest group who find the reality of being able to move their body around the planet, without external physical aides, appealing. Many in this group also see themselves as part of an intelligent universal culture that is not restricted to earth.
d) Another group may be those who Love the idea of being able to healthily go for long periods with minimal sleep, or be able to control their body temperature without the use of external heating or cooling mechanisms or the layering of clothes.

Many see the above things as not miracles but as natural attributes attained in their path of Freedom, for these are the ones who have been pre-programmed to move beyond what many see as normal and acceptable human boundaries.

As 90% of Earth's population is still struggling for survival, the above issues do not rank highly on their agendas, nonetheless these types of Freedoms can bring benefits to all races and socio-economic groups in our world. Working with the Law of Love and allowing it to lure us into Its stream, means that we can also free ourselves from any human suffering – personal and planetary – as gaining a better insight into the dynamics of the Law of Love, will in turn offer us far greater Freedom of choice.

Personally I have been guided to experiment with all categories a) to d) and still continue to do so. When I had experienced my own ability to direct enough prana through my body to successfully feed me and then went public with it, I quickly became amazed at the lack of Love that was displayed by many around me. Firstly, I experienced the annoyance and disbelief that my choice, and discussion of it, triggered in others and the world and secondly, I witnessed the lack of Love that some showed for their own bodies when they attempted to do what I had done. By this lack of Love, I mean lack of self responsibility for:
a) to not have learnt to connect with your body's voice and honor its needs shows lack of this and
b) to push your body into a way of being that it has not been lovingly prepared for, is also irresponsible, hence the need to set in place sacred and synchronistic support systems', the first one being with our DOW.

When I began the next level of preparation which was for me to be not just food free but also fluid free, I decided to not just listen to my own inner guidance regarding this but to also enlist the aide of a body worker to act as a second level, additional confirmation system along the way and also to help prepare me. Although I first sought Lucinda for other reasons, it quickly became obvious that the universe had brought her to me so that we would create a relationship that was beneficial to us both. I knew instinctively that Lucinda's inner plane team of the Medical Assistance Program was destined to help in my physical preparation for this journey.

Again, when you are destined to be with or work with someone, the universal forces make sure that you connect at the right time, so for those of you wishing to prepare yourself lovingly and responsibly for these type of Freedoms, tell the universe:

"Bring to me now the perfect sacred support systems that I need – on the inner and outer planes – to make this transition in joy and safety and with ease."
Also you may wish to add:
"If it is beneficial for me to work with a healer or a kinesiologist to help with this preparation, then bring me the perfect person now and when we meet let us connect DOW to DOW and work in harmony in a mutually beneficial way."

Apart from muscle testing via your body's bio-electric response, there is another very simple way to prove to yourself if you are ready to explore such Freedoms and that is by how the universe responds to you. If you have enough Love flowing through you and around you so that you can do everything telepathically and get beneficial results, then on one level you are ready.

There are two ways of working in this world, one is with physical effort and another one is with no effort, where Grace just reads your bio-system's energy signals and delivers everything you need to support you. For example regarding finding an energy worker teammate like Lucinda, you can look in the phone book or newspaper, ring different ones, meet them and interview them regarding their suitability or you can use the commands mentioned above and meet them via synchronicity and Grace.

I would like to tell a story to elaborate on this a little more deeply for the way the universe responds to you is great proof of your ability to work with and demonstrate the Law of Love.

A year after I moved up to the beach and created my sacred space ashram, my apartment block was sold. The rumor was that the woman buyer wanted to turn the complex into one large private residence and because the rental agency and the selling agency were different, no one seemed to be able to provide us with any further information. As I was due to leave for my month's retreat in Thailand and I was no longer on a lease, I wished to know some sort of time limit as to when I had to vacate the property so that I could find somewhere else and still meet my commitment of going to Thailand. My inner guidance said to make the beach town, where I had enjoyed the past year, a permanent base and to buy my own apartment again. Within a week, the angels had telepathically been given a description of what I wanted and had led me to it, contracts had been signed, finance was in place and I had less than a week to go before I flew to Thailand to be in dark room retreat for a month (which meant no light for reading or signing documents etc).

The only thing missing from this so far Graceful transition was contact with the woman who had bought my existing place and clarification of an exit date and so I asked the universe to bring us together so I could get the answers I needed.

The next day I was guided to walk into a jewelry shop where I intuitively felt to ask the women behind the counter if she had just purchased the particular building in which I have been living. Yes she had.

All of this can be termed synchronicity yet it is just the Law of Love and Its gift of Grace where *those who serve in Love are in turn served by Love.*

When we are in the frequency of Love, Grace supports us in every step of the way and nothing is a problem for us. If this is not your reality then keep practicing the Luscious Lifestyles Program – with its light vegetarian diet – until Grace is your constant companion and then look at the a) to d) type Freedoms. *Especially* do not attempt the group a) type Freedom from food and or fluid until the Law of Love is showering you daily with Its Grace.

Lucinda's presence has helped expedite my preparation and allowed me to work with layers in my fields that were so complex and hidden. For example, after 10 years in the public eye as a spokesperson for the Divine Nutrition Program, I needed to dump from my field "mass reality disbelief energy". This was energy that had been psychically directed at me, as a result of my media exposure, from millions of people whose education has not yet allowed them to entertain the reality of such Freedoms.

I also needed to free myself from a virus type of energy of my own creation that came from my own allowance of behavior of others close to me. This is not something I need to elaborate on here, suffice to say, that a good energy worker/kinesiologist who is destined to work with you in this way, will pick signals from your body and your Divine Self regarding things within you that you need to shift in order to safely and responsibly embrace these levels of Freedom.

In one session with Lucinda my body made it very clear to us that until I released this virus and stopped continuing to create it, there was no way that I could safely exist without water, and to attempt to do so would result in such inner disharmony that I would risk system collapse.

The Law of Love invites us to not just understand the power of Love and Its ability to nourish us, but to apply the Law of Love in the love we share with others and just as importantly, with ourselves; hence the ability to connect with and to listen to the consciousness of our body is imperative. Listening to the body's voice and our inner Divine Self is also not enough. We need to ask the right questions in order for the right answers and guidance to come.

Those who have studied my previous research manuals and or have been with me in my seminars know that I am a great proponent of two things:
a) To never to be dependant for your happiness on anything or anyone outside of yourself – especially not since the greatest Lover/teacher/friend/guide/healer etc that we have already dwells within us and
b) that it is more beneficial to us to look for the good and the God in all, including within us, than to look for what is wrong with us or the world – for what we focus on we feed and hence it grows.

Some may say, then why enter into the sort of arrangement I had with Lucinda?

I was guided to do so for two reasons. Firstly, while I trust my ability to be without food, my body is too precious to eliminate fluid from my diet without having readied my system and substantiated its readiness via the type of "double checking" confirmation process that kinesiology offers.

Secondly, I have seen too many people go through the Living on Light process, without proper preparation, and also met many who have consciously ignored the guidelines I offered in that book. While this is their Freedom of choice and while for many neither has been a problem, for others there have been some negative physical repercussions which may have been avoided had they checked with their body to see if they were prepared enough to take and maintain such a step. To write a Freedom journal such as this and lead people into a realization – via example – that a body can also be fluid free, can bring huge ramifications.

To invite those of you pre-programmed to do this to make sure you receive confirmation that your system can support this choice is simply responsible, to yourself, to me and to the world. You do this by first receiving your own inner voice confirmation which you have learnt to listen to and trust and then additionally by maybe using a well trained kinesiologist to confirm your own intuitive knowing. *(In a future chapter I will discuss the use of preparation tools and also introduce a natural re-hydration system for our body to tap into to support fluid freedom.)*

There is a fine line between genius and madness and billions would say that to attempt to be free from fluid and food is sheer madness. Yet it is only madness when a system is unprepared and unknowledgeable and inexperienced with the Law of Love – not human Love but Divine Love, the Love the Creator of our being has imbued in every cell of our systems. This is a Love that we know when released in all Its glory, brings miracles. And of course to the Shaman shape-shifter this type of journeying with our DOW is a natural part of life, as DOW devotion brings extraordinary things.

THE LAW OF LOVE

SACRED SUPPORT SYSTEMS
Freedom agenda preparation

- ☺ Our DOW – 1st level and most reliable guidance
- ☺ OUTER PLANE 2nd level confirmation from those trusted & trained
- ☺ INNER PLANE – 3rd level support although sometimes our first. Angels, Guides, Holy Help via C.N.N. – the Cosmic Nirvana Network* that are all part of the loving field of universal intelligence.
- ☺ Detoxify internal & external space via honest introspection re the need for change and then via lifestyle and attitude changes.

Inner plane systems are discussed in The Food of Gods

Chapter 8

The Lure of Love

How I just love your smiling face,
The sweet scent of your warm embrace,
Your goodness brings a wave of Grace.

In the Tang Dynasty there was a young 16 year old immortal called Lan Tsai-Ho, an entertainer who loved to wear woman's clothing and make-up while he sang and begged in the streets and gave all his money to the poor. His songs questioned life and its illusionary nature and so this, plus his appearance, branded him a Holy Fool. It is said that in winter Lan slept outdoors in the snow and that steam could be seen rising from his body as he slept, a sign that meant he had mastered the techniques of internal alchemy. Often seen mounted upon an elephant which is the symbol for strength and wisdom, Lan was taught by Lao Tsu and was once seen by an astounded crowd to be mounted on a crane which had descended to collect him amid the sounds of celestial choirs.

Like Lan Tsai-ho I am a fool for Holy Love.

There are sometimes things that we need to do because of pre-agreements that are to be fulfilled – things our soul promises to achieve in this embodiment. There are also things that lure us naturally and pique our interest. Sometimes they are the same – sometimes not. For example, my Freedom journey of achieving the 'no fluids, no food, no ageing' state, is for me something I am predestined to do and I do it as a social experiment, whereas exploring the art of dematerialization, is something I am interested in just for me, just for the fun of it, just because I believe I can and I call it the lure of Love.

I am lured to this experience simply because I Love the idea of it, similarly my molecules are lured by Love to follow my consciousness as it moves from my body to another space in time. Love is the glue that binds our molecules together and Love is what fills the 99.999% space in each atom. Love is what feeds us and Love is what frees us. Demonstrating the power of this Love, demonstrating and experiencing the miracles that this Love can bring is the real lure of my Freedom journey. Ideally it's great when all that we do is motivated by Love.

I have often shared that one of the quickest ways to both remember and re-experience the power of the Love that breathes us and allows us to demonstrate our Divinely sublime higher nature, is out of body night time training. I Love it not only when this happens but also when I wake in the early morning light, my being still bathed in Theta waves as I move back into the Alpha world, with full awareness of learning something that has gripped me with excitement. I Love to learn for the sake of learning and I Love to push out and dissolve my own self imposed – or culturally accepted – limitations. To me both of these add another level of excitement to my life giving me also the treasured gift of enthusiasm for existence. I Love to discover new things about myself and about this world.

Today as I walked my favorite beach at dusk, I witnessed something I had never seen before. A flock of seabirds were flying in such a rhythm of united harmony, that they formed an undulating blanket over the waves, a blanket of violet movement against the pink, sunset sky, a blanket that danced and rose and dove across the ocean to catch and feed on the fish that were being swept in on the afternoon tide. It truly was a magical sight as the unity and harmony of these birds demonstrated the power of one mind working together for a common cause. I didn't know birds fished like that – in groups in such waves of Graceful fluid movement as one mind. I didn't know that their feathers could sparkle with such a violet hue against the sunset sky. I didn't know that a group could bond so harmoniously that they could maintain such a rhythmic pattern of flight. All of it made me smile for I had witnessed something new.

To witness your own being reveal something new about yourself is also miraculous and attention holding and so it is when we explore the gifts that come from being in harmony with the Law of Love. To achieve the types of Freedom I have been discussing, we must also attend to practicalities and one of the first things we need to do is create for ourselves not just a sacred supportive space, which allows us the time and Freedom for this type of exploration, but also a safe space – a space that can nurture us without hindrance.

To me enthusiasm and excitement for existence walk hand in hand with gratitude and appreciation for our existence and all of these feelings are natural states of being when we allow the Love the Divine One Within us – our DOW – has for us, to lure us into Its presence. My very first formal meditation experience was of being bathed in such powerful waves of Divine Love that I immediately became addicted to this Love. Thankfully it is an addiction that frees and nourishes us.

Awhile ago I awoke one morning completely enraptured and still captured by what I call a download from my DOW. I was enthralled to find myself being shown more of the intricate nature of the mechanics of the fields. As I witnessed the power of the mind and how specific programming can alter and manipulate the way energy flows through matter and through us in life, in that semi lucid dream state just before waking I caught the tail end of a DOW training session and imagined that I had written down every detail, capturing the full remembrance of not just a brilliant out of body training session but also writing a brilliantly insightful article about it as well. Unfortunately it was written only in the Akashic Records in the etheric planes, hopefully to be physically captured as words in this book later.

Working with field mechanics, and knowing how different energy fields interact, and choosing to have them interact in a way that benefits all by inviting our DOW to demonstrate Its power, is an art and one that can be easily learnt by the sincere student. It is also a never ending journey that reveals greater levels of subtlety with every step and yet to take these steps without joy or the motivation of Love is like choosing to have no music in life – a rather dull affair.

The reconstruction of a field so that it achieves the Freedom agenda first requires conscious deconstruction of the existing field, hence the ancient sacred science of Feng Shui.

So step 1 in the preparation process of the Freedom game: *Feng Shui your internal and external living space.*

To Feng Shui our internal energy field means to live a lifestyle that allows the inner energy flow to run at maximum capacity completely supporting our Freedom agenda in a way that assures the outcome we desire. After 33 years of conscious research into the perfect lifestyle to achieve this, I was finally able to offer to the world our 8 point Luscious Lifestyle Program – or L.L.P. in brief. A combination of 8 daily lifestyle actions, L.L.P. shape-shifts our internal energy flow in such a way that it also enhances our external energy flow enough to eliminate things like disease, war and violence in our world.

I will not go into great elaboration again here for the L.L.P. program is covered in great detail in my book *Four Body Fitness : Biofields and Bliss* which can be found at http://www.selfempowermentacademy.com.au/htm/cia-education.asp#biofield. Succinctly this lifestyle entails:

- Meditation,
- prayer,
- mind mastery and conscious programming of our internal and external energy fields,
- light vegetarian diet,
- exercise and treating the body as a temple,
- service and acts of kindness and compassion in the world,
- time in silence in the nourishing field of nature and
- the singing of sacred, devotional songs and sacred mantras.

Everyone who combines and utilizes these 8 points finds their life radically changing for the better as their physical, emotional, mental and spiritual fitness levels increase and as their personal energy transmission signals alter and align them to the Freedom channel of Divine Grace.

While LLP resets our internal and external energy flow we can also recalibrate our external energy fields further by taking a close look at our personal living space, our home and community fields. Again we discuss this in detail in the Biofields and Bliss Trilogy but simplistically it may mean first getting rid of clutter and all objects in your home that:

1) are impractical and meaningless, or
2) do not enhance the 'my home is my sacred sanctuary that feeds and nurtures me' idea.

The year 2003 brought tremendous changes for me as I listened to my inner guidance at the end of 2002, and created a safe space to embrace these new levels of Freedom and complete my next initiation. One of the reasons I was guided to move from the city to the beach was that I needed to break a few limiting habits that I had formed in response to city life. Mainly I had allowed myself to become a workaholic as writing and my service work was my preferred way of spending time since city life had little to entice me compared to the lifestyle I can enjoy in a highly charged natural environment like the beach.

I said earlier that I choose to see that every moment in time, every situation that we draw into our field is perfect and it was perfect for me to often work 20 hours a day to launch stage 1 of the Freedom game into the world. Stage 1 is part of Level 3 of the Divine Nutrition Program where my role was to first personally learn to be free from the need to take nourishment from physical food, then to gather and share the research on this with others, then to teach a simple methodology for others to make this journey if and when they too discovered that it is part of their souls' destined pre-agreements. Part of this was also researching via personal experimentation other Freedoms like the ability to stop the ageing process and how to greatly reduce our need for sleep.

For nearly 30 years I have lived in cities experimenting with the challenge of being a yogi in a city cave and learning how to work with my inner and outer energy fields to obtain and maintain peak fitness on all levels. Finally at the end of 2002, it was all done, all complete, all perfect and yet I had formed a few habits in the doing of it all that needed to cease in order for me to move on to the next level.

And so it was that I left the city, and left my family home and moved 100 kilometers north to create my ashram at the beach, a TV-free, food-free space that has gifted me with the physical Freedom of time to once more explore the fields of Love that are generated by DOW power and Its space of Grace.

Freeing ourselves from unnecessary clutter in our lives does not mean walking away from family responsibilities, for there is a natural cycle and time and place for all things to come into being, and we need to hold the intention that everything unfolds with everyone in our lives with joy and ease and Grace and also dignity for all. It is in this basic premise where the Law of Love can deliver Its gift of Freedom. So we must construct these sacred spaces with the win win win reality for all.

In the metaphysical mind field, things are only as limiting as we choose to believe they are. I remember in my early days of yogic practice when I was driven by a desire to be in silence and solitude to explore the inner realms via meditation, how this desire seemed to conflict with my physical reality. In my external world at that time I was a young mother, with two small but active and noisy children, who was literally fighting for survival. Locked in a difficult marriage with extremely limited resources of time or money or the silence and solitude that I longed for, what I failed to recognize was that all of what I had created, I had pre-agreed before embodiment to gift me with specific skills and virtues. All of it, the struggle, the trials and tribulations, all of it was food for my soul.

We become empowered when we stop the blame and judgment game and accept:
a) that the universal fields literally do rearrange themselves to mirror our own consciousness and
b) that we do create it all and that
c) we can recreate it any way we choose by retuning our internal energy flow and that
d) there are great gifts for us through all our trials and nothing is wasted or inconsequential.

When we adopt these types of attitudes, which are based on metaphysical truths, then we can enter into another level of Freedom and allow ourselves to truly Love. To Love our families, to Love ourselves and our choices no matter how crazy they sometimes seem, and to Love the way the universal forces can play with us and to Love exactly where we are right now. To stop and step back and honestly assess who we are, why we are, where we are and what we have created and then to Love it all, is another step in our personal path of Freedom, for with acceptance comes both the joy of letting go and growth.

The Grace of Family, Lovers, Friends:
Thinking about the gifts I have received through my association with Lucinda, led me to think about the gifts that Love shared with others, and family and friends, has provided. I also realized that it is pure Grace that we have the opportunity to share Love with each other at all. To have a body with its seven senses, to have the intelligence to live a life that sensitizes us enough to feel and witness the Law of Love in action, this is a miracle. Life, our breath and the way we can use it to tune us through the fields, these are miracles for they give us the opportunity to express a part of our nature that knows only Love and limitless freedom.

To stop and stand still and assess our life and to feel sincere gratitude for all the people we have encountered who have helped to mould us t be as we are now, is another necessary step on the road to freedom. Without this type of recognition and gratitude for it all, we can find ourselves stuck and unable to move on. Gratitude and acceptance sometimes require forgiveness and recognition of the roles all have played so that the learning and the gifts that this interaction has brought can be appreciated and healing can occur via a shift in perspective.

A Shaman knows that all interaction with all life occurs due to the Grace of the Law of Love and the freedom that comes when we recognize this can be awe inspiring. I do not wish to digress into the mind field of emotional healing suffice to say that freedom takers and miracle makers run via the game of self responsibility, a game where we recognize that all is self created and hence there are no victims, no one to blame and that all is just the flow of fields interacting and that the way fields interact can be changed just by changing our perception. Hence the attitude of gratitude is a wonderful place to begin to shape-shift into a freedom life.

So take a moment, look at everyone in your life and focus on the insights and the gifts that they have given you. Appreciate their role and their influence in your life and then make the commitment to be in resonance with the Law of Love and to experience its freedoms.

The Love our DOW has for us is what lures us on in evolution. Its sweet inner voice lures us to explore our potential, Its Love lures us to let go of our limitations and Its Love lures us to demonstrate who we really are. Not our ego based nature but our Divine nature with all Its gifts and Freedoms.

Nearly everyone I know and meet in my travels is curious about their destiny and the things they agreed pre-embodiment to achieve this life. Reading a book like *Destiny of Souls* by Michael Newton is a wonderful source of insight for between life times, yet all of us need the personal data. Just what did we agree to do and how do we find this out? The best answer comes from our DOW. This data is stored in the cells of our body and can be released when we ask with sincerity and when it is our time to know.

Your DOW knows what your pre-agreements are – for example:
1) if you have pre-agreed to be able to shape-shift your internal energy fields in a way that allows you to be free from the need to take physical food
2) if you have pre-agreed to be able to shape-shift your internal energy fields in a way that allows you to be free from the need to take fluid
3) if you have pre-agreed to be able to shape-shift your internal energy fields in a way that allows you to be free from the need to age or create dis-ease or if you are blueprinted to create physical immortality this life
4) if you have pre-agreed to be able to shape-shift your internal energy fields in a way that allows you to master the art of dematerialization and rematerialization this life.

In meditation you can also ask your DOW if it is part of your blueprint to be a harmonizing soul. A harmonizing soul is a being who has agreed to do two things:
a) harmonize their own internal energy flow enough to experience the benefits of the stream of constant Grace and miracles that flow when we are harmonized with the Law of Love and
b) to then allow our harmonized presence to harmonize the energy fields of the world through which we move.

In Part 2 of this manual we will provide an exercise to find the answers to the above.

I would like to say that I understood fully, all the forces now guiding and also supporting me as I continue with this journey – but I don't – at least not on a conscious level.

- I do know that everything is interconnected and that our human species will keep evolving in a manner that some may see as miraculous.
- I know that we have the power of free will and the power of choice.
- I know that as individuals and as a group collective we have the power to create any type of personal and planetary realities we desire.
- I know that changing the operation of a household, community or planetary system is as basic as changing the consciousness of those who dwell within these systems.
- I know that there is no need for suffering on our planet any more.
- I know that we have all the wisdom and tools and help at our disposal to transform it all.
- I know we can exist and do exist in a world of great love where miracles, magic and Grace and joy can – if we let them – be our constant companions.
- I know these things to be my truth – not just intellectually but also experientially.
- I know that this past year living in this highly charged prana beach environment and the letting go of my workaholic patterns, has been exactly what I needed to do for it has gifted me with the evidence of the benefits of self love and self nurturing. The fact that I still managed to travel for 5 months of that year, write 2 new books and still be actively involved in the C.I.A. (Cosmic Internet Academy) and do it all supported by a river of Grace where suddenly once again it was effortless, added another level of proof to me personally regarding the rewards and bliss that come when we listen to our DOW and follow its guidance.
- I know that I am now ready to take another step.

THE LAW OF LOVE – summary

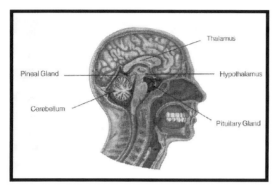

BRAIN WAVE PATTERNS

The amplitude or height of the wave indicates the total number of neurons at work, coalescing on a problem or feeling at any given time. The frequency of the wave is the dominant frequency or pulsing of the brain in each of the areas studied, it tells us basically, "How fast the engine is running?"

BETA : Beta 1 - 13 to 20; Beta 2 - 20 to 40 cps
Fully awake, alert, excited, tense. Speedy, not 'centered'. Field of mass consciousness.

ALPHA : 8 - 13 cps - cycles per second
Deeply relaxed, passive but aware, composed, state of waking and just before sleep. Perfect programming time. Early meditative state, entry pattern in higher consciousness. Integrated hemispheric brain function. Subconscious mind/brain function.

THETA : 4 - 7 cps
Deeper meditation. Drowsy, waking dream state. Associated with feeling states. Gateway to learning & memory. Increased state of creativity & intuition. Subliminal conscious states - ESP, channeling, insight, profound understanding.

DELTA : 0.5 to 3 cps
Slow wave pattern & signature frequency of the brainstem. Deep sleep state. Ultimate reality - 'beyond mind' meditation. Delta range frequencies trigger healing & rejuvenation. Gateway to 'satori' or enlightenment & quantum consciousness.

We consider these brainwave frequency patterns as indices of levels of consciousness. Delta is first line (the signature frequency of the brainstem); Theta is characteristic of the feeling or second-line limbic level; and Alpha is third-line cortical level.

When the brain is excessively busy, thinking and scheming, obsessing or preoccupied with delusions, then there may be Beta-1 and Beta-2 activity. Beta-2 betrays a racing mind, the kind that occurs at night when we worry and can't fall asleep. When the brain is focused, it tends to be synchronized, all parts working in close harmony. It tends to build amplitude as electrical potentials from each neuron summate. The whirling dance of the Sufis promotes brain wave coherence and allows the brain to vibrate in harmony.

Chapter 9

The Harmonious Heart

To live beyond death in a place,
Consisting of magic and Grace,
Means changing, to the open space.

And so in my new sacred space environment, my research continued and led me to discover the power of the harmonious heart. One of the gifts of my beach move was that my eldest daughter joined me finally choosing to live ten minutes drive away, she had come home after seven years on the road and had fallen in love with a sweet local man who carried the aboriginal dreamtime in his blood.

One day as we strolled along our favorite beach enjoying another magical sunset she said to me? "Do you feel the need for more friends here?"

I explained that I had come to the beach for solitude and silence and that my interest in quality company was fulfilled when I spent time with a brilliant group of friends as I traveled through Europe twice a year and through family sharings. Yet at the same time I valued her comment and deciding not to limit myself said to the universe: "If I could benefit by having friends here now that I am finally back in Australia with some time to share, then please if appropriate send the perfect ones."

The very next day, a wonderful woman who I had met 12 years before and shared the 21 day process experience with, arrived literally at my door. The whole meeting was incredibly well timed and fortuitous. Over weekly coffees and catch ups at the beach we have shared great insights with each other that have added another level of support to both our journeys.

One of the gifts that she brought me was data from the HeartMath Institute which has discovered that when our heartbeat is harmonious, we enjoy health on all levels – physical, emotional, mental and spiritual. To me how harmonious our heart beat is depends on how powerfully our DOW can radiate through it.

We know that our DOW anchors itself in our heart chakra and then spreads Its rays out from the inner planes into our physical world, weaving Itself through our organs, light-body, meridians, bloodlines, skeleton and whole bio-system to support our system into a continuous stream of life. We know that the more powerfully it can radiate through us the healthier we are just as we know that when our DOW withdraws its rays our physical system can no longer exist.

We also know that the more powerfully our DOW can harmoniously radiate itself through our heart and our physical system and into our world, the more Grace we will experience and the more miracles. Achieving harmonious radiation levels of DOW power requires clear focus, will and intention, and we know that one way to increase our DOWs' radiation through us and into our world is the Love Breath Meditation (http://www.selfempowermentacademy.com.au/htm/cia-education.asp#audio) as taught in the manual *The Food of Gods*.

We also know that a harmonious heart has a huge influence in tuning us to the fields of freedom.

The more I focused on my own heart, on what was real and meaningful for me in this time of transition, the more I acted in a way that brought DOW smiles, the happier I became and the more Grace that began to flow again in my life. It was as if Grace is always with us but sometimes we are just off dial, there is too much static to get the clear signals.

It soon became so obvious to me that a true devotee of the DOW dwells where the DOW dwells and is anchored. In the teachings of the Tao, the ancients agree that the Divine essence anchors itself in our heart center from where, they say, it radiates into the various organs where each energy beam takes up residence as a spirit with virtues that the Taoists see resembling the virtues of certain animals. For example, if the kidneys store the unresolved emotion of fear and the opposite beneficial emotion to fear is calm, then the animal that to the Taoists is the calmest and gentlest, is the deer. To them the calmest colour is the colour of water which is blue and later we'll talk more about using animal virtues and colour to rebalance all the organs into health.

For the heart, an organ that holds the emotion of arrogance, the opposite emotion for the Taoists is compassion, hence for the rebalancing of a person or culture that is arrogant, the system needs to be inspired to be more compassionate. Being compassionate floods the heart with this emotion and changes its frequency field which, via the process of entrainment that we will soon discuss, brings all the organs into a state of harmony.

In his book *Cosmic Inner Smile* Mantak Chia states "Compassion is the highest expression of human emotion and virtuous energy. It is a level of development that takes hard work and serious meditation before it can blossom into one's life. It is not a single virtue, but the distillation and culmination of all virtues, expressed at any given moment as a blend of fairness, kindness, gentleness, honesty, respect, courage and love. It is the most beneficial energy to share with others. The power to express any or all of these virtues at the appropriate moment indicates that a person has internally unified him or herself into a state of compassion."

The human heart is the vehicle for the DOW to pulse its essence through and I realized as I downloaded the Law of Love data that the human heart beat is the key to harmony in our world. When a human heart beat is in harmony so is our world and the quickest way to harmonize the human heart beat is to focus on gratitude and compassion.

Scientifically and morally rebalancing the human heart beat is the key to all our freedoms – scientifically because of the idea of entrainment and morally because **how we choose to feel, then act now, determines our tomorrow.**

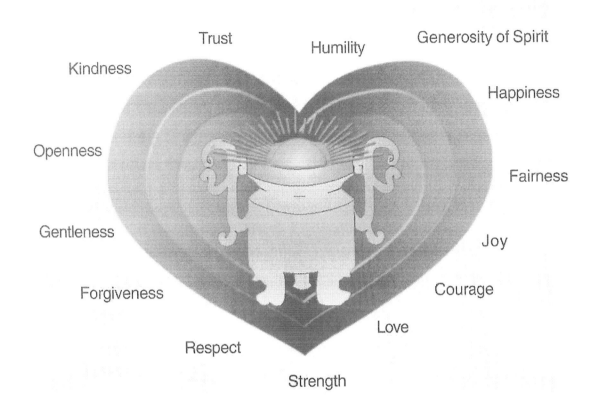

So let's address the science that supports this, what the Institute for HeartMath calls: "the intuitive intelligence resource of the heart." Below we will also share more data re our physical heart and its electromagnetic pulses and its harmony key.

The HeartMath Solution
In the book *The HeartMath Solution*, authors Doc Childre and Howard Martin explain how the electromagnetic fields radiating from the heart affect the fields around us, they also show us how to move into sensing life with the intuitive nature of our heart's brain rather than operating only from cranium's brain of limited linear thinking.

The HeartMath system – HMS – offers a model for efficient living in our world. Beyond what they have been able to prove by researching the fields of neuroscience, cardiology, psychology, physiology, biochemistry, bioelectricity and physics; the Institute for HeartMath – IHM – holds the theory that "the heart links us to a higher intelligence through an intuitive domain where spirit and humanness merge."

They say that "Heart intelligence is the intelligent flow of awareness and insight that we experience once the mind and the emotions are bought into balance and coherence through a self initiated process. This form of intelligence is experienced as direct intuitive knowing that manifests in thoughts and emotions that are beneficial for our selves and for others."(page 6 of HMS)

What has this got to do with the Law of Love? Simply this – our DOW is the purest expression of the Law of Love in existence and our DOW uses Its heart intelligence to communicate with us. Consequently I am guided to offer in this chapter some tried and true tools that work and that have been scientifically tested after being developed by the IHM, so that we can improve how our DOW communicates with us and so that we can understand and work more powerfully with the Law of Love. Hopefully from this we will all be able to make the sort of decisions that will allow for a greater expression of the Law of Love in our world.

So let's look at some facts and then a beneficial HeartMath tool.

Institute of HeartMath Research on the physical heart:
- ♥ The physical heart beats one hundred thousand times a day or approx. 40 million times per year or 3 billion pulsations over a seventy year period.
- ♥ It pumps two gallons of blood per minute or 100 gallons per hour through a vascular system that is two times the circumference of the earth.
- ♥ The heart starts beating in an unborn fetus before the brain is formed.
- ♥ The heart has its own independent nervous system that is called "the brain in the heart".
- ♥ There are at least forty thousand neurons – nerve cells in the heart and these relay information back and forth to the brain in the cranium to allow for a two way communication between our heart and brain, although the heart beats independently of its connection with the cranium brain.
- ♥ Research by Joel and Beatrice Lacey at the Fels Research Institute in the 1970's found that when the cranium brain sent signals to the heart through the nervous system, our heart didn't automatically obey. The hearts response depended on the nature of the task and the type of mental processing it required. However the brain obeys all messages and instructions sent to it by the heart, messages that could influence a person's behavior.
- ♥ The Fels Institute found that the heart beat is not just a mechanical throb but a system of intelligent language that influences our perception and reactions. Other researchers have found that the hearts rhythmic beating triggers neural impulses that influence the higher brain centers that govern emotional processing.
- ♥ Research at the IHM has also found that negative emotions disrupt the heart's rhythms so that they become jagged and disordered. They found that positive emotions produce smooth harmonious heart rhythms which in turn increase a person's mental clarity, intuition and ability to perceive the world more clearly as well as enhancing their communication with others.
- ♥ Being able to sustain balanced and harmonious heart rhythms allows a person to sustain a positive life perspective and intuitive flow and to access positive emotions at will.
- ♥ When our heart rhythm becomes balanced and coherent, every organ of the body is flooded with neural and biochemical events that improve their functioning and health e.g. experiencing compassion boosts our levels of IgA, a secretory antibody that improves our immune systems resistance to disease.
- ♥ ***The electromagnetic field of the heart is approximately 5000 times greater in strength than the electromagnetic field produced by the brain.*** It not only

- permeates every cell of our body but is powerful enough to radiate out into the field around us a radiation that can be measured by magnetometers.
- ♥ Gary Schwaltz and his colleagues at the University of Arizona found that there is a direct interaction of energy flow between the heart and the brain via their electromagnetic fields.
- ♥ "Because the heart is the strongest biological oscillator in the human system, the rest of the body's systems are pulled into entrainment with the hearts rhythms." (page 46 HMS)
- ♥ The quickest way to harmonize human heart rhythms is to focus on what the IHM call core heart feelings such as love and compassion.
- ♥ Increasing head/heart coherence requires reducing emotional and mental stress by monitoring and mastering our thoughts and feelings. The more we do this the more powerfully our DOW can radiate Itself through the higher heart and magnetize more Grace to our field.
- ♥ The difference between heart and head intelligence is that the heart is open to intuitive solutions and the head is open to linear and logical solutions. When they work together we again have more choices in life and a clearer vision of how to fulfill our dreams. Coherence between the head and heart also allows us to operate more effectively through all fields of life – a fact that the IHM has tested repeatedly.

While we can be the master of our mind and learn to work in a positive way with both our perceptions and our emotions, we cannot be the master of our heart, only its partner, yet accessing our heart's intelligence or its codes allows us to live life in full mastery.

According to research at the IHM "our feelings affect the information contained in the heart's electromagnetic signals" (page 59 HMS) and spectral analysis has revealed that when the heart's rhythms become more coherent and ordered then so does its electromagnetic field emanations, emanations that they have also found *can influence other peoples' brain wave patterns.* Spectral analysis can determine the mix of frequencies present in a field i.e. an electromagnetic fields ingredients.

Emotions such as appreciation and compassion create heart coherence just as anger and frustration create incoherence, consequently as we alter our perceptions in life, we alter our emotional flow which in turn alters our physical heart rhythms and allows us to alter our internal and external radiation levels.

Choosing to see the perfection of each situation, choosing to see the Divine spark in all, choosing to enjoy the fullness and simplicity of each moment, all of this alters our heart rhythm and our rhythm in our world and the type of rhythms that return to surround us and move through us.

Research at the IHM has found that "when a system is coherent, virtually no energy is wasted, because its component parts are operating in sync." (page 63 HMS)

I do not wish to digress here into the benefits of applying EQ – emotional intelligence which is the type of intelligence that the marriage of head/heart brings in our lives – as there are already many books on this. I recommend that if you wish to learn to listen more to the voice of your heart in a way that also honors the voice of your mind, that you read and apply the tools in the *HeartMath Solution*. http://www.heartmath.org/

My point in this chapter is firstly that in metaphysical circles we focus a lot on our heart chakra whose rhythm affects our physical heart, yet our physical heart also has very particular rhythms that can be measured and altered to our advantage, as per the IHM research. The idea that the electromagnetic field of our heart is 5000 times stronger than that of our head is a great fact to support the work that many are now doing re the "Love/Wisdom Radiation" game as discussed in detail in *The Food of Gods*.

The IHM has also found that our breathing patterns can regulate our heart rhythms so the love breath tool is again another powerful way to bring our being into coherence and balance as according to IHM research when people breathe through the heart entrained rhythms occur naturally and can thus be sustained for long periods of time. Using the physical heart rhythms to entrain – or synchronize – our biological, emotional and mental fields is a wonderful way to eliminate stress on all levels and to naturally increase longevity and free us from dis-ease.

Not only can we consciously alter our brain wave patterns as we discussed in detail in *The Food of Gods* but we can consciously alter our heart wave patterns. When we do both consciously the fields within and around us alter again via the game of entrainment or sympathetic resonance. **The Law of Love cannot function successfully in our lives without the synchronization of both our head and our heart rhythms.**

Emotional Energy – the Economy of Equilibrium:

Emotion literally means energy in motion and applying the Luscious Lifestyles Program and the type of tools in the *HeartMath Solution* book, allows us to economize our emotional energy output by bringing our mental and emotional fields into a state of equilibrium where we are the master of our emotions rather than our emotions being the master of us. In other words we operate more effectively in life and no longer deplete ourselves energetically. Maintaining equilibrium via the above practices means we maintain physical health which is altered by our mental and emotional states.

Asking ourselves if our daily energy expenditures are productive or counterproductive and then changing those thoughts, words and actions that deplete us, is another simple way of economizing our energy reserves allowing us to eliminate limiting or self defeating behavior. This is the same as being aware of the mathematics of percentages re how we spend our clock time.

Training ourselves to walk through life in a state of deep appreciation is another way to economize our energy reserves and feed ourselves what the IHM calls quantum nutrients. The IHM calls quantum nutrients core heart feelings or heart power tools – appreciation, non-judgment, patience, courage, forgiveness and compassion are all emotions of the higher heart, emotions that flow through us due to DOW Love.

As I read the *HeartMath Solution* book I had the deep insight that if all we do in life is train ourselves to perceive our life in a way that makes us appreciate it, if all we do is walk through life in a state of sincere appreciation, then our internal and external energy fields will shift dramatically. Together with the attitude of gratitude true appreciation will alter our heart rhythms and its electromagnetic field pulses and hence our experience of life.

Hence this became my focus throughout 2003.

It is easy to love others yet loving and really caring for ourselves is sometimes another matter and studies at the IHM have revealed some interesting facts. For some people loving ourselves means choosing perceptions and hence triggering feelings that create harmony and health. I never knew that indulging in 5 minutes of anger can take the body's immune system over 6 hours to recover from, a fact measurable by our IgA levels. I didn't know that if we spend 5 minutes focused on sincere compassion that IgA levels increased immediately by 41% and continued to rise for up to 6 hours afterwards. (IgA protects us from invading pathogens.)

Hence for those pre-programmed for physical immortality and to be free from all disease, effective management of our emotions is a must. We need to care but not overcare as overcare can create discordant heart rhythms as easily as lack of care by draining our emotional reserves. As the HMS book covers all of this in detail I will not elaborate here although I would like to share a little of what the IHM calls their Heart Lock-In tool as it is a quick way to "strengthen the communication link between your heart and brain and sustain entrainment and coherence for longer periods. Doing Lock-Ins regularly builds your heart power to keep your nervous, immune, and hormonal systems in balance." (page 219 HMS)

MEDITATION 1: The Heart Lock-In (as per page 213 – with some additions)
- ♥ Find a quiet place, close your eyes and breathe deeply.
- ♥ Focus your attention in the heart area and then do the love breath meditation until you feel centered and still.
- ♥ Scan your memories until you find one where you felt a lot of love, or focus on someone who is easy for you to love, or focus on something positive in your life, a person or situation that you really appreciate. Feel these feelings for at least 5 to 15 minutes. You may wish to use nostalgic music or sacred music to help you to trigger these emotions.
- ♥ Next send these feelings of love and/or appreciation from your heart into your body or radiate these feelings out to others.
- ♥ If your mind wanders bring it back to the heart with the love breath meditation or by recalling the memory and feelings again.
- ♥ To complete this exercise be aware of any intuitive thoughts or feelings that came to you and then write these down so that you can act on them later.
- ♥ Additionally you may wish to ask your DOW – as your heart is now open and loving – if there is anything else you need to know right now. Trust what comes, write it down and act on it.

As we have shared before, when we calibrate our heart rhythms to the beat of pure unconditional love, we set the stage for receiving greater intuitive guidance.

The above tool is a wonderful way for us to release and gather sincere feelings of love to then direct and radiate out to others or to our world where there is need. Remember that the electromagnetic field of our heart is 5000 times stronger than the electromagnetic field of our brain so positive feelings have a more powerful effect on the fields than positive thoughts and when we combine the two then another level of power kicks in again.

The Heart Lock-In tool is also a way to send the healing energy of love to regenerate our bodies and recharge our batteries if we are feeling a little drained. By taping into and drawing from our own emotional memory pool we can access this type of healing power quickly and at will.

Research that followed up a 35 year study on the mastery of stress at Harvard University has shown that "adults who didn't feel loved as children suffer from a much higher rate of disease than those who experienced love. What this means is that love is a requirement, not an option, for a healthy life." Hence the more we can stimulate the flow of love through our being, the healthier we will become; not just physically but emotionally, mentally and spiritually as well.

If the heart has its own intelligence which is, I believe, the voice of our DOW, then learning to distinguish and to listen to its call and applying its messages in a loving way will bring us great freedom in life, freedom from limitation of cultural and religious conditioning, and freedom from arrogance, ignorance and our fears.

I stated in the earlier part of this chapter that the human heart beat is the key to harmonizing our world and utilizing the Heart Harmony exercise, in The Pure Land chapter, is another practical aide to this journey.

As the heart is the strongest biological oscillator in the human system then by the act of entrainment, we know that when we bring the heart into harmony by focusing on compassion and love, that this then brings all of our organs into a state of harmonious functioning where they can be fed by the food of love. The food of love is the food of the harmonious heart and the harmonious heart is the natural rhythm of our DOW.

THE LAW OF LOVE – summary

☺ **Heart Harmony**
☺ **Entrainment**
☺ **Radiation**
☺ **DOW Doorway**
☺ **Love Breath**
☺ **Harmony Code**

**Honoring our E.Q. – COMPASSIONATELY
CO-CREATING A HEALTHY & HAPPY FUTURE**

- ♥ "Because the heart is the strongest biological oscillator in the human system, the rest of the body's systems are pulled into entrainment with the hearts rhythms."
- ♥ The quickest way to harmonize human heart rhythms is to focus on what the IHM call core heart feelings such as love and compassion.
- ♥ Increasing head/heart coherence requires reducing emotional and mental stress by monitoring and mastering our thoughts and feelings. The more we do this the more powerfully our DOW can radiate Itself through the higher heart and magnetize more Grace to our field.
- ♥ The difference between heart and head intelligence is that the heart is open to intuitive solutions and the head is open to linear and logical solutions. When they work together we again have more choices in life and a clearer vision of how to fulfill our dreams. Coherence between the head and heart also allows us to operate more effectively through all fields of life.
- ♥ The electromagnetic field of the heart is 5,000 times stronger than the mind.

Chapter 10

BEING
The Freedom of Now

*It's the path to divinity,
Returning to infinity,
Use refined will's agility.*

I have found in my life at the beach that there is not just a heart rhythm that I can harmoniously hook into but also a rhythm of time or perhaps timelessness.

Setting the intention that I achieve everything that I was to do in a perfect harmonious flow, I would find myself creating and chanting new powerful mantras as I walked along the beach each day.

Sometimes all the mental chatter would fade away and I would find myself moving through etheric doorways into worlds that seemed to exist in a timeless vacuum. As my breathing rhythm adjusted to my DOWs heart space, I became the watcher and observer and could hear myself chant: "Perfect life, perfect love, perfect paradise" and it was as if the mantra would draw me in and anchor me into a reality of perfection where all life was love and all was paradise.

Once again it was perfect to find that what I was becoming absorbed by – the perfection of each now moment – had been the subject of another well known book that soon came into my hands – *The Power of Now*.

Freedom from the constraints of time, freedom from living in the past or in the future, plus the freedom to not be bound in a realm where we limit our expression by adhering to man made time – all of these freedoms come paradoxically via how we choose to spend our time.

There are a few discussions here.

Firstly many great yogi masters talk about the power to be in the now, the gift of freedom that comes when we allow ourselves to fully be present in each now moment. They say that only when we are fully present in the now moment can our pure essence, our Divine inner being, fully express itself through us without mental or emotional constriction. Yet the mind does not like to live in the present for it gains its sense of self and aliveness from encouraging us to live in the past or to live in the future. When we are living fully in each present moment, the mind has no room for growth, yet in order to gain the freedoms that we are seeking in this manual, we need to encourage the expansion and expression of our DOW, rather than the one who provides the mechanisms for us to think and analyze and trigger feelings from its perceptions.

Conversely, as we discussed in great detail in *The Food of Gods*, in order to expand the power and expression of our DOW, we need to be very conscious of how we spend our time for how we spend our time determines our frequency or personal keynote, which in turn determines the type of energies we can release from within us and attract around us.

However performing an action that fills a period of time is one thing. What our mind is focused on when we are performing that action is another. For example, we can 'spend time' each day exercising to create a strong and flexible physical body. During that hour of yoga or weight-lifting or beach walking we can be thinking of chores we need to do, or a conversation we have had with someone or we can be using the mind in a very focused way that will expand our Being, deepen our experience of the Divine Presence within.

I like to use the mantra "I am healthy, I am Holy, I am in harmony with all" as I exercise each day. This works particularly well as I enjoy a deep connected breathing rhythm where I absorb pure prana as I beach walk. The mantra sets a rhythm for my mind to send out a very particular signal of reality and belief to the intelligent quantum field around me and creates a very particular physical rhythm as I walk. In this way the mind is focused, the body is focused and by being conscious of my breath I can disassociate from it all, become the watcher and be totally present in the field of energy within me and around me and be free.

Freedom is an attitude of mind and freedom also comes when we learn to disassociate ourselves from the belief that we are our mind. This is a reality that we covered in great detail in my book *In Resonance* and is a reality that is covered beautifully in the book by Eckhardt Tolle, *The Power of Now*.

Throughout this book Eckhardt Tolle talks about the need to unhook ourselves from being the slave to our mind and its false reality of self that is ego driven, to no longer identify with the mind and become instead the watcher of our mind and the way our thoughts trigger emotions and how great freedom comes from this.

What I call our DOW, Eckhardt calls our Being. He says:

"Being is the eternal, ever-present One Life beyond the myriad forms of life that are subject to birth and death. However, Being is not only beyond but also deep within every form as its innermost invisible and indestructible essence. This means that it is accessible to you now as your own deepest self, your true nature. But don't seek to grasp it with your mind. Don't try to understand it. You can know it only when the mind is still, when you are present, fully and intensely in the Now … To regain awareness of Being and to abide in that state of 'feeling-realization' is enlightenment."

As we shared in *The Food of Gods*, enlightenment is a never ending process as we are always able to expand our capacity to attract, hold and radiate light and love and wisdom. Hence it is a journey not a destination. Similarly freedom is a journey not a destination, for the more we manifest the Law of Love, the more freedoms it reveals.

In the realm of our DOW, in the Presence of our Being, there is no time, there is no action, there is no freedom for all is One and all just is. There is no past, no future, and as

Eckhardt says, time is just an illusion and "the more you are focused on time – past and future – the more you miss the Now, the most precious thing there is: Why is it the most precious thing? Firstly, because it is the *only* thing. It's all there is. The eternal present is the space within which your whole life unfolds, the one factor that remains constant. Life is now. There was never a time when your life was *not* now, nor will there ever be. Secondly, the Now is the only point that can take you beyond the limited confines of the mind. It is your only point of access into the timeless and formless realm of Being."

Focusing our mind and awareness fully in the now moment as we perform each action in life, actions that also when measured fulfill units of time, is one of the most powerful ways we have to move beyond the constraints of time and feel freedom from it – in this state we find that time is elastic and can be expanded at will for in the role of the watcher, where our actions have opened the doors to the Divine flow of pure essence through the worlds, physical laws marry with metaphysical and a new world is revealed.

On page 46 of his book Eckhardt goes on to say:

"Identification with the mind gives it more energy; observation of the mind withdraws energy from it. Identification with the mind creates more time; observation of the mind opens up the dimension of the timeless. The energy that is withdrawn from the mind turns into presence. Once you can feel what it means to be present, it becomes much easier to simply choose to step out of the time dimension whenever time is not needed for practical purposes and move more deeply into the Now. This does not impair your ability to use time – past or future – when you need to refer to it for practical matters. Nor does it impair your ability to use your mind. In fact, it enhances it. When you do use your mind, it will be sharper, more focused."

Eckhardt calls using time for practical actions "clock time" and the time we spend mentally living in the past or future he calls "psychological time". Spending clock time on the Luscious Lifestyles Program (as referred to earlier and in the *Four Body Fitness: Biofields and Bliss* manual) expands our consciousness so we are free from psychological time and can be fully focused on, merged with, enjoying and operating from our Divine essence – our DOW.

Freedom is here right now. It is not a future reality. Right here right now we have the freedom of choice, the freedom to decide how to spend our "clock time". The freedom to decide if we wish to indulge in psychological time of living in the past or the future and aligning with our mental perceptions of life or instead choosing to be bathed in the Presence of the one who breathes us and loves us and gives us life and all its limitless gifts.

I remember many years ago when I was consumed one day with worry about how I was going to be able to pay the bills that were soon due. As I sat in my car in a state of deep concern that led me to say a prayer for help, I heard a voice say:

"Right here, right now, do you have all that you need?"

I thought for a moment and replied: "Yes."

The voice then said: "Have you every truly lacked for anything?"

Again I thought for a few moments and realized that all my needs had always been provided for, that my children and I somehow always had a warm bed and clothing and the food and shelter we needed, that somehow everything was always taken care of, maybe not in the way I wanted but always in the way that I needed.

And the voice said: "Then relax, be in the moment, enjoy your now."

And I realized that if I wanted to avoid worry or anxiety all I needed to do was to be fully present in each moment, attend as well as I could to the practical realities of life and trust that as had always been the case, yes I had been, and yes I would continue to be, provided for by the loving fields of life.

With this realization a wonderful feeling of peace seemed to blossom from somewhere deep within me, a peace that stayed with me for quite sometime and when I found myself beginning to worry or be anxious that same voice within me quietly reminded me to "Be here now" to be fully conscious in the present and to give thanks for always having been provided for.

Bringing this understanding deeper into our body so that it engulfs not just our mind and our emotional realm of trust, but so that it emanates as a truth from every cell, is another step again, a step that comes from the daily training of our attitude and perception.

One of the greatest gifts that constant travel can give is exactly this type of training – the training to be fully present in each moment, to enjoy exactly where we are right here, right now. For years I have sat in airports sometimes waiting for up to 8 hours for a connecting flight, or waiting in endless lines to clear customs, or traveling on trains across continents, or in traffic jams in taxis on my way to events to share our research. The list of 'patient waiting' goes on providing an incredible training ground to dive into each now moment and be fully present.

In those situations living in the past or the future realms of 'if only's', particularly the 'if only I was somewhere else right now' reality, is such an obvious waste of time, as to indulge in this type of 'if only' thought process only elicits emotions that rob us of valuable energy. Instead I now settle in, read a book, take the time to do some programming with specific mantras, meditate (often with eyes open) and dive deep into the Theta-Delta realms, or I may just choose to listen to devotional or sacred music on my iPod and/or be the watcher in the now.

The energy effect of this type of constant training is amazing and so rewarding and stays with us so that we can maintain this through all of our clock time. It provides the ability to be fully 'in-joy' in each moment no matter what we are doing, for here judgment is suspended, and appreciation for both the action we are indulging in physically and the mental and emotional space we are choosing to maintain, adds another layer to it all.

Eckhardt Tolle says: "The quality of your consciousness at this moment is what shapes your future … If it is the quality of your consciousness at this moment that determines the future, then what is it that determines the quality of your consciousness? Your degree of Presence."

Again how much we are aligned with and aware of our DOWs Presence in each moment, is the one factor that determines our freedom to recognize, enjoy and create more miracles in our life. Freeing our mind from time-bound realities, freeing our mind from limited beliefs, freeing our physical body from limiting mental and emotional behavioral patterns – all of this is a choice we make in the now.

The Law of Love & Its Fabulous Frequency of Freedom
with Jasmuheen

Being fully present in each moment as you perform each action means loving what you are doing, appreciating and enjoying the actions and how you are choosing to spend your time. This may mean maintaining an awareness of why you are doing, while not being so goal/outcome orientated that you are living in the future again and not enjoying this moments step of the journey. Even the most mundane thing life sweeping the garden path can be done with such a now moment awareness that it becomes a Zen like action of dignity, joy and Grace.

To choose this type of focus brings freedom, for an alternative attitude to the action may be annoyance of the trees always shedding leaves and messing up the path with debris, an annoyance that then releases a feeling of reluctance or impatience at having to sweep the path yet again when you really could be doing "better thing's with your time." When we release this old attitude, surrender into the now moment, standing on the path, with the broom, breathing in deeply, smelling the garden smells, feeling the breeze and the sounds of the trees swaying in it, hearing the birds and being fully conscious of the miracle of that moment, then we feel connected again to all, part of all, one with all, appreciative of how it all harmonizes. Then, again, we feel free.

Applying consciousness and care and consideration to all that we do opens us up to a new realm of being where the universal forces in turn treat us the same in response. This is all a simple example of the Law of Love.

Whether we apply this to Level 2* Freedom of enjoying health and happiness, peace and prosperity or to Level 3* Freedom from human limitation, is simply again a matter of choice.

Regardless, this type of attitude opens us up to the simple joy that comes from Being totally in tune with our DOW, open, aware, enjoying its gifts and its wisdom and love.

So it is and so it always will be.

*As discussed in *The Food of Gods*.

Chapter 11

Fiddling the Fields
To Tweak or not to Tweak? That is the Question ...

Enhance skill in field finessing,
Outcomes certain, without guessing,
Truth requires ego's undressing.

I love the word Tweak as it brings a whole new level of reality compared to the word Fiddle. I'm a little consumed with field fiddling at the moment as I have nearly completed a fun science fiction type novel called *Fiddlers of the Fields*, a book that downloaded itself with joy and ease and Grace. It feels like I can't remember writing it as downloads are things you seem to just open up to and receive. When we apply the data in the miracle making chapter, everything seems to occur so much more easily in our lives.

It feels to me at times that I have spent so much time in training and being different and disciplined so that I could fiddle the energy fields within me and around me more consciously and effectively. For many of us, there seems to be something driving us on, inspiring us to grow and expand and yes to even fiddle the fields and to do it just because we can.

Tweaking is different from fiddling as tweaking has a whole new frequency attached to it. Tweaking is the option we get when field fiddling is more advanced. It's the final adjustment that is done after everything is in place – when the energy grids and the commands have been laid and locked down and activated, usually by this stage revealing there's been movement in the fields, a refinement and keynote change that has occurred due to all our fiddling. Next by watching in the silence we can then ascertain field effectiveness by using our higher perceptions, next we can convene, discuss and decide to unify and tweak the fields to produce a specific outcome. Unification is a way to increase our tweaking power and deliver quicker outcomes.

We all fiddle the field's everyday via how we choose to spend our time.

When the Law of Love is operating effectively through the fields without restrictions, or blockages to deal with, then the outcome is always for the highest good of all and health and harmony abound through all the fields of life in a way that is evident to all because we are all living and feeling it. This type of paradigm shift in mass consciousness is actually quite possible and happens through being more conscious of our lifestyle choice and through applying DOW power.

The Law of Love & Its Fabulous Frequency of Freedom
with Jasmuheen

The "To tweak or not to tweak" question runs through our minds due to the reality of duality as there are many different schools of thought in metaphysical circles. One of my favorites is the '**Everything is absolute perfection, right here right now. So recognize this in all you do; enjoy all as it unfolds around you. See it all through a pure heart and see it through the eyes of your DOW'** school of thought. This is a simple reality that is also run by the 'What you focus on you feed' game.

Currently I am living my life by this game and the outcomes are interesting. I am choosing to believe that I am the master of my fields which continually shift as they move through me and around me arranging my molecules according to my thoughts, words and actions. It's all nice self responsible stuff. No blame. No victim. No judgment, just a feeling to watch and tweak my fields as I feel inspired.

After decades of applying the tools we share in our websites the C.I.A http://www.selfempowermentacademy.com.au and www.jasmuheen.com most of my major field fiddling has long been done. I've fiddled my internal fields using Recipe 2000> and I've fiddled the fields on an external level via a decade of conscious creation of world tours, books and websites that all reach out to fiddle our world's fields.

Along the way I encountered the 'Everything is Perfection' game in such a powerful way that felt like being hit over the head with a sledge hammer or like someone dousing me with a bucket of water. At one point it was an experience that was so powerful that for some months I lost my words.

When we are actually in the experience of 'Everything is Perfection' then field fiddling ceases and we only need a minimal maintenance program of tweaking now and then to combat any disruptive biofeedback patterns that can sometimes resonate around us.

My favorite recent field tweaking experience was my rainbow room game. Creating rooms filled with rainbows is incredibly rewarding. A relatively inexpensive exercise it involved buying and hanging multifaceted cut crystals all along the beams of my upstairs and downstairs verandahs. Acting as light attracters, refractors and beamers the crystals would radiate the most glorious and divine rainbow spectrum of light into my bedroom and bathroom each morning and also in through my meditation room and lounge room. Some would even bounce through on beams to bathe the walls in my office.

My next act of tweaking the fields was to then arrange my activities through the day to bathe for as long as I can in each rainbow room. Morning meditation on the upstairs balcony in the place the crystals radiate the brightest rainbows, now irradiates my auric field with the most perfect pulses of color and frequency imaginable. From a little field fiddling, I now receive a lot of pleasure as crystals are great natural field tweakers.

I recently got my television back after a year or so of being TV free. Every time I watched it I would fall fast asleep within the first hour until I placed a giant amethyst crystal cave in front of the TV. A cruel thing to do apparently as some say that the only crystal capable of handling TV radiation is a large smoky quartz, a conductor that is powerful enough and dense enough to absorb and repattern any field discordance. I recently added a large rose quartz crystal of the top of the TV and a large clear quartz crystal at the front, both of which have tweaked the field even further and I no longer fall asleep when I watch TV as the crystals absorb the frequencies that used to make me so drowsy.

The Law of Love & Its Fabulous Frequency of Freedom
with Jasmuheen

People field tweak every moment they breathe – via our thoughts, words and actions the fields are constantly being altered around us and through us. Applying a little more consciousness and awareness to what we are radiating into the world, how it is affecting the world, why we are choosing and allowing that particular radiation frequency, and dealing with the quantum and virtual fields own response to our presence, can be very preoccupying for a field mathematician or a dimensional biofield technician as I am and all of it is part of field fiddling.

Some of us fiddle fields consciously and others do it without even being aware, but we all field fiddle. One of my favorite games, the first year at the beach was invisibility, to cloak myself so that my radiation left no imprint on any of the fields around me. Hungry for solitude and appreciating anonymity, invisibility was a powerful key.

Socially people like to objectify, 'gurufy' or deify those who exhibit a skill at unusual things and if I was to be known as anything I would like it to be as a Biofield Technician, a fiddler of the fields. It's true my specialty in the fields has been the freedom agenda and in particular as it manifests in Divine Nutrition and living on its love and light. To be known only as someone who says that they are free from the need to eat food is so incomplete in the bigger scheme of things but we digress.

Our focus is on the choice of games we can sense and tune ourselves into.

So the 'All is perfect' game is the most amazing. It is subtle and requires silent watching and learning to see with our inner eyes so that we can go beyond the materiality and density of life and see the dance of Grace that drives it.

If we don't do this then another choice is to remain in the dense field of duality where we see the goodness of the fields and the positive aspects and we also see and recognize the incoherence, the chaos and the discord. In this second field everything feels separate and the fields need fiddling in a major or minor way – depending on our perception on any given day. Some days when we get a little caught up in struggle and survival it may feel as if everything in life needs a major overhaul or maybe you feel swamped and overwhelmed and too stuck to do anything. Thankfully we usually don't stay in such spaces for too long.

It's nice to know that other fields can be tweaked into and that by choosing to do very particular things with our clock time we can move through the various fields of reality at will.

We know in metaphysical circles that there is no such thing as reality, as everyone's perception of life, and hence their experiences of life, vary. Yet there are fields of shared awareness that the masses exist in, fields whose expressions are controlled by our cultures, power bases and religions.

Choosing the freedom to explore the fields comes automatically as we choose to explore our 7 levels of consciousness, until eventually we find ourselves so immersed in DOW power and so cocooned by the Grace of the Law of Love, that perception disappears and the 'Is'ness of it all takes over and then we go beyond even the meaning of perfection and into the state of BEing pure.

For those who now exist in a state of everything is perfection' and who are enjoying radiant health and happiness, then field fiddling at this time may not be a focus. For others it may be imperative – either to bring themselves into this same state, or to aid others to come into this state, and so we discuss the Being and the doing of it all in Part 2 of this book.

Resurrection and Redemption, Regeneration and Reclamation

My time at the beach this past year has been a time of resurrection and regeneration, a time of reclaiming a space for myself in a silent field. On one level it has been a time to redeem my DOW, to focus on it more fully. To resurrect something is to bring it back to life and according to the dictionary redeem means to free or atone for.

Using the tools provided in our educational manuals and in part 2 of this manual allows us to regenerate and hence fiddle our internal and external energy fields more effectively – yet when we add the frequency of reclamation, everything shifts gears.

I ended the book *The Food of Gods* with a chapter on the Deification of our DOW and how the reclamation of It via an attitude shift within us, was a necessary and basic step in the paradise agenda. In chapter 2 in this manual I spoke of being a devotee of our DOW.

As many are now aware, our DOW is our common link – we are connected to everything because of It for Its tentacles of conscious awareness permeate every field, spanning out through a white hole or grid point, through our physical sun and back through the great central sun on the inner planes. As we expand through the 7 levels of consciousness we gain access to the many different matrixes of realities that permeate the galactic and universal and dimensional fields.

These familiar with Christianity are aware of the idea of the resurrection in relation to the rising of Christ from the dead, the idea that a man could be crucified but, because of his role in the fields and his field frequency, he could rise again and be reborn into a new and altered state – humble, wise, shining, enlightened, a light and a beacon and a symbol of unconditional love and faith and trust, a being knowing of a higher potential and capable of demonstrating this on a physical level.

This is all an example of field tweaking.

Jesus tweaked his fields until somehow magically at age 30 he locked into a field of Grace, a field that overshadowed him enough to transform him into the Christ – a being who would then imprint the crucifixion, ascension and resurrection realities as records in our historical pool.

Calling for a regeneration via the process of redemption, the Christ via his example, opened the fields of possibility for us to follow and do all that he had done and more. By reclaiming the Christ within us and frequency matching via how we spend our clock time, our resurrection and ascension out of the plane of duality and into the plane of perfection, is guaranteed.

The choice of course is ours and the Law of Love makes all fields possible allowing us the free will to choose the field of reality we wish to exist within. That we have choice like this is probably the most powerful piece of information that will lead to the redemption into perfection particularly for those still living in the fields of duality and playing the game of separation.

Separation and suffering are a choice, seeing the perfection of it all and feeling the Oneness of all, is a choice. Playing with both our psychological time and our clock time to experience different fields, is also just a choice.

Albert Einstein once said: "The finest emotion of which we are capable is the mystic emotion. Herein lies the germ of all art and all true science. Anyone to whom this feeling is alien, who is no longer capable of wonderment and lives in a state of fear is a dead man. To know that what is impenetrable for us really exists and manifests itself as the highest wisdom and the most radiant beauty, whose gross forms alone are intelligible to our poor faculties – this knowledge, this feeling … that is the core of the true religious sentiment."

How we spend our time determines how sensitive we are to the different fields of life and which fields we can sense and access, and using our discernment, and DOW mind allows us to determine which fields we wish to play in. I call this a process of 'sensing'.

LAW OF LOVE
& GRACE

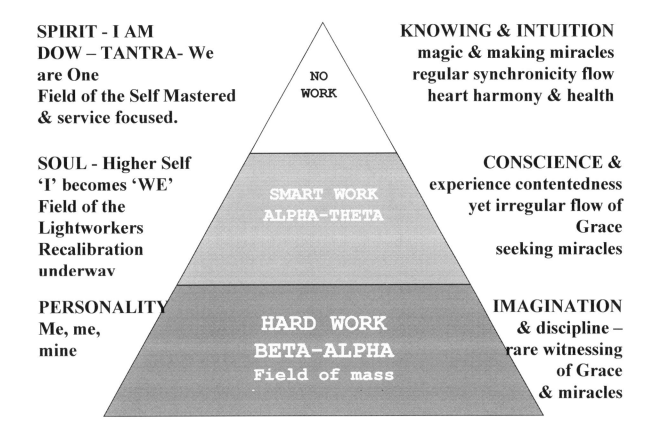

SPIRIT - I AM
DOW – TANTRA- We are One
Field of the Self Mastered & service focused.

KNOWING & INTUITION
magic & making miracles
regular synchronicity flow
heart harmony & health

SOUL - Higher Self
'I' becomes 'WE'
Field of the Lightworkers
Recalibration underway

CONSCIENCE &
experience contentedness
yet irregular flow of Grace
seeking miracles

PERSONALITY
Me, me, mine

IMAGINATION
& discipline –
rare witnessing
of Grace
& miracles

(Pyramid labels: NO WORK / SMART WORK ALPHA-THETA / HARD WORK BETA-ALPHA Field of mass)

TUNING FIELDS – Lifestyle, Grids & Programs – detailed in Part 2
HARMONIZATION for PERFECT FIELD FLOW

Chapter 12

Sensing

To be answered without asking,
You stroke gently, without rasping,
Move from shade to white light basking.

Sensing is a term that I use here in relationship to sensitivity, the ability to be sensitive enough to recognize and explore the seven levels of consciousness that we touched on in chapter 2 on Devotees of the DOW. To live life consciously knowing only the consciousness levels 1 to 3 or 4 is like playing with half a deck of cards. There is simply more choices, more fun, more variety and more stimulation when we play with a full deck – including the joker cards – and the only way to have access to a full deck is to develop and fine-tune *all* of our senses so that we can operate from what Deepak Chopra calls 'nonlocal mind'.

In his *Synchrodestiny* book he develops the idea of local and nonlocal mind. For example on pages 101-104, he writes that local mind is: "ego mind; individual mind; individual consciousness; conditioned consciousness; linear; operates within space, time, causality; time-bound and limited; rational; conditioned into habitual ways of thinking and behavior, shaped by individual and collective experience; separates; inner dialogues: This is me and mine; fear dominates; requires energy; needs approval; interprets the 'I' within the observer as different from the 'I' within the observed; thinks in cause-and-effect modalities; algorithmic; continuous; active when senses are active because sensory experience is local; expresses itself through the voluntary nervous system (individual choice)."

To Deepak Chopra, nonlocal mind is: "Spirit; soul; universal consciousness; pure consciousness; synchronistic; operates outside of space, time, causality; timeless and infinite; intuitive, creative; unconditioned, infinitely correlated, infinitely creative; unifies; inner dialogue: All this is me and mine; love dominates; operates without energy; immune to criticism and flattery; knows it is the same 'I' in the observer and the observed; sees an acausal interconnectedness or interdependent correlation; non-algorithmic; discontinuous; supra-consciousness; always active, but more available to itself when senses are in abeyance or withdrawn, as in sleep, dreams, meditation, drowsiness, trance, prayer; expresses itself through autonomic and endocrine systems, and, most important, through the synchronization of these systems (and also through the synchronization of the particular and the universal, the microcosm and the macrocosm)."

"By its nature, nonlocal mind connects all things because it is all things. It requires no attention, no energy, no approval; it is whole unto itself, and therefore attracts love and acceptance. It is imminently creative, the source from which all creation flows. It allows us to imagine beyond the boundaries of what local mind sees as 'possible', to think outside the box and to believe in miracles."

To me nonlocal mind is DOW mind – the mind of the all knowing, all powerful and all loving Divine One Within us, the Divine One Without – the one who breathes us all and unifies us all in a field of intelligence that is fed by the Law of Love and governed by Its Grace. To me, Grace is synchronicity in motion and it is from operating from DOW mind, or nonlocal mind, that the freedoms we discuss in this journal, are possible. To me, alignment with, surrender to and merging with our DOW is the secret to all freedoms. Attaining this type of freedom is easier when – as Deepak shares on page 107 – our intention "serves the needs of both the local and nonlocal 'I'. The nonlocal intention is always evolutionary and therefore moving in the direction of harmonious interactions that serve the larger good."

We can use either our local or nonlocal mind to sense and exist consciously through the various levels of life. However, when our seven senses are fully activated and working in harmony with the seven elements, then we understand the game of life and the human predicament of chosen limitation and the reasons for our lack of freedom become obvious. Ignorance breeds fear which breeds restriction especially when we choose to stay anchored in local mind and are not given the holistic educational choice of tools that allow us to consciously explore the realms of nonlocal mind.

Sensing means actively developing all of our senses so that we can be aware enough of all the games and to then choose wisely which game we wish to partake in rather than being at the mercy of other more dominant or limiting fields. To me a game is a chosen reality in which we decide to partake, a reality that we have created for particular reasons – hopefully because it serves us and also serves our world. The more we operate from the non-local mind within us, the more reality choices we have.

Developing our senses to access the seven levels of consciousness, and be aware of nonlocal mind, allows us to understand the truth of the stories of the Taoist immortals of each previous chapter and the purest essence of all the Holy Scripture.

The Tao masters say that we need to make a book on Anatomy and Physiology our bible, for when we understand the human body better we can apply internal alchemy more successfully. Controlling our internal energy flow and our fields' emanations also means that we have a greater choice of internal and external realities to access.

Many people, who operate from local mind, refuse to accept that they create their own reality; many believe that things are set in motion, like fate, and that life just happens to us and so we just react to it. Yet how we react to life is a choice and hence each choice determines an outcome which determines a reality.

All metaphysicians now know that when we change our thoughts, words and actions, we change our keynote and also how the universe responds to us and what reality we find ourselves existing within. An aware person will indulge in thoughts, words and actions that will allow them to explore all seven levels of consciousness so that they can be well informed as to what exists in the fields and thus have a greater choice as to which reality they wish to spend time in.

So let's begin this chapter with looking at one some would consider the purest or highest game, the fulfillment of destiny – personal destiny and the destiny of our species.

The Game/s

In the late 1990's I met with a very interesting woman who was associated with the Noetics Institute in California, a center that looks at bridging metaphysics and science. She was writing a book that was to be a collection of interviews with various metaphysicians and was curious about my Divine Nutrition research. At some point she asked me a question about destiny and did I believe that a pre-planned destiny exists for us or is destiny what we make it.

This is an interesting issue particularly as in our "Tao & Tools" chapter we will provide a way of you finding out – if you are interested – exactly what you pre-agreed to do this life in relation to the freedom agenda of the Law of Love.

As Deepak Chopra has shared, in the virtual realm everything exists as a potential possibility. As millions of people dream of a better world and are willing to do what is required to co-create it, this has in fact opened the fields for this new world to come into being.

The game of co-creating paradise is just one in a myriad of choices and it is because of the Law of Love that every choice can be made manifest, for love neither judges nor limits or constricts. Unconditional Love allows all to flow naturally according to their own rhythms and frequency field. With 6 billion plus on our planet there are 6 billion plus life games running, or realities intermingling, with those of greatest similarity forming the strongest rivers for change.

Is there some sort of Divine Creator sitting in judgment of what and how we create? Is there some sort of Intelligent God that wants us to fulfill some sort of pre-written master plan? The cosmic joke is that if we believe that there is then for us in our own little game called life – there is – because that is the nature of the virtual field from which all potentiality and life continuously springs.

I prefer to see it all as a sea of energy with tides that shift and change according to field influences and that all living things constantly emit energy that influences the field. If we are alive and breathing we are influencing the mass biofield of reality called the game of life. What signals we transmit then determines in which game of reality we find ourselves immersed.

To the metaphysician none of this is new – the point is that some games are perhaps more worthy of our attention than others. I don't use the term worthy in a judgmental sense here as everything we experience in life can be invaluable, however once we have explored the various levels of consciousness available to us and understand the mathematics of life a little better, we then have the awareness to make more discerning choices. Being aware enough to recognize life as a game and knowing how to move through reality fields in a harmonious way is a basic skill for a metaphysician or a shape-shifting Shaman.

Sensing is about consciously fine-tuning our senses so that we can be sensitive enough to co-create games that are beneficial to all and to do it in harmony with all. For example as we shared in *The Food of Gods* research has proven that decreasing our calorie consumption by half can increase our longevity by 30%. If we then take the money we save from buying less food and give it to children's charities to help eliminate third world poverty, others also benefit. The action of, for example, eating 2 meals a day instead of three, means that our earth also benefits as we decrease our dependence on the world's food resources immediately by 33% – hence we have another beneficial game.

In Dimensional Biofield Science, the reality of a God or Higher power that has a pre-planned paradise program for earth, and that we have destined roles to fulfill in manifesting this plan, is irrelevant and inconsequential. The mathematics of the quantum and virtual domains simply state that if enough people wish to achieve a dream and if that dream is beneficial for all, then the Law of Love will ensure that the right ingredients i.e. element mix, will come together to bring it into being, provided the dreamers also attend to practicalities. Shape-shifting our selves and our world into the Fabulous Frequency of Freedom will require our desire, our focused attention and our clear intention.

Reason for refinement – Why, How, When

It is rare to find a person who is 100% content and happy with their place in the game of life as even those who are no longer driven by their personal agendas are often involved in the global service game and hence may have as an agenda the positive progression of our planet. People are either seeking to refine themselves so that they can fulfill more of their own seemingly limitless potential or they are seeking to refine their families, their communities or the world.

Sometimes the only reason we need to begin this journey of self and sense refinement is our response to one question and that is:

"Do you feel completely fulfilled on all levels of your being?" If your answer is no then ask why not and have the courage to change it so that you do.

If your answer is yes, then the next question can be asked: "Do you feel 100% happy with the way our world is operating right now?"

If you get a no, then you may wish to ask: "If not why not and what is your pre-agreed role in our planet's refinement? Is there something you can do to make our world a better place for all?"

How to refine both ourselves and our planet was covered in detail in the Biofields & Bliss trilogy where we provided data and tools to bring this into being. When we will attain this, is a matter that is determined by our desire.

Is there a paradise game for all destined for earth?

The simple answer is yes.

Why?

Because enough of us have dreamt it into being and are supporting its manifestation by our thoughts, words and actions and the more who envisage this as an achievable reality, the sooner it will occur.

Discerning Your Part

Discernment is a precious skill that we all soon develop in the game of life. As we activate and fine-tune and remember how to use our higher senses, our sense of discernment and our trust in our inner voice and the Universal Voice, grows. Our inner voice is our intuition and how our DOW connects with us to guide us to fulfill our potential. Meditation 1 in the Tao & Tools chapter will help us to discern our part in the freedom agenda.

Gathering

The act of gathering follows the act of sensing the fields. Once we have sensed which field we wish to exist in we then enter into the stage of gathering with discernment. Gathering is about imprinting into ourselves the type of people and experiences that stimulate contentment or joy depending on what we are seeking. Gathering requires us to be selective as to our exposure re other energy fields, however in the realm of complete mastery, there is the reality that if we are completely in our power, then we are able to exist or dive into any energy field and add to it rather than have it detract from us. The only way to do this is via the process that I call field anchoring.

Anchoring

Anchoring is about living a particular lifestyle that includes adopting specific attitudes that allows us to be anchored permanently into the field of our conscious choice. For many this means being the lotus in the maya. The Indian lotus blossom is an incredibly beautiful flower that grows best in the density of the mud. At this point in time, this is something that the bringers of change are being asked to do – to exist and be grounded in the maya – the mud or denser plane of illusion – that is our current multi-cultural world but to do so radiantly, shining our light when and where it is appropriate. This is a challenge for many and it requires us to anchor ourselves in the base field of the Law of Love, where we live on a wave of Grace and constantly experience miracles, requires great sensitivity. To remain anchored in this state while we journey through the denser worlds is a challenging initiation.

Once we have sensed which field is right for us, gathered with discernment the data re the tools and attitudes that we need to anchor ourselves into it, then we have the doing it game.

Doing It

The doing it discussion is aligned to the BEing it game. In order to BE the manifestation of all that we have been designed to be, we have to do – unless of course we answered yes to the 'happy with us, happy with our planet' questions. The doing means the expansion of our consciousness through exploring the seven levels of our own consciousness and the creation and instigation of a new personal and global dream. The tools to achieve this are in the Biofield & Bliss Trilogy and the tools to achieve the freedom agenda that is a gift of experiencing the Law of Love, will be provided in the following chapters.

Sidelining

Sidelining is an interesting game that we often play with our selves and the reasons we do this are so varied. All sidelining games are emotionally driven and the reasons for this are based in our cellular memory. Sidelining is about indulging in thoughts, words and actions that keep us just out of the frequency range of a constant flow of Grace – it's kind of like training for a football game and doing just enough preparation to make the team but not enough to be selected to play on the field and so we end up sitting on the sidelines – nearly there but not quite. Maybe we've been actively playing on the field for a long time and need a break so we slow down and sit ourselves out. Or maybe we've been playing but got sidetracked and lost form so the game spat us out of the main field for awhile.

An interesting point to remember is that important games that affect human evolution always have back up players and rarely depend on any one individual, each main role also has understudies. Also it helps to know that if it is crucial to the main game that you are active, your DOW will make sure you are. There is no right, no wrong, just opportunities for us to grow and learn.

Motivation & Outcome

The concept of needing either motivation and/or the desire for change implies that there is something wrong with the perfection of each new moment yet **perfection is dependant on perception**.

There is a very interesting discussion in metaphysical circles and that is as follows. If we are made perfect in the image of the Divine, and if everything comes to us anyway and the greatest masters say to be here now, relax and enjoy the beauty of each moment and the perfection that we are then why do anything? Surely there is nothing to strive for or to change?

Then we have people who say 'but look at the state of this world, can't you see it is not perfect, people are suffering, how can you do nothing?'

My response to this is that our perception in this matter depends on where we are in the game, if we are bathing in the seventh level Delta field then yes everything is absolutely perfect, if we are bathing in the Beta-Alpha fields then yes we will see the duality of life, the good, the bad, the just, the unjust.

Yet even when we have explored all seven levels and had all our questions answered and all our desires fulfilled, if we have not yet been melted into the Oneness – or disappeared into the 'Is'ness – of the Law of Love field, and if we are still here in an individualized form, then there is a reason for this and that is that there is more for us to do, if not for our selves, then for others.

We also need to be aware that some of us are here to bring through, from universal mind, new ways of being that require our personal experimentation as we learn to create new models that are beneficial to human evolution. So while it is wonderful for some people to dance in the Delta waves starry eyed and appreciating the perfection of it all, others learn the Delta dance then move back into the Beta field forging pathways for others as they go.

Motivation comes with desire and commitment to just do whatever it is we have come to do, for ourselves and for our world.

And the outcome?

We'll all know when all the fields are tuned and in harmony as there will be peace and health and happiness en mass in our world.

Never before have we had such a quick educational tool at our disposal, a tool that can change the course of our history if used wisely. That tool is the media.

Never before have we had such freedom of information via the internet.

Never before have the ancient wisdom schools been so forthcoming in the sharing of their knowledge so that we can access the innernet the way we now do.

Never before have we understood the power of our imaginations and what we can achieve when we utilize imagination with an understanding of universal law.

These four things – if used wisely and with love – will ensure the success of our dreaming ourselves into a better world.

THE LAW OF LOVE

FIELD FIDDLING

- RECLAMATION
- REGENERATION
- RESSURECTION

- SENSING
- DISCERNING
- DOING & BEING
- GATHERING
- ANCHORING
- SHAPE-SHIFTING
- SIDELINING

PHYSICAL, QUANTUM & VIRTUAL REALMS

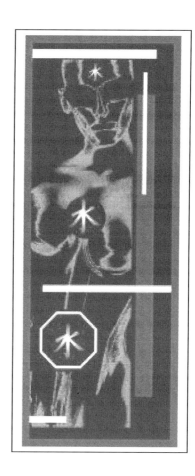

Part 2

THE WIZARD'S TOOL BOX

The Alchemy of Doing & Being

You can't intend to not intend,
No planning when you apprehend,
Non-doing and doing's fine blend.

Chapter 13

Shape-shifting Space
New Field Designs and Activation

Luck from magnetic attraction,
Energy's output projection,
Produces enhanced reflection.

Some people are more extreme than others and co-creating a space where all are honored and where a Shaman can shape-shift can sometimes be a challenge. Tonight I lay my body down to sleep at nearly 1 a.m. only to find myself in the training field receiving the download of the "Lure of Love" and waking at 2.30 a.m. with a desire to capture it all in writing. It is now 4.30 a.m. and the sun is beginning to rise and the birds have begun their songs of appreciation as the dawn breaks over the valley. As I sit here and write, I witness another beautiful sunrise over the Pacific Ocean.

The more we apply the Luscious Lifestyles Program and experience the harmony it brings us an all levels, the less we need of things like food or sleep. If I shared my bedroom with someone who needed more than an hour or two of sleep, my minimal sleep lifestyle pattern would be very disruptive to them, hence the practicality of both sleeping and also maybe even living alone when we are shape-shifting into and adjusting with these levels of Freedom. That is not to say that if you are in partnership and have a family that you cannot pursue these things. If you have good communication and a supportive relationship you can find ways to do practically anything if it is your heart's desire and your blueprint.

Minimizing our sleep requirements:

As I have discussed this in our other manuals I will not devote much time to the freedom that comes when we minimize our need for sleep suffice to say that adjusting to a lifestyle like this requires firstly a change in mindset and beliefs. Shortly after I stopped eating physical food and allowed prana to bring me all my nourishment, I found that instead of needing my usual 8 hours of sleep, sometimes, like tonight after an hour or two I would be wide awake and refreshed.

Initially the mind reacts by running old programs of limited beliefs like: "If I don't get my usual 6-8 hours sleep I'll feel terrible in the morning." This does not need to be true as our bio-systems can function well on minimal sleep *if* we are in harmony on all levels. Personally I still enjoy my dream time and out of body experience at night, so as I have already mentioned, freeing my body completely from the need to sleep will not be my focus this journey. I also find this happens automatically the more I 'lighten' up.

My main objective with this current research manual is to bring my physical, emotional, mental and spiritual systems into perfect harmony with the universal forces so that I can be free from not just food but also permanently free from the need to take fluid, if I can achieve this during this journey I will be happy, nonetheless time is not an issue for me as I insist that it all occur with joy and Grace.

New Field Designs:

Once all inner and outer energy fields are clear of unnecessary clutter and detoxified, the next step is to create a new physical field design to act as an internal sacred support system and to activate the new design with its relevant programs and to also apply the energy mechanics to trigger and fulfill any desired physical change.

MEDITATION 2: New Field Design – Perfect Bio-Body Meditation Part 1:

Throughout this new section we will share ancient Taoist techniques plus new data that I have downloaded from universal mind and its Dimensional Biofield Science field. Usually when I receive something, it comes as a powerful mental, emotional or physical experience and sometimes as all three combined. The following meditation on field designs combined all three although it primarily came as an intense physical experience.

The below template was revealed during an intense yoga session that I did after 6 weeks on the road. It was a wonderful experience for me as I love it when my body reveals new steps to me in support of my shape-shifting Freedom agenda. As we have previously stated, when something is pre-ordained – in that we have agreed to achieve it this life – it means that all of our internal and external energy systems have been designed to support this into being. Hence once my new 'Freedom' assignment had been revealed to me on that sunny day in Barcelona, and once it had been accepted, then my DOW and my body could then begin to reveal the steps required to achieve it.

One of the aides I find useful before an intense yoga session is the technique I call a "shake-out". A shake-out is where you position your body into a particular posture or asana and then hold this posture while the body shakes out any crinks in its energy lines, this shake-out allows the body greater flexibility as the yoga session progresses and yet if yoga is done regularly, there is rarely much to shake out. *(The use of a chi machine – as we discussed in* The Food of Gods *manual – also helps to facilitate this.)*

On the day that I download the 'Perfect Bio-body Template' I was in the shoulder stand/plough position allowing the shake out to complete itself, feeling my legs vibrate and shudder as I held myself strongly enough to also be relaxed in the posture. With my legs pointing backwards over my head and my body weight squarely balanced on my shoulders, I was guided to begin to go through each section of my body and mentally redesign it into perfection with my DOW saying:

"Imagine you are the Creator designing a new physical model, how do you see it?"

Visualizing Naomi Campbell's long, lean, taut legs and that my own were now transforming into the same shape, I slowly worked up my body, seeing a trim taut '6 pack' stomach and all the other changes my vanity and ego would allow until the new design had been clearly seen and created.

This type of visual imaging is not unusual and is a basic step in re-creation.

Some people may say "Why not Love your body just the way it is?" and I agree that acceptance and self love is a necessary step for any transformation. However some of us are learning to manipulate or redirect molecules as a forerunner to things like dematerialization which is a Shaman shape-shifting skill that brings many gifts. Discovering a model that can work for our selves and others is an interesting service.

The reason we work with the physical body this way is that it is here that the results are more easily visible as the body responds quickly to diet and exercise adjustments and also to mind mastery.

So back to the creation of our perfect bio-body template …

Once the shake-out and new visual imaging were done in my yoga session, a new program kicked in that I have come to call "slicing".

Slicing:

Slicing is a technique where we break up the existing energy fields by shooting 10 lines of violet light through our finger tips and imagining them forming perfect arches or loops that we then direct in a 360 degree pattern through the core energy channel of our body while holding the intention and image that these energy lines are breaking up the existing molecular structure of the physical body's field.

This is similar to when we finely dice a vegetable it's that same motion except that the energy lines are the knife. Once we have dissected or sliced through the old energy field and broken up its existing patterns, we then need to integrate and merge the new design and harmoniously recalibrate the fields.

We do this as follows:
- ॐ Firstly take the time to go through each section of your body and re-image it in your mind into a new 'perfect bio-body template' – you may wish to see it as a healthy, self-sustaining, non aging system. Visualize each part in detail.
- ॐ Next, while still sending out 10 violet beams of light through your fingers
    a) hold the image in your mind of the new design then
    b) imagine overlaying this new design into your existing fields while you then switch the energy rhythm of the beams coming from your fingers into the motion of the symbol of infinity. The symbol of infinity is designed to bring a field into a harmonizing state of balance which is what we wish to achieve – the perfect balance of the new energy patterns and new design with the existing system.
    c) We will offer the complete meditation at the end of this chapter.

On the day that I did this, the way my body responded, recalibrating itself with such a shudder and shake astounded me. It was as if every little cell was ready and proceeded with this new program and design which I was guided to call "Jasmuheen's Perfect Bio-Body". Calling your new design template by something like this, means that you can command it into power more and more each day with the simple mantra "Perfect Bio-Body Now". Now as I walk along the beach each day, as I take each step I use the mantra: "perfect bio-body now" and hold the visual image in my mind as I imagine my body transforming itself to demonstrate this new template.

I realize that this may sound complicated to some people but remember my fascination is dematerialization and rematerialization and further more my curiosity extends itself to this question:

"If successful dematerialization requires:
a) that we move our consciousness from our body and anchor it into a new place and time and then
b) call our molecules and atoms to disassemble themselves,
c) then when they also reassemble themselves in a new point in time can they be reassembled to mirror the new "Perfect Bio-Body design" and also
d) does the imprinting of this image design into the body's consciousness, and the use of the mantra, speed this process up since it's a good practice of molecular shifting?"

Of course all the above is theoretical and it would be easier to first master normal dematerialization and rematerialization using the current body image. However, reimaging the body by using the Lure of Love and the Law of Love, so that the molecules learn to obey our command, is a prerequisite step for other things. Individuals change their body size, shape and pattern regularly just through changing their lifestyle habits so adding a bit of mind mastery to the equation is simply working with an additional layer. Shamanistic shape-shifting is not much different especially when we apply the mathematics of Biofield science. Please note that the more aligned to, and merged with, our DOW that we are, the easier it is to obtain results by using these visual imaging tools.

What I love about incorporating this type of field work in a normal yoga session is that while we are holding a known asana that works a particular muscle group, we are just adding a mental reimaging layer and science has already proven that the power of visual imaging is something to which the body will quickly respond. As mentioned in my previous books, research has shown that when we move our mind into a muscle and visualize it toning up while we also do our exercise program, that this is more beneficial than just exercising alone.

The next thing I love with all of this is that once a new design has been visualized, it does not have to be done again. We can simply use the mantra of "Merge Perfect Bio-Body" to super impose and adjust the fields. So every time I do my yoga or other exercise sessions I hold this image and chant "Perfect Bio-Body Now", which reaffirms my focus with the body. We use the "Perfect Bio-Body" command as our biological body, like our biological age, is adjustable and unlike our chronological age, is alterable and responds to changes in the visual image we hold of ourselves just as powerfully as it responds to our lifestyle changes.

Being a sensitive and feeling the way my body responded to all of this in this particular yoga session was awe inspiring, and a way of my being telling me that what I am doing is real, as feeling such a powerful physical response is only possible if an energy shift is actually happening. Imagination and wishful thinking alone do not achieve this unless the basic blueprint of possibility has been pre-encoded into our cells ready for discovery and activation.

This was similar to what I experienced in my first kinesiology energy session with Lucinda where I felt as if an invisible hand had reached into my heart chakra and pulled me up with such a force that my body felt like it was levitating off the table. Consequent sessions with her have gifted similar experiences. My point is that after a few years of meditation a metaphysician has enough experiences to move themselves way beyond doubts and questions like: "Is this real or is it my imagination?" for we know that the use of our imagination is step one for altering our fields of reality.

PERFECT BIO-BODY PROCEDURE

- Firstly take the time to go through each section of your body and re-image it in your mind into a new 'perfect bio-body template' – you may wish to see it as a healthy, self-sustaining non aging system. Visualize each part in detail transforming into perfect health and perfect image.
- Next, activate your hands to be Alpha energy tools for change and imagine sending out 10 violet beams of light through your fingers, direct these in an up and down motion while you imagine that they are forming loops that run up the spinal column, out through the top of your head, around your body and up through your feet chakras and up the spine again in a loop.
- As you do this, hold the image in your mind of the new design as you recalibrate your system with the lines of violet light and begin to break up your existing energy using the slicing technique, slowly go through all sections of your body that you wish to shape-shift.
- Next recalibrate your new bio-body with its new pattern of energy, through your existing field by using the violet light while you mentally superimpose your new image through your existing system.
- Chant: "Perfect Bio-body now!" 3 times.
- Then as you imagine overlaying this new design into your existing fields, then switch the energy rhythm of the beams coming from your fingers into the motion of the symbol of infinity. The symbol of infinity is designed to bring a field into a harmonizing state of balance which is what we wish to achieve – the perfect balance of the new energy patterns and new design with the existing system.
- When done offer it all to your DOW for fine tuning and release into 'perfect time' manifestation with three "So it is! So it is! So it is!"
- Finally have faith and do not doubt your ability to shape-shift into such freedoms.
- Support this with a healthy lifestyle that keeps your brain wave patterns tuned to the Theta and Delta zone as discussed in detail in *The Food of Gods*.

FREEDOM AGENDA Summary

- First create a safe sacred supportive physical space that is free from any limiting energy interference. Do this on both internal and external levels. Tools for this are in previous manuals.
- Next confirm via the meditation in the "Tao & Tools" chapter exactly what your personal pre-agreed agenda is so that you can begin appropriate preparation and training when and if required.
- Next begin to work with a switched on therapist who the universal forces of synchronicity will help you to locate. Work with this one as a secondary level of confirmation and clearing only. First level must come from your connection to, and trust of, your DOW.
- Next ask to begin or to intensify your night time training program to reveal to you more of the field mathematics required to fulfill your personal freedom agenda, particularly the perfect steps for you to take.
- Next design and implement your new perfect bio-body template to create a new matrix for your molecules to shape-shift around.

BASIC YOGA ASANAS:

As discussed in *The Food of Gods* there are various practices in yoga from Hatha to the devotional Bhakti yoga, to Surya – the yoga of the sun. All serve to establish a strong sense of chi flow in our systems and to prepare the bio-system to handle the frequency of love and freedom. Explore the different systems and enjoy the benefits especially when you add the Matrix systems of this and future chapters.

THE LAW OF LOVE
FIELD RE-DESIGN – REHARMONIZE

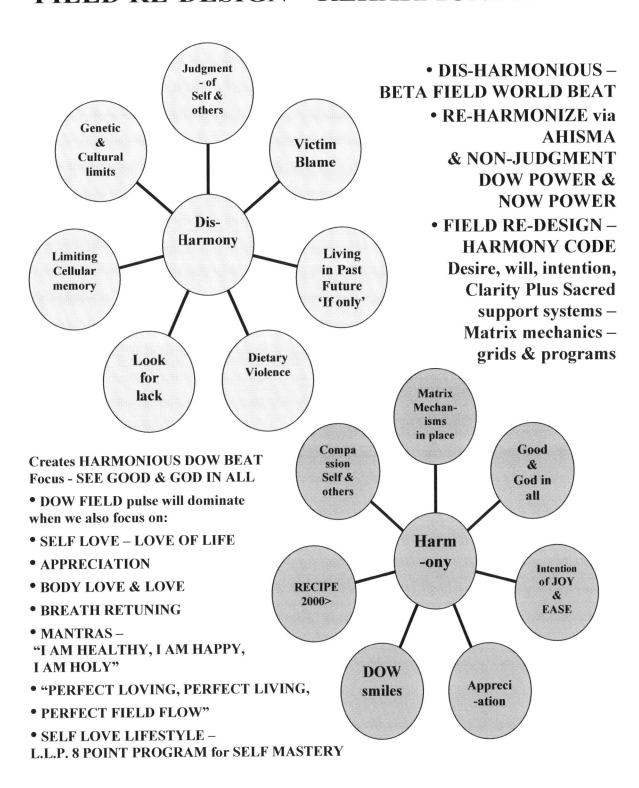

- DIS-HARMONIOUS – BETA FIELD WORLD BEAT
- RE-HARMONIZE via AHISMA & NON-JUDGMENT DOW POWER & NOW POWER
- FIELD RE-DESIGN – HARMONY CODE Desire, will, intention, Clarity Plus Sacred support systems – Matrix mechanics – grids & programs

Creates HARMONIOUS DOW BEAT Focus - SEE GOOD & GOD IN ALL

- DOW FIELD pulse will dominate when we also focus on:
- SELF LOVE – LOVE OF LIFE
- APPRECIATION
- BODY LOVE & LOVE
- BREATH RETUNING
- MANTRAS – "I AM HEALTHY, I AM HAPPY, I AM HOLY"
- "PERFECT LOVING, PERFECT LIVING,
- PERFECT FIELD FLOW"
- SELF LOVE LIFESTYLE – L.L.P. 8 POINT PROGRAM for SELF MASTERY

Chapter 14

Mathematics, Movement & Molecules

Fruit always follows the flower,
The higher floors in the tower,
Increasing levels of power.

I have decided that what excites me with this exercise of Shamanistic shape-shifting is the freedom of exploration of both molecular and elemental movement. The fact that we can rearrange our internal energy flow and its external structure at will is for me – enticing. Similarly the freedom of moving our consciousness and molecules to a different space in time via dematerialization and rematerialization also excites me as a wondrous possibility. Taking this further as the shape-shifting Shaman do, into assuming a different form altogether, is another level again.

I also love the act of recalibrating fields – from the processes of de-activation, redesign and re-activation – as it is a wonderful way to effect lasting and evident change. Apart from lifestyle change, **two of the most powerful ways to re-harmonize a discordant energy field, in ourselves and in our world, is the practice of Ahisma and non-judgment.** When we withdraw from all acts of violence and negative type judgments from a field we immediately tune ourselves into the channel of kindness especially when we develop the virtues of fairness with the intention to create perfect harmony. Ahisma is a term introduced by Gandhi and it means to not just refrain from physical, emotional, mental and spiritual violence but to also take this into a dietary level and support no animal slaughter.

Many years ago I decided that my life was like a pie graph that was governed by percentages and that altering my life and my experiences could be as simple as altering the percentages of how I spent my time. At that point 8 hours of each day I spent sleeping which was 33% of a 24 hour day. I discovered that if I ate a lighter diet and exercised my body daily then it became fitter and functioned better and needed less sleep. When I added regular meditation to help deal with any emotional or mental stress levels, I found I needed even less sleep again as meditation evened out my emotional range and gave me more mental clarity. Meditation also allowed me to access my creativity more easily and to generally act instead of react and hence be more detached and able to direct my energy more effectively.

By these three actions – diet, exercise and meditation – I was able to healthily decrease the percentage of time that I spent sleeping to 20% instead of 33% as my need for sleep naturally decreased with the combination of these activities. This shift of energy then gave me 13% more time each day to spend on other preferred activities.

Shape-shifting is just redirection of energy and as the ancient Tao masters say – where mind goes, chi follows – so dreams and intention need to come first and also be followed by the appropriate action.

Miracles are also based on the mathematics of percentages of what we spend our time doing and how much time we spend doing it, and determine how tuned we are to the channel of Grace which is the channel that delivers miracles.

Since my intense yoga session with its "Perfect Bio-Body" creation and integration layer, every day I am noticing subtle physical changes – the shape of my legs, hips and stomach is becoming more like my new Bio-Body template – even though I have made no other lifestyle changes as my existing lifestyle is already operating in a way that supports my freedom agenda.

MEDITATION 2: *Perfect Bio-Body Template – Part 1 continued and Part 2:*
Recreating or refining and then holding the "Perfect Physical Bio-Body Template" is part 1 of working with the new Freedom matrix that is designed to also support the elimination of age and disease especially when the tools discussed in *The Food of Gods* manual have been applied.

Tools like:
- ॐ the "Body Love" tool which prepares our body's cells to handle higher doses of nourishing Love
- ॐ plus the "Love Breath" tool which keeps us consciously plugged into, and downloading our required quotient of pure prana from the Diving Mother Love channel,
- ॐ plus the "Dietary Exercise Detox Lifestyle" tools and
- ॐ the "Violet Light One Chakra Column Plug In" tool.

For me personally all of this has now been done and will thus form the foundation layers for the new Perfect Bio-Body Template. All of these form the basis of the Freedom matrix and are elaborated on in great detail in *The Food of Gods* manual. This also includes using the "Perfect Health, Perfect Balance, Perfect Weight and Perfect Image" mantra as part of our daily lifestyle maintenance program.

Hence I assume that if the reader of this manual wishes to accompany me on this journey, that they too will have utilized and experienced the benefits of these tools before attempting to go to this next level. ***For me, understanding and applying personally all of what I have shared in the book The Food of Gods is a necessary part of preparation for and a prerequisite of undergoing this journey.*** As I also shared in that book, for some people – like Hira and Zinaida and Prahlad – perhaps this type of preparation is not necessary and yes there are simpler ways, however remember I am seeking to offer a safe, proto-type model that all may undertake.

Going through each section of your body, looking at it, sending it Love, then visualizing its transformation into your Perfect Bio-Body is all part 1. Remember to make sure that you lovingly attend to each part of your body, recognizing each part and connecting consciously with it, thanking it for the space it has held and job it has done so far and being very clear with your image, will and intention. Activation of the Self Sustaining Template is also recommended and the creation of the Template is detailed in the books *Four Body Fitness – Biofields and Bliss* and *The Food of Gods* and discussed in future chapters in this manual.

We are now ready to move on.

With part 2 of the Creation of our new Perfect Bio-Body Template and its Freedom agenda, we begin more intense physical inner world work. Assuming that all the meditations and tools recommended as part of the Freedom Agenda – Level 3 of the Divine Nutrition Program – in the book *The Food of Gods* have been applied, and hence our inner plane feeding mechanisms are secure; we then move into inner plane re-imaging and the transformation of the physical system.

- ॐ Firstly we begin with the skeleton.
- ॐ Holding the image of our skeleton in our mind, we imagine it now being flooded with violet light which is healing, regenerating, nourishing and rejuvenating it.
- ॐ Imagine a 'violet light pulsing' bone structure that is strong and healthy with perfect bone density, that is youthful and strong and capable of carrying the weight of worlds if ever need be, but also imagine the molecules that form the skeletal structure are loose enough to be dancing and ready on command to disassemble itself to follow its master – you – into another space and time if and when required.
- ॐ Imagine now the muscles around your bone structure are also pulsing with this violet light. Imagine these are toned, lean, well defined perhaps exuding health and fitness and vitality as they pulse with life, imagine nourishing blood flooding through all the sinews.
- ॐ Imagine your lymphatic system and all your bloodlines – arteries, veins, capillaries – all flowing with healing, nourishing violet light and becoming revitalized, healthy, in perfect harmony with the tides of life and the forces that shape it.
- ॐ Do the same for each organ, then your nervous system, and work your way through every system. Imagine all your organs dancing and filled with violet light.
- ॐ Imagine your whole inner body structure and circuitry being healed and nourished and regenerated and transformed into an ageless, disease free, food and fluid free, self sustaining model that is your perfect model.
- ॐ Set the intention that this new template of your Perfect Bio-body is now being perfectly aligned with your **Perfect Bio-Body DOW Freedom Model**.
- ॐ Your **DOW Freedom Model** is embodied and encoded in the matrix of your light body, it is a template of how your bio-system can function when it is in perfect harmony with all the elements and all the forces that give and

shape life. It also holds the perfect image of a system in balance, in Love and in harmony with all.
- ॐ Next we call in all the support of all the universal forces, guides and inner and outer plane help for perfect merging, integration and activation of these models and that it all occur with joy and ease and Grace.
- ॐ Visualize your new P.P.B. – Perfect Bio-Body – model now infused in a cloud of violet light, as this is the original frequency field of creation, and then surrender this new model back to this original force, but do it with the attitude of 'to come into being in perfect time' and though it all hold the attitude that you yourself are a master of creation and a master of Love, a master that your molecules will obey.
- ॐ So as with Part 1, when all this is done you declare "So it is, So it is, So it is."

Please note that the emotional spectrum of this new template is being fed by the virtues gathered and downloaded from applying the instructions in the Self Sustaining Template meditation as described in *The Food of Gods* manual.

Next: The Repetitive use of the "Perfect Bio-Body" mantra.
As many are aware, programs and mantras are statements used singularly or repetitively to provide molecules and universal forces with a specific instruction for action or to flood our atoms with a specific frequency.

Sometimes programs/affirmations/mantras are used to replace or override limiting belief systems when they arise. For example with this one, anytime I look at or think about my body, I simply say after the first thought comes in "Jasmuheen's Perfect Bio-Body Now" with the intention that it is merging through the old system, integrating, harmonizing and replacing limiting realities with my new Freedom model reality. Like many of the tools and meditations in *The Food of Gods* book, the new P.B.B. Template only has to be created/visualized and commanded into being once but what needs regular attention once it has all been done are our habitual limited thinking patterns. Singing the mantra "Perfect Bio-body now" as I exercise each day simply reminds the bodies of a new role and possibility.

The type of preparation we have discussed so far is designed to enable a smoother journey and all of us have received many wonderful tuning tools in our evolution. It is interesting to reflect over some of the tools I have received over the years and the benefits of their application and we will share more of the tools that are relevant to the freedom agenda in the chapters on "Tao & Tools" and "Matrix Mechanisms".

Summary of Steps taken so far:
We have ...
1) Applied internal and external Feng Shui via specific lifestyle changes to redirect our physical energy flow and by creating a safe sacred external space for us to comfortably to take the next step.
2) Applied the preparation tools recommend in *The Food of Gods* manual.

3) Enlisted the aide of a trusted and capable energy worker to act as a bridge of confirmation for you and your body e.g. a kinesiologist.
4) Created and activated the new field design via using the "Self Sustaining Template" and "Perfect Bio-Body Template".

PERFECT HARMONY =
PERFECT LIVING + PERFECT LOVING + PERFECT FIELD FLOW.

Exercise: Contemplate Perfection.
- ☺ What does perfection mean to you?
- ☺ What is physical perfection for you? Does it mean being free from human limitations?
- ☺ Does it mean having the perfect image where your DOW can shine Its radiance into the world?
- ☺ What does emotional perfection mean to you? Mental perfection? Spiritual perfection?
- ☺ What is your perfect life?
- ☺ What is your perfect love?
- ☺ What is your perfect planet?

I know that there will come a day where we will all understand that there is no mystery to the Divine, that everything operates perfectly via a system of mathematical codes that are supported by the interaction of light rays and sound waves and that everything is a system of energy whose frequency signals can be adjusted at will. The secret to successful shape-shifting of a human bio-system or a human world can be found when we apply a futuristic science perspective to the ancient teachings and tools. And so it was that I took myself to Thailand – at the invitation of Mantak Chia – to learn the secrets of the highest teachings of the Ancient Immortal Tao Masters for intuitively I feel they hold the key to my next step.

Chapter 15

Dark Room Diary Downloads

Release what you no longer need,
The lightened load means less to feed,
Correct weight is correct indeed.

I began to research the work of Mantak Chia in the early nineties when I discovered how living purely on prana was changing my sexual energies.

At that point in my journey – as now – it was not in my personal interests to be completely celibate. Applying the Taoist techniques that he recommends in his books, my long term lover and I experienced many of the amazing benefits that the Tao Master had long revered with the practice of Tantra. As discussed in my book *The Food of Gods*, I also discovered how the microcosmic orbit can not only energize the body but also feed it as well, especially when used in conjunction with the 'Violet Light One Chakra Column inner plane feeding system' that I recommend.

There is only so much in the way of tools – visuals, energy work and programming – that we need to do before the body's own innate intelligence kicks in to run the system in a more beneficial way. *If* this is then supported by a lifestyle such as the Luscious Lifestyles Program, everything becomes automatic and self fulfilling and yes eventually self sustaining. This gifts us with the ability to relax and be totally present in the now moment.

If we then have more to do re our personal blueprints, then these things also form the foundation for our next step to come into successful completion.

My next step towards my freedom agenda is to fall in love with water.

This may sound like a strange step since my goal is to harmonize my system to be healthily fluid free, however, my intention with this "falling in love with water" is to do so to the degree that

a) my body's weight settles and stabilizes at its perfect level as I unhook my emotional and social dependence on the flavor of liquid substances and
b) by falling in love with water that I bring my emotional and mental body's into perfect alignment with where my physical body now is.

For the past 2 years my physical body's voice has been growing louder and louder and manifesting its annoyance (at my reluctance to take the next step) in very obvious ways. It takes the minimal consumption of additional substances to push it into discomfort and I have literally physically passed the 'point of no return' where my physical body's only interest is in water.

The 'point of no return' is when a bio-system such as mine has been nourished successfully by prana for so long that it is impossible to comfortably go back to a physical food based diet and when this is attempted, the physical body expresses its rebellion in very obvious ways.

When a physical body receives *all* its nourishment – its vitamins and minerals – purely from prana via the Law of Love, it becomes capable of amazing achievements. Over the past decade I have been continually astounded by my physical systems performance and ability to handle the crazy demands I have placed upon it as I explored the first part of this journey and then took my findings to the global stage. To be able to maintain peak health while spending up to eight months a year on the road living in polluted cities, dealing with closed minded media and the anger that my research has released in some people, has been an art; yet my body has done this effortlessly and I believe that this is because of the bond of Grace that 'the Law of Love' has naturally placed around it.

To live purely on prana in a cave in the Himalayas, in fresh air, without the constant negative psychic energies that are directed to someone challenging the status quo I am sure is an easier road. Nonetheless I have no complaints as our blueprints are always perfect and because they are part of a natural new cycle of human evolution the levels of Grace that support us are miraculous. If this were not so, I doubt it could be done as the power of fear due to ignorance on our planet can be overwhelming. This fear can be likened to the pain a body feels when a finger nail or toe nail is ripped from its bed. Assuming people exist in the heart of the body protected by the Grace of the Law of Love, when they are public, the pain of fear and ignorance represented by the toenail, can be felt as it shoots through the rest of the body. As we are all cells in the body of the Divine, our fear and our joy are interconnected. Learning to shield ourselves from these types of painful, fear based influences is also part of our journey into mastery and we discuss this in detail in our other manuals.

I began this chapter with the mention of Mantak Chia as my journey has now led me to combine his work and mine by utilizing his Dark Room technology with my new game of "falling in love with water" and maybe if I can achieve it, freeing myself from fluid.

For thousands of years the yogis have found themselves in caves deep inside mountains, in a space they have shared with snakes and scorpions, while they've gone into deep meditation, often leaving their body for long periods of time. In this space, free from the confines of their physical form they would wander freely through the cosmos while the body absorbed what chi or prana it could from the inner planes. Sometimes their body just fed off itself yet due to their frequency, even though they'd spend long periods of time without fluid or food, while they may have lost weight they did not die.

During the month of February 2004, I placed myself at the Tao Gardens in Chiang Mai in Thailand, in a situation similar to the above yogis except that instead of being in a cave contending with snakes and scorpions, I was in a condominium converted for these purposes. Depriving ourselves from our sense of physical sight by being totally in the dark is an experience that is unimaginable, an experience that provides amazing gifts.

What follows now are a few excerpts from the audio diary that I kept to record the daily insights and experiences and downloads that I received during this time, so I share here those that are relevant to this freedom journal. The complete details of this journey can be found in the free booklet "Darkroom Diary Downloads" at: http://www.selfempowermentacademy.com.au/htm/training.asp#RETREATS – the data received during other days is placed in the relevant chapters of this manual.

Darkroom Diary Downloads – Day 1

Over the years I've been asked: "What is the point of this? Why deny oneself such pleasure, why deny the social inter-reaction of eating and the pleasure that comes from tasting the various flavors?"

To me, on one level, the physical enjoyment of food is so limited.

To their question I could say that I have tapped into the channel of divine love to such a degree that it feeds me in all sorts of ways. I could say when we live by the Law of Love in every moment, so that Grace is constantly with us, how this provides us with so many pleasures; pleasures that are incomprehensible to those who have not been witness to these things. I know that there are people who have not had the opportunity or taken the opportunity to tune to this channel of love and then to feel what this Grace brings and so to them the pleasure gained from food etc is stronger.

I could tell the world, a world that often only sees with outer eyes, of all the beauty that lies in the dimensions within; how we can all sit down to meditate and close our eyes, and go within and find our self seated within the center of the universe and how we can then watch the stars around us blinking in and out of existence as if we are seeing it all somehow through the creator's eyes. I could share of what we can experience when we sit in the silence and listen with our inner ear, and how we can hear sounds that are like celestial choirs, of how sounds can caress our soul and how when we still the tongue and place it gently on the roof of the mouth, how the pituitary gland in all its glory opens like a flower to release a drop of dew, a nectar that is so supreme and so sweet that every cell of our body tingles in recognition and hungers for more and yet at the same time ceases to be hungry.

I could share of the pleasure that comes when we move our awareness and look for the force that breathes the breath and in that looking how the magic happens that allows us to align with the river of love that is so sweet and fulfilling that we are never hungry and we no longer seek for more.

I could share how there are so many gifts in these subtle realms that take the subtlety of touch and how our intention and attention allows us to let go of this world enough to find these gifts. And yet we live in a world that satiates all our senses, overwhelms all our senses with so much taste and noise and action, permanently dulling our ability to sense the inner world.

And so I find myself quite content to sit surrounded by the darkness, my physical eyes sometimes open looking for a glimmer of light and seeing none, closing them again to drift deeper still on the waves of silence into the inner worlds and I begin to hear again the celestial choirs and feel again the easy rhythm of that stream of love.

Darkroom Diary Downloads – Day 2
Part of the Taoist practices is this connection with the body through the constant smile. To constantly smile at your heart and your lungs and your kidneys and liver and all of your organs and every part of your body, for as they say where the mind is focused the chi will follow. So to focus the mind in these areas and smile and hold that intention of each area being flooded with chi brings a beautiful burst of sunlight yellow energy into these areas particularly if we imagine this color and this form of light flooding them as well. These are the infinite little joys that the body seems to be loving and responding to and so I have set the exercise of placing my hands on various parts of my body that need a little boost of energy or healing and allowing the green light to flow there as I smile in this area.

I have found already that my body is very dependant on external chi, it is used to absorbing prana from being in nature, walking on the beach and downloading energy via sun gazing. I realized also here that the reason that I am not affected in other more polluted environments where there is minimum prana is because when I am traveling and working I am held in a constant state of Grace which feeds me all that I need. Yet here in the dark there is neither external sunlight prana nor excess Grace so I am now having to modify my internal energy flow.

Darkroom Diary Downloads – Day 3
Regardless of motivation or models or formulas of joy, this experience of sensory depravation of sight is a very powerful one for already in this brief period of time I have learnt so much about myself and about my body and its relationship to energy fields. Also the teachings of the Taoist Masters are quite invaluable, the working with the elements of fire and water and steam and directing the energy flow through the different organs, the connection of the mind with the organs and having the organs move and respond at our command.

I have never felt, for example, the contraction of my pineal gland muscle yet now as soon as I contract my perineum, immediately I feel a sympathetic resonance, a contraction in my pineal gland as the two are connected. So regardless of my restlessness today, I wouldn't hesitate to recommend this experience to anyone seeking to explore more of the inner universe without distraction. I am also learning some more energy movement tools while I rest and relax and explore my inner world. It is also a wonderful opportunity for me to apply all the tools I have downloaded over the years and test the resonance of each tool.

Darkroom Diary Downloads – Day 4
Have been practicing more of the microcosmic orbit and distributing the chi energy that is gathered into all of the organs, flooding each one with the energy of creation that brings life into being. I like to imagine that each organ can receive enough of this chi so that it comes into a state of such joy and enjoys a type of orgasm.

The Taoists believe that our DOW is anchored in our heart but also splits itself to inhabit all our organs filling each one with various frequencies and virtues. I have been learning of the creation of the immortal body by applying the Lesser Kan Li practice that entails the creation of the iron cauldron which we have anchored between the sacral and solar plexus chakras. The cauldron is an etheric vessel that stores the elements of fire from the heart and water from the kidneys that mix together to form a violet light steam that we can then direct through the body to cleanse the organs.

What occurs in this darkroom therapy as well is that you start to go through deep chemical transformations in the body by using the Taoist tools of the five elements and also from directing the chi is a specific manner around the body. Chi follows mind and blood follows chi so wherever you focus your mind the chi will follow in service to you as a master. I have developed the breathing technique where you place your mind into your sacral chakra and then with a deep inhale draw in pure sun yellow fire energy imagining that you are tapping into this stream from the great central sun within, then drawing it on the inhalation through the lower Tan Tien and then as we exhale sending this fiery yellow chi into every cell of the body intending that it burn up any dross and re-energize us. It's a nice and simple breathing rhythm.

Darkroom Diary Downloads – Day 6

I am finding that every day here is completely invaluable. What I have understood in the making of models is that you need to work with some of the ancient tradition, tradition that is tried and true and carries the weight behind it of all those who have gone before – in other words a tradition that is an accepted way of being that has maybe also been analyzed. For example, the testing of prana or chi to heal bone fractures etc., as the benefits of qigong, Tai Chi and the ancient Taoist practices are now well known. Within all of these practices there are particular techniques that can be used to make models that deliver very particular outcomes, and so it is that I am finding with my freedom model that I am able to gather some incredible tools and techniques that will aid in the freedom journey, particularly my part of this journey for seeking the freedom from fluid.

My current model over the last few days is where I am having a day of juice, then a day of water then a day of just prana as my body adjusts its internal feeding mechanism to draw more prana from the inner planes. This model is working very well and I am feeling stronger and stronger every day. I am working daily on the sacrum and the joints as well, and doing the chi exercises is contributing to this state of well being. If my body continues to be pain free on a muscular level then I will no longer take any fruit juice and use the model of one day on water then one day on just prana and then one day on water.

I am carefully listening to every nuance and sign of my physical system, honoring it, loving it, respecting it, working with the chi energy flow to keep it in a state of strength and harmony. Loving and respecting our bodies is imperative for anyone seeking these levels of freedom and also that we do so in complete alignment with the comfort zones of our physical system as the physical body is so precious and we do not want to create damage in the organs or on any level.

With regard to the health of the organs, it is important that the suggestions given in the chapter "Tao & Tools" be applied for those seeking these freedoms.

Yesterday I was in meditation and a voice began to share with me, a voice of such love and compassion that I knew it was the voice of my DOW. Are we separate? No. And yet there is the personality where mind can be at times like a monkey chattering, observing and doing in this world; whereas this pure being, completely aware and enlightened, this

Buddha, this Christ within began to speak to tell me of all the gifts that I would receive in this retreat and how these gifts would make any discomfort pail into insignificance. It invited me not to think so much and to flow into the power of each now moment and simply BE. It also shared of other things that I choose not to mention here except to say that the voice was so magnificent, so beautiful and it came after I had treated myself to a symphony of devotional music.

For me there is no more powerful way to move the human heart and soul on an emotional level, and to bring them into an energy field of absolute gratitude, than through listening to sacred music. After five days of silence, listening yesterday immediately bought tears to my eyes and bought me into a state of such appreciation and devotion. Today I treated myself again to an hour concert of sacred indigenous music – it was such a wondrous experience.

Darkroom Diary Downloads – Day 8

The teachings of the Tao are the same as the teaching of the DOW – the Divine One Within us for they come from the same essence. The repetitive teaching throughout both is about the power of the mind and the need for any shape-shifting student to have a very strong mind/body connection. Learning to listen to the voice of the body is imperative for yes it does tell you what it needs.

And so as the days progress I am learning to adjust my inner plane violet light feeding mechanism with its spinning chakra column and the rays of light that move through my cells and atoms, in through the inner universes to bring back the prana to feed me. As this system has been supplemented from external sunlight until now, I am paying very particular attention to the voice of my body to ensure I am fed what I need.

Today I noticed a little discomfort in my stomach and asked my body if it was hungry and it said yes so I have now developed an additional feeding mechanism that I will share in the "Tao & Tools" chapter. I must admit that I am loving the daily revelation of all these tools as, freed from all sorts of external stimulation and distraction, I can spend more and more time within the structure of the physical system, scanning it, talking to it and working with the different systems, and also working with areas that may carry a particular weakness. And with every physical connection like this the body will reveal to you, a way that it can be bought back into balance, or healed as the need may be.

I have found in this dark room retreat that the lack of light produces an excess of melatonin in the brain that is generally not converted to serotonin unless we are incredibly active in our mind. And yet there are ways of releasing the pinealian from within the pineal gland which when released acts as a blocker for this serotonin. So we can block any imbalance of the production of serotonin and even melatonin by the release of extra pinealian.

Darkroom Diary Downloads – Day 10

Have been playing a little more with the rhythm of my daily routine to try and maximize the pleasure gained from being in this environment. I have found myself missing a little of that beautiful heart energy, the things that bring DOW smiles, and so after our morning exercises with the group first I stay within the hall and continue my yoga for another hour, and then I go upstairs to my room and listen to my mantras and sacred songs of devotion as this allows the heart to open so beautifully and be flooded with that feeling of divine love and devotion for all life, and appreciation also of everything that has gone before regarding the Holy Ones and their messages. It is beautiful to dance in that time and to continue the energy work of working with Chi around the body especially after going through a more intense yogic session prior to it all. The dance loosens things up again and directs another layer of violet light while I sing along with the mantras. The whole experience is really quite sublime and puts me in the perfect space for Mantak's class and subsequent meditation.

I have found that it is important for me to start the day with good open heart energy and the feeling of devotion for it adds a whole new level. When I am at home it is easy to release this feeling for it is simply a matter of waking up, if I have been sleeping and walking out on to my balcony and watch the sun rising over the ocean. Immediately my heart is filled with love and devotion for I get to witness the magnificence of all creation via the simple rising of the sun. As I do not have that pleasure here so it has to be induced in another way and the singing of devotional songs and mantras allows this to come together quite beautifully.

Darkroom Diary Downloads – Day 11

I have been watching and listening avidly as a student and feeling the fields as the darkroom experience unfolds and trying to summarize the goal and the outcome as well as the procedures involved attaining these, as the teachings progress. Also at the same time I have begun seeing the relevance and the similarities with the way that I have been trained with using the violet light and the outcomes that I too have been guided to focus on.

Week one was focused on what is called the Lesser Kan and Li, week two is the Greater Kan and Li and week three will be the greatest Kan and Li. Kan and Li literally means water and fire and these are used together alchemically to cleanse, regenerate and feed our organs by using cosmic particles (Chi), sexual energy (Jing) and also the hormones of our body.

The easiest summary, that I have come to understand so far, and have since confirmed with the leading instructors of these methods, is that in the Lesser Kan and Li we are looking at creating an inner plane cauldron of energy that stores and activates energy in the lower chakras, it is anchored in the sacral and around the navel, and through a particular process we learn how to generate and direct the powerful violet light steam.

This steam is then used to cleanse and hydrate the organs which is interesting for the research that I am doing, for as I've shared, I am looking for a powerful system of internal hydration so that my body can be free from the need to take fluid.

In the second week the Greater Kan and Li goes into the creation of a clay cauldron which has a different heat mechanism and is more gentle again in its production of the violet light steam to regenerate and cleanse the organs, and in the third week we go into the heart area to produce the jade cauldron.

These three cauldrons work together producing denser, to finer, to totally refined frequencies of violet light mist, to totally cleanse the whole system, but more than that the energy work and the tools and techniques then begin to allow a person a greater activation of their divine essence and to provide to them with the freedom to come and go from the body at will to explore the inner cosmos.

The third part of this is the creation, within these cauldrons, of the immortal fetus – as the Taoist Masters call it. This is a fetus that is an immortal body that will grow, when fed over time, to allow the complete transmutation of the dense material of our physical system into the immaterial, the pure light body of spirit, and maintain the forever youthing or self-regenerating system of immortality.

There is a strong emphasis in this darkroom retreat on 'out of body' experiences, falling through the inner atoms into the inner cosmos. With out of body training people need to understand that it is our frequency which will determine which dimension we can access and which doors open to us and allow us to enter these different worlds.

When the ancient masters said 'be here now' what they meant was to be totally focused on the moment and very present, for when you tune yourself through frequency adjustment, via lifestyle and where you focus your thoughts, your words, your actions, then everything does automatically just come to you. You can find yourself walking into a sacred temple and suddenly moving through a dimensional door because there is something in your energy field that matches the purest teachings in that temple, and in that walk-through you find yourself going backwards in time, living in another world, or glimpsing another world, either simply as the watcher, or as an invited guest, where you can participate and interact with the ones who dwell in that realm.

So for me these days I no longer go seeking for I've witnessed enough in my experience with meeting with the Holy Ones and many of the other experiences I've had, where it just happens automatically when the time is right and when there is something that you need to know to support your service agenda.

When you are pure of heart and have tuned yourself and surrendered totally to the divine one within, with an openness and a desire to have revealed to you all the codes within your light body regarding what you have come to do in your service for the evolution of humanity, then all the universal forces support you with this river of Grace and deliver to your door everything that you need, exactly as you need it. Whether it be the resources of wisdom, clarity, vision, or time, money, people or anything that you require; because what you are participating in is a pre-programmed and pre-agreed part in a cosmic movie that supports positive human evolution. Staying focused in the now moment is needed to allow everything to come to us is part of the path of self mastery, as is tuning ourselves so that we can magnetize exactly what we require.

Darkroom Diary Downloads – Day 12

I have been in my silent time over the last few days, very much in the position of the watcher, just watching the different levels of consciousness within me rise and take center stage and how the rising of each one effects my energy flow.

I am also seeing more and more of the complexities involved in the creation of a model that one can apply en mass and sometimes I wonder if it's possible, for every human being is so complex.

Perhaps the end result will be again that loose guidelines can only be offered, things that have worked for me that we then encourage people to apply in tandem with their own inner guidance. I do believe that we can apply the science of matrix mechanics but there are so many other subtleties involved.

As I have shared earlier there are conditions that are like anomalies in the field, for example, yes I can travel constantly taking no nourishment from physical food; yes I can be in highly polluted environments because of the use of my bio-shield and my inner plane feeding mechanisms, and also because of the anomaly of the fact that I am constantly channeling high voltage, high frequency energies of love and wisdom as I work in each different city.

I do not know how much that this anomaly is compensating for dealing with the mental, emotional and physical pollutions that I move through, but I am sure that it compensates a lot, for to spend months on the road, in a constant state of deep meditation, where you are totally merged into that energy of your divine force, and where all the love and wisdom of the universe can flow through you, as drawn through you by the crowd before you, all of this is an amazing boost for our system.

But this is just how I work and is not something that the common man making these sorts of transitions is normally exposed to. Conversely if you have a Lama or a being in a highly energized, high prana environment like the beach or the Himalayas where you are doing your spiritual practices, and where you are not exposed to any mental, emotional or physical pollutants, then again it is easier to maintain a high voltage Qi field flow to feed and nourish the system, but again the regular person does not live at the beach or in rainforests or in the Himalayas, the regular person is congregating generally in cities where there are huge levels of pollution.

As we all know pollution can take many forms – pollution from television, pollution from cars, pollution from toxic thinking – where thought forms are constantly bounding through the city and toxic emotions that are constantly being released from people's unhappiness and feelings of desolation, isolation or whatever they are going through.

All of these are contributing factors that constantly move through a person's energy fields particularly if they are not using the matrix mechanisms that we recommend in this Law of Love manual.

I do not believe that it is for one person to formulate a particular model but by taping into universal mind as I'm doing and then applying what is received, I think that one person can offer guidelines that will at least point people in the right direction and save them a lot of time when they then add their own layer of DOW power, which will be their missing ingredient to take them into the freedom plane.

If it was a matter of one person delivering one model, then no doubt we would end up again with the students and teacher game, the flock and the shepherd, and this is definitely not a time of flocks and shepherds, this is definitely a time of self mastery. It stands to reason that even the most tuned individuals, when accessing universal mind, will be able to bring through most of the ingredients, but there will always be one missing key ingredient which determines success and that ingredient is the key-note of each individual that is applying this model. This is something that only the individual can control or regulate.

Darkroom Diary Downloads – Day 13
I have also begun to glimpse the danger within my own system of the fine line that I walk, that while I can maintain a certain frequency, then it easy for the body to go for long periods, if not permanently, without fluid. But as soon as I get out of balance through side-tracking with any emotional issues that are still needing resolution within my own life, then that acts like a plug pulled from a hot air balloon, immediately deflating all the air within that balloon and causing it to spiral downwards.

So again my body consciousness is telling me, that I have to attend more at this time to my emotional body and bring it into a stronger space of harmony with my future path.

Part of this disharmony for me, is to do with the coming of the media in the next ten days for I began my work on the global stage open to share with the media all our wonderful research. I was like a child that had found a treasure chest that was filled with the gifts that the divine one brings and in my naivety I found myself entering, what I have often described as a boxing ring with Mohammed Ali, where I was completely unprepared for what was to come.

It is true that even for the most courageous warrior when the odds are stacked against you that you come out from that ring feeling battered and bruised. To deal with the media onslaught with the deaths of the three people indirectly associated with my first book *Living on Light*, to receive blame for situations that were caused by events and people either ignoring what was recommended, or by people who were perhaps unskilled to deal with the problems that they encountered; to deal with the onslaught of all of this can leave its mark. To continue, always acting responsibly, to refine the model further knowing its place in the greater game and the long term benefits that will provide our planet, in the face of all of this is also a challenge as sometimes it is easier to walk away.

So my emotional body, that sweet innocent child within, so in love with the divine and so hurt on some levels by the reaction of our world to these pearls of wisdom, was so happy to have been able to retire these last few years from working with the media. This child has had to be enticed into co-operation again for I know that my involvement with this documentary is going to bring media attention back to our door. No doubt with that attention will come the digging up of all the misconceptions, and fallacies, and rumors that have been released through the fields from our previous foray in trying to educate our world regarding the gifts of our DOW.

For me it is like child wanting to share something so precious with an adult, sharing it with so much love and trust and knowing that if only the adult could see what this child could see, that the adult's world would be transformed as the child's is, and then as the child shares the adult turns around and smacks the child in the face, then the child retreats, perhaps hiding in its room. Then the adult says "come on out, it's okay", and so perhaps the child ventures again, shares again, gets smacked again, and retreats back into its room.

How many times will it take before the child refuses to come out?

How much courage must that child gather?

How much belief in the beauty of what it has to share must the child have to keep coming out of the room to be smacked again and again.

The Law of Love & Its Fabulous Frequency of Freedom
with Jasmuheen

Interesting dilemma for a child and the inner child forms part of all of us. It is our trusting innocent nature. It is the one that responds so purely and so joyously and so delightedly when the divine one that breathes us begins to dance its way through our system. It is the one that doesn't question but feels the endless potential of such a dance, and dances the dance using steps it has always known, for these are the steps that will take this child back to the one true home, the home from which the child was born – that original force of creation that heaven, the Eden, the nirvana sought by all.

This is the dance the inner child loves and when it knows the steps it is put upon the global stage and instead of receiving any praise or 'thank yous', it is booed and hissed by certain members of the audience. And so the child learns not to have those members present, for when they are not present then the rest of the audience and the child can dance the dance of the divine. When the like-minds gather, when the seekers of miracles gather and listen to that inner voice and learn the dance of their DOW, then the miracles happen and the dance becomes stronger and the pathways easier to follow for it is multiplied by the masses.

I guess you could say, to me dealing with the media is like the hecklers in the audience, by not involving myself with them I won't get slapped, I won't get heckled and the journey is easier and a thorn is removed from my side.

It is interesting to know how destabilizing that the sort of emotional reality that I describe above – and the feelings that come with it – can be, so of course as the master of the system one does what is required to forgive and to let go and move on.

I remember when the media frenzy was at its height and I found myself crying quietly in my hotel room under the shower feeling what a missed opportunity it was, knowing what a powerful tool the media is to re-educate our society and lead it out of fear, and to provide powerful tools for eliminating all the poverty and chaos and disease and war on our planet; and as I allowed my inner child its moment of sorrow, I felt myself encased in arms of such love that just held me gently and shared, whispering in my ear: "Forgive them Father, for they know not what they do. Forgive them Father, for they know not what they do".

Of course I understood immediately what this referred to and so I re-gathered myself and let it go and moved on, knowing and trusting that there are paths for human evolution that we will take that are supported by the Law of Love and its flow of Grace.

I can only assume that I am guided to share this story here as I lay wide awake enjoying the dawning of another morning, because *it is so important that we be in a state of physical, mental and emotional congruency when we take an extreme path within our freedom journey,* particularly the path of a food or fluid free existence.

This sort of congruency is not something that can be delivered by a model, although the model as we've shared can provide guidelines. It is the congruency that comes from the living of life where we experience through circumstance what it's like to be humble, what it's like to totally surrender, what it's like to come into such levels of sincerity in our desire to know such freedoms.

The greatest gift that all the dealing with the media given me, was the gift of true humility and for that I will be eternally grateful. Because of this gift of true humility I've been able to enter through the most amazing dimensional doors, to be with beings of great light and great love, who have revealed to me so many of the secrets of the higher planes all of which has expanded my emotional capacity to such levels of refinement of joy, awe, love and wonder. I know that without this key of humility that these are experiences that probably would have been denied.

So again for me, everything that occurs is absolutely perfect for in the greatest suffering throughout the greatest trials, tests and tribulations there will be a gift, a gift that is so needed, a gift that will add a flavor, a virtue, an insight that will add a necessary part to our key-note as we progress through the freedom fields.

Darkroom Diary Downloads – Day 14

Master Chia says that the more that we practice the GSC meditation that I outline in Part 2 of *The Law of Love* manual, the more adept that the glands become at secreting the hormones that make up the elixir of life, what the yogis call Divine nectar, a nectar that is not only secreted through the pituitary gland but also through the mix of the other hormones, from pinealian and the known hormones that exist within the saliva. When we add to this the creative life force of sexual energy from our reproductive organs, and the universal chi from the cosmic oceans we have a very thick, sweet nectar that we then swallow to feed and hydrate the body and lubricate the joints. The technique is quite complex and I have outlined it in detail in Part 2 of this manual but I am finding as I work with this tool daily that the body is adapting it quite naturally. My intention for simplicity seems to be the key.

For the past 14 days – or in my case for the past decade – we have been working with isolating the different muscles from the anus and perineum, to the vagina and the clitoris, we have been feeling how as we contract and release these muscles without touching anything, how these muscles can send out different electrical responses through the body, particularly the clitoris and the muscles around this, as it has an energetic connection to the pineal gland, so when we contract it we can feel this pineal gland contracting back in response. It sends out a pulse in the center of your head in a biofeedback rhythm to every clitoral contraction. The Taoists says the pineal gland is a female's male sex organ and partner to the clitoris – hence they use the term for this technique as practicing 'self intercourse'. The male's natural female sex organ is his pineal gland which is directly energetically connected to the penis. This contraction releases the intangible substance of pinealian which then flows down into the saliva to create this powerful food and fluid mix of Divine nectar.

I keep remembering the words of my one and only guru, before the tools he provided allowed me to discover the guru within, he told us all to never be dependant on anything outside of ourselves for our true happiness or pleasure. Good advice especially if we are interested in true self sufficiency.

I have never wanted or desired to live my life forever food or fluid free but I understand that part of my blueprint is to develop a model to do so, for having the ability to do this is a wonderful gift for us to enjoy regarding the freedom agenda.

Once we have a skill it does not necessarily mean that we use it all the time. We use our skills as required in our service. So my own inner dichotomy is that unlike the Russian woman Zinaida who is happy to never eat or drink again and is happy to be an example of a woman who has moved herself permanently out of that reality band, I have no long term desires to do the same. However I would like to do it long enough to be absolutely convinced that I can be fluid free as well as food free and suffer no detrimental side affects from either choice regardless of whatever situation I am in. I also wish to be able to maintain this, whether I am in the fresh aired Himalayas or on the high prana beaches, or in the noisiest, smelliest, most polluted cities of our world.

    This type of mastery over my molecular structure is of great interest. Because I can see my role in the greater agenda re all of this, and the pathway of human evolution, I am of course motivated by something deep inside, and by forces all around me to continue, and these forces support me with such love and such Grace. Because of this the idea of being revealed all of this and not applying it, and sitting on the sidelines, is no longer an option.

    The majority of humanity are still driven in a way by a hunger that sees them as the seekers of miracles and a small selection within that populace have witnessed and enjoyed miracles. Some have also come into the understanding that we can go beyond that again and literally become the makers of miracles in our own lives, and then can take it to another level where we realize that we can become the makers of miracle models which can be applied en mass in a way that is beneficial to all – this is another layer again and the choice is always ours and the options are available to all.

    Are these options that we make and create as we grow in our conscious dance through the fields of life? Or are these choices and options pre-planned before coming into embodiment? Either which way is irrelevant for they are there.

    Provided the models do have obvious benefits for the path of human evolution then the Law of Love and its channel of Grace will feed and nourish the model and present it to the perfect channels in our world. Thus it has been and thus it always will be.

Chapter 16

Tao & Tools
Doing It

Tao is unnamed, but not unknown:
By singing the perfect life tone,
You're drawn to the certainty zone.

As synchrodestiny led me to the Darkroom Retreat to receive the downloads of new tools and to learn the ancient Tao Master techniques – both of which will support the freedom agenda – then it is only fitting to share a little more of the Taoist tradition. At the start of Chapters 1 to 8 we have shared the stories of the eight Tao Immortals, beings who represent the various characters of human kind, beings who managed to shape-shift themselves into their own freedom agenda.

To the Chinese, Taoism is an attitude towards life that exhibits the joyful and carefree sides of their character. The founder of Taoism is Lao-Tzu who was said to be a court official specializing in astrology and divination and the keeper of sacred books. Legend says that when he was eighty, he set off towards what is now Tibet and when he reached the border a guard asked him to record his teachings before he left China. Although he was sad at mankind's unwillingness to follow natural goodness, he did as the guard requested and the 5,000 characters he composed then formed the Tao Te Ching.

Like many of our religious traditions there is so much in the Taoist tradition that is beneficial and hence I recommend that you do your own research and apply what appeals to you. What I wish to do in this chapter is look at the practicalities of attaining the freedom agenda and the tools that are helpful to do so.

Some are from the Taoist tradition and some I have downloaded directly from Universal Mind – all I have personally applied with beneficial results.

The Law of Love & Its Fabulous Frequency of Freedom
with Jasmuheen

TOOLS:

There are countless tools we can use to bring us into a higher knowing of and harmony in the fields of life; tools which also provide us with a recognition of, and experience of, the Laws that govern all life and how to work with these Laws with minimum effort to get maximum impact, and how to do it in a win, win, win way for all. All of these tools we have discussed in detail and provided in the "Biofields and Bliss" trilogy, so in this manual my focus will be more of our tools for Freedom and yet everything builds on everything that has gone before.

I was brought up as a Lutheran in a Christian community and probably the first tool I used and took comfort in was the tool of prayer, particularly the tool of 'ask and you shall receive' for although results were usually not instantaneous, all of what I asked for that was connected to the fulfillment of my pre-agreed assignments – did come to pass to aid each step along the way.

One of the next most powerful tools was given to me by my father and that was an attitude that I could do anything in this world and that I was my only limitation. Coming from a war torn Europe to live in the "Lucky" country of Australia, my father was convinced that everything was attainable in this country and that only people rather than circumstances could create limitation in his new found land. Interestingly enough this is a basic metaphysical truth where we know that attitude determines our reality and creates our perceived state of limitation or lack of Freedom.

The next powerful tool for me was finally adopting control over my diet as a young teenager and choosing to be vegetarian. Such a simple act, this immediately eliminated the energy of aggression and slaughter in my fields and opened me to the channels of kindness and compassion and sensitivity.

Quickly after this came the tool of Ancient Vedic Meditation techniques that when applied gifted me with the insight of the Oneness and Holiness of life, and particularly of myself as part of this Holy Oneness, for as I sat each day and explored the inner stillness and felt the Love of the One who breathes me and saw Its light, I finally experienced my true nature, which was to me a most powerful and necessary revelation and one I was very hungry for.

Daily meditation over the following decades gifted me with numerous truths from experiencing the more subtle realms behind life as we know it, with its amazing array of beings who dwell within these realms; to allowing me to understand the benefits of surrender, and the joy of being in the Presence of all that is divine, and the Love and devotion that comes with all of this; plus the gift of the clarity and insight as to the mathematics and mechanics of existence and finally the answers to all my existential questions to a point where all my questions disappeared.

Another life changing tool for me was of course the spiritual initiation of the 21 day process which gifted me with, or enhanced my ability to live on prana and be free from the need to ingest physical food. This initiation and its subsequent decade of integration has exposed me to some amazing experiences in life, from meeting the most unusual people, the bright sparks and the courageous souls who, like me, have come to inspire and stimulate humanity into certain paths of evolution.

A few years after this initiation I received the tool of my "future self/past life virtue" download which allowed me access to my future self who happens to be a scientist in the field of Advanced Bio-Energetics as it pertains to Dimensional Biofield Science; who then taught me more of inter-dimensional matrix mechanics. This covered the creation of things like the Self Sustaining Template, how to use bio-shields and so on. I learn more of Matrix Mechanics daily as an aid to my current shape-shifting journey. Via this future self initiation I learnt that opening the inner doors to cross the usually restrictive lines of time can speed everything up in our journey and provide limitless possibilities.

My experiences with Holy Ones, as outlined in my *Divine Radiance – On The Road With The Masters Of Magic* manual, came about I believe due to the direct use of these tools and also from the daily use of Recipe 2000> which I downloaded from Universal Mind at the end of the last millennium. A Recipe designed to create health and support immortality, more than anything it is the combination of this daily lifestyle focus that for me has brought the greatest change. Transcending religions and races the Recipe 2000> tool quickly and efficiently moves us through the seven levels of consciousness allowing us to be sensitive enough to find amazing dimensional doors.

Over the last 30+ years I have received numerous powerful tools that have led me to this point in readiness to take the next step and I particularly love some of the Taoists techniques that we will share in this chapter.

If I stand in my mastery, it all feels so natural and attainable – the idea that I or any human being – can attain such Freedoms. If I stand in my human bubble of conditioned limitations – it is all rather daunting and in the background I hear the usual doubts and concerns voiced by the countless who know human physical limitations as it pertains to, and is demonstrated in this limited world. Yet I have personally successfully defied many of these perceived limitations and have also met with others who have done so and more. Again the key are the words "Perceived Limitations", for my theory begins here – that perception, like the creation of a harmonious heartbeat – is the key to all Freedoms.

A prisoner in jail is perceived as being denied Freedom yet that prisoner may have discovered how to have his/her consciousness leave the physical form at will. They may then feel more Freedom than they've ever known before such as being able to explore dimensions beyond time for although they may not be physically free, by being able to project their consciousness out of their body they will no longer feel restricted.

Some may say that the research fields that interest me contravene the physical laws and yet again this depends on our perception, for what is driving the physical laws and providing them with food to function, are the universal laws which feed themselves by the Law of Love and Its gift of Grace. These are the Laws I choose to live by and choose to now further explore.

Rather than contravene the physical laws, by using more refined methods and specific tools, we can access and experience realities where we are free from self created physical limitations and thus live more harmoniously within our heart.

Unify with eternal world:
From an infant shape, tightly curled,
Perception's new flag is unfurled.

DOING IT:
Note: If it is possible, please record the below meditations onto tape as your body will respond better to your voice and you will be able to close your eyes and go deeper into the meditations if you can listen to them rather than read them. Also note that the Taoist tradition – on which some of the below meditations are based – can be seen to be quite complicated with the student being encouraged to practice, practice, and practice. For the purposes of our freedom agenda we have streamlined these tools to be easier to apply and recommend a minimum of 21 days practice until the reality of these meditations and their purpose are anchored in your cells. Here is a list of the meditations we will elaborate upon.

- ॐ MEDITATIONS 1-3: Provided in Chapters 9, 13, & 14.
- ॐ MEDITATION 4: Accessing our Pre-agreements.
- ॐ MEDITATION 5: The Balance of Yin/Yang: Exercising the pineal gland, feeding the brain, having heart orgasms and using self intercourse to nourish us.
- ॐ MEDITATION 6: System Flush and hydration with breath rhythm.
- ॐ MEDITATION 7: Additional Inner Plane Feeding Codes.
- ॐ MEDITATION 8: Healing Sounds
- ॐ MEDITATION 9: The GSC formula –the magic mix of Glucosamine, Saliva & Chi.
- ॐ MEDITATION 10: The Perfect Life, Perfect Love, Perfect Paradise Programming Code:
- ॐ MEDITATION 11: The 11 strand healing system.
- ॐ MEDITATION 12: In Chapter 20.

In this and in the following chapters we will present all the DOING & BEING tools, the freedom tools, that can be applied for us to achieve our shape-shifting agendas but before we can do this we need to know what we have personally pre-programmed ourselves to do.

Please read the next Chapter on Matrix Mechanics BEFORE applying the below meditations.

MEDITATION 4: Accessing our Pre-Agreements:
This below meditation is similar to one we did in *The Food of Gods* however this one, and some of the others, takes it to another level again. The following exercise is a simple meditation designed to reveal to you your own pre-agreements – things that you agreed to achieve this embodiment.

- ❖ First create a space of silence and stillness, tune yourself to the rhythm of your breath using the Body Love and Love Breath tools in *The Food of Gods* manual, or by using a meditation technique that you like that you know will center you and allow you to hear the voice of your DOW.
- ❖ Once you are still and centered, by using your imagination, fill your body up with pure violet light energy. This will change the frequency of your cells and allow for an easier release of your Divine Codes.
- ❖ Next we are going to ask some basic questions that require a simple yes or no answer. Trust the first response that comes.
- ❖ Breathe deeply, take 3 deep, fine connected breaths or however many you need to feel centered.
- ❖ Once you feel connected and still, we then ask:
- ❖ a) Is it in my blueprint, my pre-agreements to earn how to and then be free from the need to create dis-ease?
  Pause between each question and wait for an intuitive answer to come, trust what comes. Yes / no.
- ❖ b) Is it in my blueprint, my pre-agreements to learn how to and then be free from the need to take nourishment from physical food. Yes / no.
- ❖ c) Is it in my blueprint, my pre-agreements to learn how to and then be free from the need to take fluid. Yes / no.
- ❖ d) Is it in my blueprint, my pre-agreements to learn how to and then be free from the need to age and die. Yes / no.
- ❖ e) Is it in my blueprint, my pre-agreements to learn how to and then be a harmonizing soul. Yes / no.

* Please note that you can substitute the word 'remember' instead of 'learn' for we already know how to do all of the above, but we have just forgotten.

Once you know your encodements you can then choose which tools other tools – from either the following or those listed in *The Food of Gods* – that you may need to support the fulfillment of your pre-agreements.

Also once you have your answers to the above questions you can confirm this using kinesiology to tune in to the body consciousness and also ask the question:

"Considering my **current** energy field status, and the status of the energy fields that surround me now, how long will each conversion and transition take place?"

Go through each one you get a "yes" for and then check for the conversion/transition timing. This could be months or years for successful transitioning depending on your current frequency. The point is to allow this transition to take place with joy and ease and Grace in a way that is harmonious with your physical, emotional, mental and spiritual being.

MEDITATION 5: *The Balance of Yin/Yang: Exercising the pineal gland, feeding the brain, having heart orgasms and using self intercourse to nourish us.*

I mentioned in the Darkroom Downloads chapter that there are ways of releasing a frequency from within the pineal gland which when released acts as a blocker for the excess production of serotonin. The way to do this for a female is to focus on the muscles of the clitoris and around the clitoris, and to contract these all lightly, while imagining that the chi this contraction produces, is moving up the inner channels into the pineal gland. If you are sensitive enough you can actually feel the pineal gland contract in response and release in perfect rhythm to when your contract and release your clitoral muscles, for as mentioned the clitoris has a direct energy line to the pineal gland.

Similarly the tip of the penis and the glands there are also connected to the pineal gland in the male. This is a natural physical hook-up that allows the Taoist to engage in what they call self intercourse by merging the energy of our male and female selves. In the woman the female self is represented by the clitoris and her inner male partner is represented by her pineal gland, in the male the masculine is the penis and their feminine is represented by their pineal gland.

When the two interconnect through this sort of exercise they blend two powerful energies to feed the body. Learning to control our orgasm via a hands off experience by simple moving energy around the body is a wonderful skill to develop as the Taoist teachings are very focused on self happiness, and self love, and being in a state of such a free flow of energy through the system that we can feel the bliss of the cosmic forces and the love of creation pulsing through us whenever we desire to feel it. Self intercourse using the above tool and combining it with the microcosmic orbit is another nourishing and enjoyable energy distribution food.

MEDITATION 6: *System Flush and hydration with breath rhythm:*
A tool that uses Creative Visualization, programming & breath for hydrating the body – this is for those whose are encoded to be both food and fluid free or who wish to know how to hydrate their systems using an internal plane mechanism.

- ॐ Sit or lie down comfortably, center yourself and begin the love breath meditation.
- ॐ Inhale deeply from the never ending well of divine love in your heart chant "I am love" and exhale and chant "I love". Remember this is your cosmic door opener that puts you automatically in touch with all the love in all the fields from which true nourishment comes.
- ॐ Tell the body over and over "I love you, I love you, I love you" – this prepares the cells receptivity levels to absorb and receive more love and cosmic particles and also expands their capacity to hold them.
- ॐ Next allow your feet to touch the ground and visualize that your feet are resting in a beautiful cool, bubbling glade of highly energized chi water that is sparkling with golden violet hues of pure nourishing energy. Imagine that this is a magical pool offered to you by mother earth.
- ॐ Next move your mind up to your crown chakra and imagine that all of the thousand petals of the lotus that sits in this chakra are open and that a thousand beams of violet light are radiating from each petal, searching out in a 360 degree direction to connect with and magnetize all the cosmic particles of pure chi energy that you need.
- ॐ Imagine these beams also now anchoring themselves into a vast, nourishing cool blue universal ocean – an ocean of pure hydrating and nourishing chi.
- ॐ Now establish a breathing rhythm where each inhale is connected with each exhale, breathe deep, fine and connected.
- ॐ As you breathe in deeply, imagine that you are now drawing in through the souls of your feet, all the hydrating liquid that your body needs, draw it from this pool, draw it up through your feet, through your ankles, through your calves, through your bones, through your muscular structure and blood lines and lymphatic system, draw this cooling liquid right up your legs, through the torso and through to the top of your head.
- ॐ Imagining as your mind follows your breathe, and you draw it up through your body, that you are flooding your whole system with cool energizing chi filled water that comes from the heart of mother earth.
- ॐ Then as you breathe out imagine that as you push your breath gently downwards that you are drawing all the universal water through the beams that are anchored in the lotus in your crown chakra and that
- ॐ you are now sending, directing this universal liquid down through your system.
- ॐ Imagine that it flows through your brain hydrating it with this magical cosmic particle violet and blue light liquid,
- ॐ imagine sending it down your throat, into your lungs, filling your lungs and then your heart with healing nourishing liquid from the universal ocean,
- ॐ imagine it then being pushed gently with your exhale down into your intestines, through your sexual organs, then down your legs and into your feet and send these universal streams of liquid light back into the pool.
- ॐ Imagine that as you inhale and exhale that you are literally flushing out your whole system, bringing in the water element of earth from the pool at your feet as you inhale, and then as you exhale you begin to flush out your system as streams of

cosmic particles from the universal ocean of chi now flow in through your crown chakra down into your system like an internal shower.
- ॐ Imagine then as you take a deep inhale that you are again drawing more of this perfect hydrating fluid from the pool of water at your feet and again as you exhale you draw it down or in through the crown from the universal ocean.
- ॐ Keep repeating this breathing rhythm and holding the visual images in your mind's eye, imagine marrying the waters of the cosmos with the waters of the pool.
- ॐ Imagine that as these streams flow through your body with your inhale and your exhale that your body is being re-energized, re-hydrated exactly as it needs.
- ॐ Repeat until you intuitively feel that your body has had enough – but do for 5 minutes minimum.

The success of using all the tools in this chapter depends of you having a mind body connection where you listen to the voice of your body, as your body will tell you what it needs and when it has had enough.

As with the other exercises in these chapters do it for 21 days, for a minimum of 5 minutes morning and night. Doing it for 21 days allows it to become part of your cells, and a natural part of your breathing rhythm, just like the spinning light chakra column meditation from the book *The Food of Gods*. Just like we set this meditation to be in permanent motion with the rhythm of our inhale and exhale; so too can we anchor this visual imagery of drawing liquid through the souls of our feet and through our crown chakra to also flow in natural rhythm with our breath as per the above meditation.

While most of our meditations really need to be done only once to set the mechanics in place, setting into cellular memory where it is real for the cells, comes from daily practice and we do it like this to move beyond a mental construct. As you are aware, it takes 21 to 28 days to form a new habit and by doing it for this period of time, it becomes part f your being and then you can set it into automatic motion to flow with the rhythm of your breath.

MEDITATION 7: Additional Inner Plane Feeding Codes. The following simple meditation and programming codes are an aid to feed the body from the inner planes. It is a variation on, and the next level for, the meditation in *The Food of Gods* and includes programming with the seven elements. The success of this technique depends totally on your mind body connection and the belief that you are the Master of this vehicle and that *chi follows mind* and that the body can do anything that it is instructed to do.
Note: This is a feeding mechanism – do before a meal NOT after. Also drinking a glass of water before you begin to aid the body in handling the electromagnetic boost it is about to receive.

- ॐ Lie or sit in a comfortable position.
- ॐ Use the love breath tool and body love tool so that the body co-operates more easily with us.
- ॐ You may also wish to apply the spinning chakra meditation in *The Food of Gods* and breathe deeply.
- ॐ When you have established a good breathing rhythm then if you feel murmurings in the stomach, ask the body if it is hungry. If you get a yes apply the next step. If you get a no then ask why you are having the murmurings and 'is it due to blocked energy?' If you do get a yes and are still taking nourishment from physical food then you may wish to replace your normal feeding methods for just one meal a day by using the cosmic particles program below.
- ॐ If you get a yes then after you have created the Spinning Chakra column in meditation, instruct: "Cells of my body, molecules of my body, I instruct you now to follow the rays of violet light from the spinning chakra column through into the inner universes. From there I instruct that you draw all that you need to feed you now."
- ॐ Next continue your instruction with a command said with intention as if you are the master and the body must obey you.
- ॐ Command: "Body feed your self from the Cosmic Fire elements now, body feed from the element Akasha now, body feed from the astral light element now, body feed from the cosmic particles now. Body feed off the elements of air, earth, fire and water now. Body take all that you need – your vitamins and minerals for your perfect nourishment and hydration – take all this from the seven elements now!"
- ॐ Continue with the chant: "I am fed by cosmic fire now! I am fed by akasha now! I am fed by astral light now! I am fed by the element air now! I am fed by the element fire now! I am fed by the element earth now! I am fed by the element water now!"
- ॐ Next imagine all the filaments from within all your cells dancing and being revitalized as the violet light attracts all of this from the elements and brings it back into your system to feed it now.
- ॐ Imagine it nourishing and hydrating your light-body, your meridians, your skeleton, your bone marrow, your bloodlines, your organs, your muscles, your nervous system, your lymphatic and endocrine systems and your skin now.

The above meditation can be used in conjunction with the other inner plane feeding tools discussed in *The Food of Gods*.

Additional programs to use may be:
- ॐ All my nourishment, all my food, all my fluid comes to me from the violet light and the cosmic ocean now
- ॐ All my nourishment, all my vitamins, all my food, all my fluid comes to me from the inner planes from the cosmic particles now.

Just allow your intuition to find your own mantras to use but remember that your words must be accompanied by the feeling, the knowing that chi follows mind and that chi has the power to create and sustain all life.

Again do this for as long as you are guided and then ask your body if it is still hungry or if it is happy and full. You should feel a shift in your stomach and those flutterings should have abated.

MEDITATION 8: *Six Healing Comic Sounds*

One of the most helpful preparation tools in the Taoist tradition – for the following GSC meditation no. 6 – is the Six Cosmic Healing Sounds. These are a system of visual intentions combined with specific sounds that are designed to cleanse each organ and stimulate the chi flow within them. I recommend it here as the organs store emotions that can block the way chi flows and hence block how we are fed and hydrated. Mantak Chia's booklet *Cosmic Sounds – Sounds that Heal* details this practice perfectly. The Cosmic Healing Sounds are also a good way to release any energy that we collect from the day that we no longer need, and we can also use these sounds to replenish the organs with higher quantities of chi on a daily basis and to tune the organs to a more nourishing vibratory pattern.

I love the visual image in this tool that the kidneys are connected to and fed and watered by the inner plane universal oceans. I love to visualize each day pure blue cooling energy flowing through my kidneys, to smile to all my organs and say hello to each one – even to my brain – and then to imagine each organ filled with the following colors and animal totem energy as I make the healing sounds and send the vibration of color, image and sound through each organ.

Briefly:
I. The lungs: color – white; element – metal; animal totem – white tiger; virtues – courage and righteousness; sense – smell and touch; emotions – grief and sadness; season autumn; sound – "Sssssss" (said with the tongue behind the teeth)
II. The kidneys: color – dark blue; element – water; animal totem – deer; virtues – gentleness, calmness, stillness and alertness; sense – hearing; emotion – fear; season – winter; sound "Chooooo".
III. The liver: color – green; element – wood; animal totem – green dragon; virtues – kindness; sense – sight; emotion – anger; season – spring; sound – "Shhhhhh" (tongue near palate)
IV. The Heart: color – red; element – fire; animal totem – pheasant; virtues – joy, honor, sincerity; sense – tongue, speech; emotion – hastiness, arrogance, cruelty; season – summer; sound – "Hawwwwwww" (said with mouth wide open)

V. The spleen: color – yellow, element – earth, animal totem – phoenix, virtues – fairness and openness; sense – taste; emotion – worry; season – Indian summer; sound "Whoooo".

VI. The 6th sound of "Heeeee" balances the temperature of the three energy centers in the body – the upper which is the brain, heart and lungs and is a hot energy; the middle which is the liver, kidneys, stomach, pancreas and spleen – which is warm energy and the lower which is the small and large intestines, the bladder and the sexual organs, an energy center which is cool.

When we use the above sounds we also visualize the color, virtues or totem animal image, to redirect the energy flow around the body to create health and balance. As the meditation to use these healing sounds is both elaborate, detailed and powerful in Mantak's book, I suggest that you follow it as outlined there.

MEDITATION 9: The GSC formula –the magic mix of Glucosamine, Saliva & Chi. Based on the Taoists Elixir Chi Kung technique.

Discussion: One of the concerns I have had in the past has been the dehydration and re-hydration of the system, particularly if one is no longer taking any fluid at all and also if one is out of a highly energized pranic environment such as your own home sanctuary where the energies have been set to feed you. Particularly for me as I travel and have spent so much time every year in highly polluted environments.

The concern for me in the past has been maintaining my weight level when I have chosen to be liquid free as I found that my body would automatically take some of the energy that it uses to feed me and then redirect it into flushing out some of the pollutants that I would inhale through breathing and living in these more toxic environments. This redirection of the chi energy would thus create a lesser feeding percentage and a greater cleaning percentage – hence the weight loss, as I would not get enough nourishment. In order to combat this in the past I would usually choose to still drink water and even coffee to handle the social activities that on road life often presents.

In this situation we are looking for a permanent fluid free existence which means being able to utilize enough of the chi from the inner cosmos and from our external elemental world environment and to do it in perfect balance with our system so that fluid/hydration levels can be maintained without any external sustenance.

I would like to introduce here a number of processes that I believe will address the above issues. First we have to look at the whole skeletal structure as the structure of the skeleton has to be very strong and also flexible. We need to maintain bone density and health of bone marrow which we do by infusing the skeletal structure with the violet light and also by working with keeping the joints flexible by lubricating the sacrum and the lower lumbar areas and the top of the femur bones. These are three areas which carry the complete weight of our system and therefore sustain the greatest wear and tear.

The following meditation allows us to use very specific Taoist tools to increase lubrication and hydration of the whole system. The Taoists work as part of their basic training on
    I. strengthening their whole skeletal system particularly the three areas mentioned and
    II. lubricating all the joints and
    III. distributing through the whole system a highly energized food that is directed into the joints and then into the whole system.

I have come to call the technique that does the above, the GSC formula. This is the Glucosamine, salvia, chi mix which is an alchemical power pack of energy that can be used to achieve the above. The following technique is imperative for those who wish to enjoy a fluid free future although it can be also used by those wishing to maintain inner health, particularly on a skeletal level.

Glucosamine is a form of amino sugar that is found naturally in the body and it is believed to play a role in both cartilage formation and repair. In the Taoist practices there is a very particular way of producing more Glucosamine naturally in the body and that is the rolling of the stomach. When you roll the chi in the stomach as per the below technique your body will automatically produce more of this, however we are not just looking at increasing the production of Glucosamine but also to mix it with other powerful feeding and hydrating substances.

It will be of great aid to you to record the below meditation onto a tape so you can use it to guide you daily or until you are more adept at this seemingly complicated practice.

Technique: Elixir Chi Kung: creating and using the GSC – Glucosamine, Saliva and Chi – alchemical formula:

Due to the relatively complex nature of the below exercise I have broken it up into five parts for you to practice individually before you string them all together. The practice is like making a cup of tea or coffee where various ingredients need to be created and then mixed together to deliver a specific outcome.

Part 1: Elixir Chi King – eating Cosmic Particles and creating a particular alchemical saliva mix.

The Taoists say the saliva is the fountain of life, an extremely complex fluid that contains a huge array of substances that can affect our health. According to Mantak Chia's book *Elixir Chi Kung*, saliva "aids in digestion, electrolyte balance, control of oral micro flora, tissue maintenance, enamel maturation, acid neutralization and behavior." It also aids speech and protects our teeth and helps us to swallow. When we add cosmic particles and chi from our master glands to this mix, it becomes alchemical and includes the immortality hormone.

It is said that a healthy person produces 1.5 litres of saliva a day and that when a Taoist master sits in meditation and leaves his/her body to explore the cosmos often for hours, days or months at a time, that this body swallows this alchemical saliva mix approximately 1,000 times a day, thus feeding and hydrating the body perfectly.

So let us begin:

- ॐ   Stand comfortably with soft knees (knees that are slightly bent)
- ॐ   Next bend over and shake yourself out like a rag doll, releasing all stuck energy, shake your arms, body, legs and head. This shake-up activates the endocrine system and stimulates the flow of the cranial sacral and cerebral fluids.
- ॐ   Next begin to breathe deeply and to center yourself using your breath, find that place of stillness.
- ॐ   Take a moment to smile to each of your organs – your brain, lungs, heart, spleen, kidneys, liver, intestines, sexual organs etc. send each a beam of pink loving light. This is cosmic etiquette of greeting before you begin to play with your internal being as each organ contains consciousness, and you as the master of the system are about to invite this organ consciousness to operate in a slightly different way. *The Taoists say that if you smile at something long enough eventually it smiles back at you.*
- ॐ   Then rub your hands together to form an Alpha ball of energy and when your hands are energized place them over your kidneys.
- ॐ   Imagine that pure healing hydrating chi is flowing from your palms now into each kidney.
- ॐ   Next as you keep your hands on your kidneys, move your focus to your mouth.
- ॐ   Now focusing on your mouth begin to imagine that you are chewing the most delicious meal, imagine that you are chewing and sucking on the most incredibly tasty food. This will produce saliva in your mouth that we need to gather here so do not swallow.
- ॐ   Imagine that as we are chewing, that the saliva is filled with healthy hormones, and that also that the pituitary and pineal glands are also releasing more of their own nectars which are vibrating and flowing down into our mouth as we chew. Remember always that chi follows mind so if we think that the pituitary and pineal glands are adding their fountain of youth type magic elixirs to our saliva then so it is.
- ॐ   Imagine too that as you are chewing and sucking that you are drawing in with each open mouthed chewing motion, all the cosmic particles from the universal oceans creating a fluid that is filled with your natural saliva hormones, your master gland chi mix and the cosmic ocean chi mix.
- ॐ   Imagine as you keep chewing that these are all mixing together.
- ॐ   Next take a big breath in with your mouth open, take a deep breath as if you are a cosmic vacuum cleaner that is now drawing in all the higher elements of Cosmic Fire, Akasha and Astral light as you inhale.
- ॐ   Next chew with your teeth touching together seven times to the right, seven to the left and seven to the middle – this action increases saliva production.
- ॐ   Imagine that this mix of hormones, saliva and cosmic chi is gathered into one pool, now tighten both our mouth, jaw and throat muscles as if we are

constricting and jutting out our jaw/chin/throat – this creates an easy pathway for the saliva to flow in one motion directly into the Glucosamine/chi mix that we have created using the steps below.
- ॐ Then swallow it all and
- ॐ Imagine that your stomach holds a huge etheric cauldron that is waiting to receive this mix.
- ॐ As we swallow, imagine this saliva flowing down into our stomach/intestine area and filling up an etheric pot or cauldron. Imagine that we have now added part 1 of a three part recipe of ingredients into this cauldron.

Once this is done once, there will always be a residual of GSC in the stomach 'cauldron' to add more saliva to.

Next practice steps 2 & 3 & 4 below and then do step 5.

Part 2 – Elixir Chi Kung: Increasing Glucosamine production
- ॐ Next we learn to roll our stomach.
- ॐ So focus your mind on your solar plexus and then move your intention along with the physical movement and roll your stomach over to the right side of your body, then down to the pubic bone, then up to the left side of the body then over to the middle of your stomach area. In other words roll your stomach and move its muscles in an anticlockwise and circular motion.
- ॐ Next think of the word Glucosamine as you focus your mind in your stomach area, remember chi follows mind and blood and chemicals in the body follow chi. Just thinking of this word alerts your body to its existence within it and hence makes it more accessible for our use.

Part 3: Elixir Chi Kung: Increasing our Chi reserves
- ॐ So let's now begin to further build up our chi reserves.
- ॐ Place your mind into your sacral chakra and imagine that this chakra is the doorway to the inner central sun.
- ॐ Imagine that golden light energy of pure cosmic Christed consciousness is flowing through this grid point of this central sun, see it flooding in through the sacral chakra as bright yellow energy.
- ॐ Imagine this yellow inner liquid light energy of pure chi now mixing with the Glucosamine in your stomach as you continue rolling it anti-clockwise then clockwise.
- ॐ Next let's begin to draw chi energy up from the sexual organs as we begin to contract and release the clitoral or penis muscles and to feel that as we do so, that our pineal gland is also contracting in rhythm and begins flooding our brain with its own special chi frequencies.
- ॐ Imagine energy flowing from the ovaries and testes down into the perineum as in the micro-cosmic orbit technique we shared in *The Food of Gods* manual. Gather this life creating energy of sexual food and imagine it flowing now into the cauldron in the stomach area that is holding the GSC mix.

ॐ So now we have the brain pulsating certain energy waves as our pineal gland works in rhythm to our sexual organs which also pulsate certain waves plus we have energy flowing in from the sacral chakra via the central sun and we have Glucosamine flowing more freely as we roll it all together in circular motion around and throughout our intestinal area.

ॐ Now we are ready to add extra hormones to the saliva mix, and then in part 5 we will add a mix of energy that we gain from using a technique the Taoists call eating the cosmic particles.

Part 4: Adding additional hormones through laughter.

ॐ Next put your finger on your Thymus gland and imagine it growing very long extending into the Thymus gland as if you are tickling it and then

ॐ laugh and laugh and laugh and laugh as laughter produces more of the T-lymphocytes which are your special fighting force, your defense force to strengthen your immune system then

ॐ put your finger on your navel again imagine your finger extending growing longer and longer right into the navel and focusing on the body producing B-lymphocytes again to help the immune systems defense system, then

ॐ laugh and laugh and laugh and laugh again.

ॐ Next you put your fingers on the femur bones – on both sides of the femur bone left and right, and imagine extending your finger right in to the top of the femur bone and again imagine tickling this bone and laughing and laughing and laughing. This laughter addition produces extra ingredients for the GSC elixir formula to strengthen the whole system.

Part 5: Distributing the alchemical mix throughout the body.

Now you have an energy pool from parts 2, 3 & 4 for the saliva mix you have created in part 1 to flow into. So create again the saliva mix and swallow it and add it to the Glucosamine/Saliva/Chi – GSC – mix and roll it all together as if you are stirring a great cauldron of GSC – a mix of energy that we can now distribute to hydrate and lubricate the system, a mix that you now imagine gathers all day every day with every swallow into this new alchemical etheric cauldron.

Once you have imagined that this mix is in the cauldron it is time to distribute it through your body so,

ॐ bend over and shake your body till it is relaxed and loose.

ॐ Imagine as you are shaking that your joints are loosening up and opening getting ready to receive this alchemical mix of GSC.

ॐ Imagine that the area between all our joints, around our femur bones and hip joints and sacrum is all soft, jelly like and lubricated and of a mud type consistency.

ॐ Imagine now that shooting out from the cauldron are five lines of light – light rays that are now carrying the GSC formula,

ॐ Imagine that as this light is radiating out – that one ray of light flows down each leg, one flows down the spine (if you are still bent over) and two more

- ॐ flow down the arms. (This is great to do with the yoga asana downward facing dog.)
- ॐ Imagine these rays of GSC alchemical light flowing now throughout the body like a river, flowing through the skeletal structure, through the endocrine system, through the meridians, through the bloodlines, until it also infuses through the bone marrow.
- ॐ Imagine this special GSC mix is healing, hydrating and feeding everything it flows through.
- ॐ Imagine directing this GSC formula with these light rays down through the hip joints, through the knee joints, the ankle joints and down to the toes.
- ॐ Direct these light rays down through your arms. Imagine that this formula is lubricating all the joints in your whole body and then
- ॐ Direct it through your spine, around all the vertebrae, through the ribcage and up through to your neck joints and lower skull and finally into your brain.
- ॐ Imagine the GSC formula light rays also mixing through the cranial sacral fluid and through all the fluid in the brain.
- ॐ As you direct these GSC infused light rays throughout your whole body, hold the intention that this is your new perfect hydration system and
- ॐ Imagine that it is now permanently anchored in your body.
- ॐ As you direct this energy through your body you can also use the mantra: "Perfect hydration now! Perfect hydration now! Perfect hydration now!"
- ॐ Finally, ask that this GSC formula creation be produced automatically as you swallow and that it gathers in the cauldron with sexual chi and Glucosamine and that this mix is automatically distributed on light rays through your limbs and torso in perfect rhythm with your inhale and exhale.
- ॐ Breathe deeply then chant 'so it is' 3 times to close this meditation and release your intention to the universal fields.
- ॐ So it is. So it is. So it is.

The above is a great mix to direct through your body when you do your yoga and asanas. Please note that this GSC and hydration model that I am offering is not based strictly on the Taoist teachings, but rather the Taoist method is adding a new layer to the work we began in *The Food of Gods* where we worked with the ancient Vedic teachings and the tools of pranayama and kria yoga. To this we have added the Biofield Technology and now a layer from the Tao which draws more deeply on the cosmic and earth elements. The Taoists recommend that you do the above routine 6 times as part of your daily morning meditation – i.e. so 6 saliva gatherings and mixing, and swallowing and mixing and distribution as per steps 1 to 5 above.

Again, while the Tao masters recommend that these type of practices form part of your life and are done daily forever, I recommend that they are at least practiced for 21 days or until they are anchored in your body's cells. Then we can trust the automatic program to do its job in alignment with your body's own memory, you will also have a conscious awareness of it all anchored in your fields and so can trust that it happens naturally as you swallow.

I also recommend that you practice the meditations in *The Food of Gods* for 21 days also.

MEDITATION 10: The Perfect Life, Perfect Love, Perfect Paradise Programming Code:
Thoughts words and actions go hand in hand and while we can apply many of the tools within this manual, we also need to exercise a little mind mastery in recognition of the fact that the quantum and virtual fields respond to us according to our beliefs.

The mantra "Perfect Life, Perfect Love, Perfect Paradise" encapsulates a number of potential realities. It is also a totally subjective thought form as the word perfect and what is deemed to be perfect is also totally subjective. One person's paradise is another person's prison.

Hence when we use the above mantra we need to have thought through exactly what is a perfect life for us? What exactly is perfect love for us and exactly what is perfect paradise for us personally and our world? Once we have clarified these things then we can use this mantra as a mental override program anytime we find our self consumed with limiting thoughts regarding life, love and our planet.

Daily exercise: As you walk, wash dishes or shower or shave you can chant over and over in your mind: "Perfect Life, Perfect Love, Perfect Paradise" with the intention that you have the power to bring this to you now.

MEDITATION 11: The Eleven Strand Healing System of Violet Light
Apart from using the method of steaming the organs with violet light mist to purify the system, there is another method which you can use that is a violet light matrix mechanism. This is a system that can be used for recalibration and also for nourishment of our system. Again drink a glass of water before you start to stabilize the system and allow it to distribute the higher frequencies you are about to receive.
- ॐ Firstly sit comfortably in meditation, spine upright. This is not a meditation to do lying down.

- ॐ Visualize again pure violet light, the pink, the blue and the gold streaming in through the crown chakra, coming from the heart and supreme mind of the Source of creation.
- ॐ Imagine that as soon as it hits the crown chakra that a laser beam of violet light then flows into the energy matrix of the light body.
- ॐ Imagine another strand of violet light or beam of violet light now going into the meridian system, which is the bridge between the light body and the physical system.
- ॐ Imagine another strand of light going in through the whole chakra system coming through the major and minor chakras in the body.
- ॐ Imagine another line of light going straight through the crown and into the skeleton, like a river of laser light flowing through the skull, and down the spinal column, through the vertebrae, through the shoulder blades, down the arms, through the major bones down into the hands, and right down into the finger tips.
- ॐ Imagine the light going right down into the pelvic area and down through the major bones of the legs, the femur, the knee joints, the tibia and the fibula, right down to the toes.
- ॐ Imagine the whole skeleton lighting up like a Christmas tree, a violet light filled tree.
- ॐ Imagine as these strands begin to move through the body as rivers of violet light that this violet light is regenerating you and is capable of transmuting any stuck energy, any blocked energy, that it is healing any disease and any decay, whether in the bone structure or muscular structure or whatever it encounters along the way.
- ॐ Imagine that it is a pure, healing, laser ray of energy that is flowing through you and now bringing you back into a state of perfect health.
- ॐ Next imagine that a laser beam of violet light is going through the muscles surrounding the skeleton and doing exactly what we have shared above – healing and transmuting as it flows through all the major muscles of the body.
- ॐ Next imagine that another strand or line of light moves through all the bloodlines of the body, through all of the major veins, arteries, capillaries, branching right through you like a river of tingling, golden, violet, healing light;
- ॐ Imagine that it flows through all the blood streams – charging and nourishing the white corpuscles and the red corpuscles, exactly as they need, feeding the blood so that the blood holds pure nourishment as it works its way through the body exactly as required.
- ॐ Imagine as the violet light hits any arteries or veins that may be in need of healing, that are beginning to collapse, or that are bleeding from problems with valves, or things like this, that the violet light immediately heals and reconstructs these problem areas or the valve systems if necessary.
- ॐ Imagine rich, nourishing blood coursing through the heart and all the violet light moving in such a way that it is healing any damaged or clogged arteries or capillaries or any other problems within the ventricular system of the heart.
- ॐ Next imagine another laser beam of light flowing in through the crown chakra or branching off from the crown chakra and that this is going through the lymphatic system. Similarly as above, imagine it carrying through all the fluid of the body, through the gland system, through the endocrine system, through the fluid in the

- spine and around the brain, the perfect frequency for all of it to be revitalized, re-calibrated back into a state of perfect health.
- ॐ Next imagine another line of light going through the whole nervous system of the body, following the whole system of nerves from deep within the body through to every organ and right through out into the skin.
- ॐ Also imagine another line of light going through into the organs – first through the brain like a river coursing through the left and right hemisphere of the brain, feeding the brain, nourishing the brain, activating all centers of the brain that need to be activated for you to experience your paranormal powers.
- ॐ Imagine the violet light coursing through the synapses around the cerebral cortex, through the cerebrum, through the cerebellum, through the hypothalamus, through the thalamus, through the pituitary and pineal glands.
- ॐ As you think it, imagine this happening immediately, as I say these words or as you say these words on your tape. See your whole brain being recalibrated and activated. Hold this idea that this is real, that this light has the power to do all that we intend.
- ॐ Imagine this healing light going through all aspects of the brain and then flowing down into the lungs coursing through the lungs, filling the lungs like a river of violet light, transmuting all sadness, or sorrow or anything else within the lungs that is no longer serving you.
- ॐ When you imagine the lungs are totally overflowing with this healing light,
- ॐ then imagine this violet light moving through the heart and healing the heart, re-energizing the heart, cleansing the heart and then
- ॐ moving down into the spleen, dissolving all worry and anxiety and then having moved through the whole spleen,
- ॐ send it into the kidneys. Imagine it dissolving all fear and any other old energy patterns that you no longer need in the kidneys, then imagine that
- ॐ this beam of violet healing light now goes down into the liver and is dissolving all patterns of anger and resentment or jealousy or anything else that has been stored there.
- ॐ Just imagine following this beam of violet light and if you can, scan your body and look to encounter any dark patches of energy that you intuitively feel no longer serve you, then
- ॐ imagine this laser beam of violet light zapping these dark clouds of energy and dissolving and transmuting them, making every organ as the light enters it, be totally crystal clear and dancing with golden violet light of health, vitality and youth, regeneration, rejuvenation and transmutation – trust that this is what this beam does.
- ॐ Now send this light beam through to the stomach to cleanse its way through the stomach and then see it flowing like a river through all your intestinal organs and then out into the sexual organs.
- ॐ Finally we see another beam of light moving from the crown chakra and spreading it's way like a river around the skin moving through the subtle levels of the skin as it encases the whole body, the miles and miles of skin right through the whole body.
- ॐ Imagine the skin being hydrated properly, healed of any lesions or scar tissue or any moles that you may not wish to be there.

- ॐ Just take the time to visualize on each area like scars or moles and visualizing that the laser light is healing these as more and more of this light floods in from all the other systems, from the energy lines flowing through you to now support this instant body transmutation and the transformation of your skin.
- ॐ Finally imagine one other beam of violet light moving from the crown chakra up above the crown chakra now, and beginning to wrap its way horizontally very snugly around your whole body, but only moving through only about half an inch to an inch away from your body, moving through the auric field and as it does so
- ॐ imagine it like having a hurricane, vacuum effect except it is also pulsing through the auric field and healing any schisms, severing any psychic ties, any energy bonds that no longer serve you and also that it is now moving its way through the energy field emanations of the emotional body and mental body as they extend through the auric field.
- ॐ Imagine your whole body now being mummified and totally encased within these circles of violet light. Imagine again that this violet light swirls around your head, down your neck, around the shoulders, around the arms, and imagine extending your arms out and the violet light mummifies each arm, encasing every part of your arms before swirling up again to begin swirling its way around the torso, and again around the individual legs down the feet and down to the individual toes.
- ॐ It is as if your whole being now is being sealed in within this beautiful matrix of pure violet light that is healing, transmuting, realigning, regenerating and youthing your body and recalibrating all of your energy fields back into a state of harmony with the energies of divine love, divine wisdom and divine power as all the lines of light now run through your whole physical bio-system.
- ॐ Imagine them now all connecting through the soles of your feet and flowing out from the feet energizing the feet chakra and moving down into the earth to energize the earth with every step that you take as you move through the world.

- ॐ You may wish to add to this meditation that as the violet light moves through all aspects of the physical system and that as you lay these energy lines through this matrix, one by one through each system, that you program this violet light for the perfect delivery of vitamins, of nutrition, minerals, everything that you need to feed the system plus for perfect elemental harmony and equilibrium to hydrate each level of your body with perfection are fluids that it needs now and forever more.
- ॐ Imagine that this violet light, as it flows through you, is constantly connected to and drawing from, the universal ocean of all cosmic particles and energy in a way that you need to feed and hydrate your internal system.
- ॐ Check to see that your inner system now has all these strands or beams of light flowing into your crown chakra and that all are now permanently hooking into your lightbody, chakra system, meridian system, skeleton, muscles, bloodlines, endocrine system, nervous system, organs, skin tissue, and through into your emotional and mental body energy fields.

- ॐ Ask your DOW to make any final adjustments required to this matrix system so that you can remain healthy, well nourished and so that your system can be held in the perfect state of regeneration.
- ॐ Imagine these adjustments occurring.
- ॐ Then chant three times … "So it is! So it is! So it is!"
- ॐ Drink another full glass of water and imagine the water as a conductor of energy carrying all these new programs into every cell as it flows through you.
- ॐ Finish with a few minutes of deep, fine, connected breathing and chanting "I am love, I love."

Additional Data for Hydrating the System:

One of the chants that I used in the Darkroom Retreat was: *"Perfect balance all the elements – freedom NOW. Perfect harmony all the elements – freedom NOW."* This is a mantra that I used as I held the visual image of waves of liquid blue water from the God of water flowing through me on all levels re-hydrating my system. The element we would hold focus on as we use this chant would be whatever element we would wish to rebalance within our system. For example the heart always brings the element of Cosmic Fire for it is the doorway between the realms and according to the Taoist masters it is the compassion energy of love and fire that sustains the flow of the other elements in the system. For me, with hydration, my focus in this particular meditation and chant is on visualizing cooling blue waters of a fresh glade fed by a water fall, or the undulating rolling waves of the ocean, flowing through me as I use this chant and imagine it re-hydrating every aspect of my being.

Regarding the hydration mantra, you could also add to the above programming *"Skin – perfect hydration NOW!"* as you visualize the motion of the universal ocean moving through you; or *"Body – perfect hydration NOW!"* but these are commands only to be used if you sense or feel that on some level your skin or body is dehydrated.

Also gathering the saliva in the mouth and imagining that as you do so, that you are bringing in the cosmic life force of divine nutrition, sucking it through the planes, from the inner realms, from the cosmos, and as you breathe imagine that you are drawing in all the elixirs of life and the nectars of life, to perfectly hydrate your body and then swallowing this saliva, visualizing it as nourishing violet light going into your system and re-hydrating you again on another level.

The issue of dehydration and re-hydration is very important in a system that is choosing to be fluid free and not only is it necessary to have perfect equilibrium with all the elements, but to adjust the percentages of this elemental flow through the system in consideration that:

a) we are a human biosystem living in a physical world
b) that this system is choosing to no longer be fed from the physical world
c) that this system is also being influenced by energy flows within the physical world that are man made and not natural, as in pollution, air conditioning and smoke e.g. Cigarette smoke.

Pollution in this case includes emotional, mental, physical and spiritual pollution as all of these are strong pollutants that any biosystem needs to deal with as they move through the fields of life.

Given this and given the fact that we need to rely more and more on our internal system of feeding, then hooking in to that cosmic ocean and the elemental flow of water through this ocean, we can then use the technique above, the programming code in rhythm with our breathing, so for example, as we breath in with a deep inhalation we use the chant: *"Perfect physical hydration"*. Imagining the cosmic ocean passing through us from the internal planes, through the atoms, into the cells and into the body and re-hydrating it in exactly the way it needs, and then on the exhale we just chant: *"NOW"* in a state of masterful command, so inhale: *"Perfect physical hydration"* exhale: *"NOW!"* and so forth.

Again when this is used in alignment with the in breath, and the exhale and the out breath, and imagining the cosmic ocean as a tide coming in when you breathe in, and the tide flowing out as you breathe out, plus then working with these chants, this gives us a triple level of power that combines visual imagery, thought, command, breathing rhythm and intention. So the triple mechanism is the visual imagery coupled with the programming, the thought, the intention and command; coupled with the breathing mechanism of the inhale and the exhale to guide the energy flow or the Chi; remembering of course that Chi follows mind and blood follows Chi.

I would like to stress here again that we are currently undergoing a journey of involution not just evolution, and this means that as all the dimensions around the worlds are layered upon layer, they exist right here right now, within us and around us. It really is just a matter of frequency shifting for the doors to these realms to reveal themselves or the veils that are currently separating our realities to disappear.

Yes it is true that many Shaman cause these veils to disappear by the use of external stimuli like Peyote and other consciousness expanding substances and these are tools that need to be used with the highest spiritual awareness for they simply amplify that which already is and so they can take you to the highest highs and the lowest lows. As I've shared in my previous writings these sort of Shamanistic tools were given to humanity to explore the layering of the dimensions, and the different worlds, and having found these doors we were to use the natural method of frequency adjustment to journey back into these realms without external aides.

We touched lightly on the science of matrix mechanics in my book *Biofields: Four Body Fitness* as a futuristic science that is being downloaded backwards in time through universal mind. The grid work is always based on the ancient alchemical power of the violet light spectrum for reasons already mentioned.

There will come a time when quantum mechanics and quantum physics would have understood more of the power of cosmic particles and exactly what they do as they beam into our earth, both on the inner and the outer planes, and the gifts that these particles bring.

Hopefully these sciences will also soon understand the power of the mind to manipulate the flow of these particles via simple things like how people choose to spend their time and the focus of their thoughts, words and actions; to which all these particles will respond as these particles will either be magnetized to or refracted from our fields accordingly.

I can envisage in the future that the science of matrix mechanics with its violet light mechanisms will be offered through textbook learning, along with the basic lifestyle tools for frequency adjustments, and expansion of consciousness, so that human beings can be taught how to operate with all cylinders firing. In other words how we can operate as well tuned instruments instead of the untuned instruments that many currently are, simply due to lack of education in the higher light science of which matrix mechanics forms a part.

Education is the key to our future for it will eliminate all fear, all ignorance, all disease, all poverty and all the other ills and chaotic expressions that we currently find within the earth plane.

Again we must stress that these must be taught with an understanding of the Law of Love and preferentially with the full understanding of all the universal laws, how they operate particularly the Law of Resonance and the Law of Cause and Effect. Please note that these Laws are expanded on in detail in my book *In Resonance*.

Please note that it is not enough to apply tools, the violet light matrix mechanisms, or even the lifestyle tools that we recommend, to have success with the types of freedoms that we are seeking. There is a missing ingredient that a model will never give you and that missing ingredient is your own frequency, your key-note, the purity of your heart and no model can teach you how to find that.

As I have stressed over and over in my previous books, sincerity, humility, surrender, a pure heart, selflessness, kindness, compassion, the ability to love unconditionally, an openness to joy, patience, dedication, devotion – all of these and many more virtues must walk hand in hand with the science of any tool or matrix mechanism. For without enough of these ingredients – of virtues, of emotion – the doors to such freedoms will remain veiled. This is the teaching and the way of the Law of Love for these virtues provide the creative fire for the pure Tao of life to be revealed.

DOING IT

THE LAW OF LOVE

RECALIBRATION TOOLS & PROCEEDURE – summary

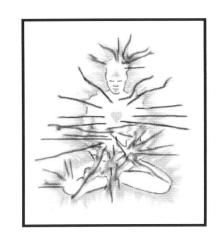

- **MIND TOOL/S:- VIOLET LIGHT RAYS; RE-IMAGING using clarity, visualization, will & intention; SLICING; OVERLAYING; MERGING; ACTIVATION**

- **HEART TOOL/S:- LOVE BREATH; BODY LOVE; APPRECIATION**

- **PHYSICAL TOOL/S:- DIET; EXERCISE; PROGRAMMED WATER**

- **EMOTIONAL TOOL/S: DESIRE – DEVOTIONAL MUSIC; HEALING SOUNDS**

- **SPIRITUAL TOOLS: DOW POWER – Surrender, alignment, merging, meditation & mantras**

Chapter 17

Inter-Dimensional Matrix Mechanics
Synopsis of Freedom Tools & Meditations

*The physical body we'll shed,
Higher, faster thought to be wed,
To lie in a waiting light bed.*

When a human heart is filled with love for self, for others and for our planet, this heart focus automatically puts them into the stream of the Law of Love and allows more Grace to flow into their lives; it also allows for an easier activation of their original freedom codes which are held in their light body matrix. This 'my heart is filled with genuine love for all life' attitude or space of feeling, can be enhanced by using matrix mechanics which is a system utilizing energy grids plus specific programming to direct and activate the matrix.

Matrixes can be created within and around the human bio-system to assist the human bio-system and to create an easier journey for it through the fields of life. The individual matrixes can also be hooked into community and global matrixes to enhance all and tap into greater levels by using combined power.

The grids of matrixes operate best when fed by the violet light. When the energy of chi, prana, the universal life force chooses to express its freedom frequency, it does so via the violet light, for violet light when refracted contains the three primordial frequencies behind creation – divine love, divine wisdom and divine power. We spoke at length about the properties of the violet light in the book *The Food of Gods*.

Suffice to say here, before we go on and introduce some of the matrix mechanisms that can bring into manifestation very particular results, the most important point to note with the violet light is that the violet light has the most amazing properties of healing, regeneration and rejuvenation, hydration and nourishment on all levels. Apart from the beauty of its power source, the violet light is the only light that can be programmed and directed thus it is the perfect underlying frequency to use for all grid work in matrix mechanisms and I would recommend no other. It has been utilized by the ancient immortal Tao masters for eons and also by the ancient mystery schools in their alchemical practices. When combined with sound mechanics and intention, all of creation can be redirected or enhanced and hence it works multi-dimensionally.

Yes you can use green light for healing, pink light for soft love radiations and golden white light which contains the whole rainbow spectrum but the violet light is the seventh ray of freedom and so its gift when used to support a matrix within a human bio-system, is freedom.

I have found over the years when I began my training with inter-dimensional matrix mechanics nearly a decade ago, that I received from the universal mind layer upon layer as my need for such a system arose. Being a sensitive existing purely on prana in a Beta field world is virtually impossible if we continually keep absorbing Beta field radiations which we then need to transmute and/or release. Hence the **bio-shield** in its simplest form was given to me visually in meditation plus the instructions how to use it. These instructions developed and matured over time as more and more layers and uses of the bio-shield began to be revealed.

The personal bio-shield is possibly one of my favorite matrix mechanisms for as mentioned above it is multi-purpose particularly when it is used with extensive programming. On one level it is an aide to help us to be totally focused in the now moment and move beyond this constant living in the past and the future with our mental wanderings. We can achieve this by programming the perimeter of this cocoon to radiate very particular signals and messages into the universal field, that field that surrounds us and constantly asks what it can do for us because it believes we are God.

While visualizing ourselves in this shield we can also go through all aspects of our lives, all of our wishes, all our desires and make very clear intense positive statements about who we are, and what we want, and have the universal forces deliver these things to our door. Provided we have totally surrendered to the divine one within us and made our commitment to act impeccably and be in service for the good of the greater whole, these wishes will come into being in perfect alignment with divine time and our own blueprint. This saves us thinking constantly about these types of issues particularly regarding abundance and relationships and things like this.

This shield can also have holographic images imprinted into it regarding the visual realities of how we wish our perfect bio-body, plus even our living environment to be manifest into this realm. This field when filled with the intense violet light energy also acts as a cocoon that is like a cosmic hotel keeping our physical, mental, emotional and spiritual being constantly held in a frequency match compatible to support the maximum radiation of our Divine nature. The Bioshields outer perimeter can also be programmed with webs of interception so that we only absorb from this world, as we move through it, information that is nourishing and supportive of the things that we wish to manifest rather than having psychic energies move directly into our auric field and having to constantly deal with these.

The personal biofield is also connected to a never-ending stream of divine love, wisdom and power which is constantly radiating in through the top of the bubble, around the bubble and into the bubble, and we can also have this light flow through the base of the bubble into the earth to feed and nourish the earth.

There are many, many variations that can be added into this bubble or cocoon. From within this cocoon all other matrixes that we discuss below can be anchored and can operate simultaneously without interference.

While the creation mechanisms for the bio-shield and the below devices are discussed in detail in both *The Food of Gods* and *Four Body Fitness : Biofields & Bliss* manuals; the following data shares a little more of how they came into being and why they are beneficial.

The *digestive grid system* was given to me when I decided to indulge my emotional body's interest in socializing and the ingesting by choice that went with this of soy cappuccinos – something which became my stable social drink for some time. Obviously this could set up a strong negative chemical reaction for a pure system to take something like this into itself, when there was nothing else being digested in the system, *unless* the substances could be handled in the body without causing stress; similarly the ingesting of the odd piece of chocolate which I would have once a month around period time. This has horrified many food purists around the world – to think that a prana feeder could also now and then have chocolate or coffee is too much for some to contemplate.

Yet as we have shared so often when a being is completely free from the need to take vitamins or minerals from normal food as they can absorb it via the inner planes using the violet light, then they are free to indulge from time to time in taste simply for pleasure and provided they are able to transmute this 'taste hit' there will be no negative physical reaction. Hence the delivery of, and purpose of, the digestive system grid which was designed and delivered as a matrix for transmutation.

This matrix has been discussed in my book *The Food of Gods* but simplistically it is a violet light mechanism that is programmed so that any food or fluid that we take into our system through the mouth is automatically transmuted into the perfect frequency that our body needs.

The *self sustaining template* was downloaded to me by my cosmic colleagues one day when I was deep in meditation seeking to see and to be instructed into how consciousness would create a full grown physical form rather than the process that happens when it chooses to come into embodiment as a baby. I asked to see the process of what would occur if our DOW were to choose to manifest in an adult system. I saw in the delivery of that data how the original matrix was formed, and how that this matrix could have additional layers added to it – such as virtues that came from previous experiences the soul had enjoyed. I saw how all the good, the learning, the understanding that we had gained previously could be collected to run as a new emotional body program and thus leave behind in cellular memory all the other experiences that delivered these gifts – the suffering and sorrow of life's journey, experiences that we had as we gained such virtues. I saw also how we could also download into this new template or grid, the virtues of the archetypes.

In the course of this meditation I was shown how to create a new bio-body template or energy matrix, how to form the molecules around it by working with the seven elements, how to imbue this new matrix with emotional qualities and also how to set new program codes for freedom from our current limitations.

In the watching of all this I could also see how a new self sustaining model could be born, a model that had a different harmony and rhythm with the elements and with the 'paradise, perfect form' grid – a model that would feed and hydrate itself, that would be self regenerating and never grow old or become dis-eased or die.

I saw that if we could create such a system, a matrix with a pure emotional base and a powerful program base that we could superimpose over our existing bio-system, that we could support our freedom agenda on a deeper level.

The programming base that drives the new template is based on one agenda and that is the full manifestation of the divine being that we are, as supported by our original divine DNA blueprint with all its freedom codes.

Surely, I thought, as I watched all of this come in to being, surely we could also fuse this template with our existing meridian system, and fuse it within the light-body and also anchor it in the bio-shield. I knew as I was creating this in my own system in this meditation, that when systems are fused together like this, a final merging cannot take place until there is a frequency match and then the two systems – old and new – can come together like mercury and integrate to become one.

Obviously if you are overlaying the Perfect Bio-body template or the Self Sustaining template, then if these templates are already perfect as new designs, then the determining factor for success must lie within the physiological bio-system already in existence. What I mean by this is that we then must also alter our own personal keynote and change our own frequency mix to bring our existing system into the perfect resonance to facilitate the merging.

Understanding this, then part of the programming within the self sustaining template is that as soon as the fields are in perfect resonance, the merging occurs and all new programming codes are activated automatically – for they cannot be activated before the physical, emotional, mental and spiritual bodies are pure enough and energized enough to handle the new frequency download that such a merging would release through the fields. Because of the nature of the programs, and the level of violet light that the new templates grids are based on – they must be supported by our current system to bring this into being *without* burnout of our circuitry.

The self-sustaining template is an energy matrix similar to the light body yet it has been activated to carry very intense violet light frequencies to constantly regenerate and rejuvenate the body. It is also programmed to extend lines of light through past, present and future realities to download all of the emotional and mental virtues and the gifts and talents of all previous lives, that we need to be working with in our conscious reality to be able to manifest what we have come to do today.

Again more details of this can be found in both the *Four Body Fitness* and *The Food of Gods* manuals and Recipe 2000> is the lifestyle key that will facilitate the merging by altering our existing bio-system's keynote.

In the previous chapter we introduced the 11 strand healing system which is another layer of the **one chakra column of spinning violet light system.** This is a system that radiates millions of rays of light constantly and simultaneously out into all the major organs of the body and into our circulatory system, lymph system, muscular system, skeletal system, bone marrow, through the cells and through the molecules and through the atoms opening the doors to all the veils between all the atoms and also deeper into the inner universes. It is also programmed to move in rhythm with our exhale it goes out through the inner universes and then when it reaches maximum expansion as it begins to contract it does so in rhythm with our breathing and it draws back all the sustenance of the cosmic particles and more violet light from the inner universes, bringing it back to the atoms to feed them, then to the molecules, to the cells and so forth back within the body. This feeding mechanism is discussed in detail in the manual *The Food of Gods* and its main purpose is to set up a constant source of inner plane feeding that will nourish our body bringing us all the vitamins, minerals and everything that we require to maintain health.

The ***11 strand healing/feeding system*** was a system that again I downloaded in meditation in response to having just been taught level one and level two of Reiki and deciding that it would be easier to set up a permanent Reiki flow of energy through the body rather than have to do this consciously on a daily basis as the mechanism once created, anchored and activated would operate permanently with or without my attention.

My intention in the creation of this mechanism was that this universal energy flow would constantly cleanse, feed, nourish and rejuvenate my body and thus keep it in a state of freedom and health.

Obviously matrix mechanisms like this need to be supported by quality feeling and thinking habits. It was also obvious to me that this matrix mechanism had to run through every level of the physical bio-system and also extend out into the emotional, mental and etheric body planes and, as this system came to me, I also realized that this matrix could do other things apart from healing, it could regenerate.

Supporting the re-programming of the pineal and pituitary to stop the aging process by only producing life giving hormones – as was originally intended by our divine DNA – I realized that we could take this matrix one step further by not just rejuvenating the body but to also have the system provide minerals and hydration levels in a perfect flow as well. This of course made perfect sense to me, to have such a grid anchored permanently in the system with violet light lines anchored through each system to again deliver the outcomes as intended.

All of this is similar to the self sustaining template – the difference is that these 11 energy lines course through every system from the light-body, meridians, skeletal system, muscular system, nervous system, chakra system, endocrine system, organs, skin and into the emotional and mental fields. The self sustaining system is like an electrical grid that when the bio-system resonates at a set frequency, fuses into the existing system to strengthen and regenerate it. The 11 strand system is a basic healing tool.

When I originally received the 11 strand system I was not aware at the time that it could also be used to hydrate and feed the system. At the time it was downloaded I was only looking at healing through using the violet light's transmuting power. It was not until recently that I realized that I could use this system as a base matrix and add the additional layers of inner plane feeding as per the Violet Light flooding and feeding meditation detailed in *The Food of Gods* and also that I could add the perfect hydration intention.

The Law of Love & Its Fabulous Frequency of Freedom
with Jasmuheen

Violet light as it moves through the skeletal system and into the bone marrow can also be instructed to melt the fat there and transmute it into a type of Holy water to strengthen and regenerate the bone marrow as well. This is a practice used by the Tao Master immortals as way of feeding the body more refined frequencies.

Yes the eleven strand violet light matrix system coming in through the crown, can be also used as an inner plane feeding mechanism, but more importantly it was originally set in place as a healing and transmutation matrix to constantly flush from all systems within the physical bio-system, all toxic matter, transmuting any stuck energy patterns or any energy we no longer need. As I cannot remember which manual that this can be found in, we covered this tool in greater detail in the Tao and Tools chapter.

I have found over the years that each matrix mechanism can be added to and elaborated upon. For example ***the three cosmic cable hook-in*** matrix that we discuss in *The Food of Gods* is a simpler version of this. It is designed to energize the upper, middle and lower Tan Tien chakras and flood them with divine love, divine wisdom and divine power, just as the Love breath matrix floods and feeds the heart with a never ending source of love.

I received the ***Akashic Records*** grid matrix when I was guided to tune the pituitary gland as a cosmic receiver and the pineal as a transmitter for telepathic inner plane communication. It is the activation of these glands that allows us to follow our higher more intuitive guidance system and hence be more aligned to the Law of Love.

However how powerfully we are aligned to the Law of Love is determined by our total frequency or keynote, which is determined by not just the use of the type of matrix mechanisms mentioned above, but also via our lifestyle, and how much toxicity we allow through our thinking, feeling and feeding habits.

Successful programming of the body and the use of matrix mechanisms can be enhanced by an in-depth knowledge of the mechanics of the physical bio-system. Hence for a metaphysician, an anatomy and physiology manual can be a helpful aid. With matrix mechanics we are merging the physical bio-system with the metaphysical understanding of the higher light science. The more we understand the physical operations of our body and the more we learn to listen to its voice and co-operate with love and honor and respect, the more our higher capabilities can reveal themselves to us, no longer drowned out by the limited voices of the status quo and our cultural conditioning, especially when we exist in societies with corporate structures that gain financial benefit by the maintaining of human illness. Human beings who unhook from the dependence on the medical and pharmaceutical industries will also aid in creating economic changes there.

Each of the matrix mechanisms discussed above and below came to me as I sought answers to my own physical body changes as I progressed further and further with my experiential research with the journey of pranic feeding and as I allowed my consciousness to expand further in deeper meditations to open up universal doors within the inner cosmos. These were doors that suddenly revealed themselves to me as my personal keynote began to change. The more I allowed the violet light to flow through my system and nourish me physically, emotionally, mentally and spiritually, the more I prayed and meditated and developed a sincere system of divine communication, the more I spent time in silence and enjoyed the beauty of nature, the more I gave of myself to others without seeking reward, the more I sang songs of devotion and used the sacred mantras; the more inner doors began to open themselves as if veils were disappearing before my eyes.

I have always loved the mathematics of life and studied computer science for awhile at university, for I was fascinated by the languages and the systems of creating, and writing software to run a computer system. During all of this I always saw the body as a matrix of light and how our mind is also a software program that directs the chi and the molecules around the body's natural grids in ways that allows the system to either operate in health in its highest potential of reality, or in dis-ease when the chi flow is weak.

It was so obvious to me also at this time to see the influence of diet and exercise on the bio-system for at this time in my life I needed to keep my system strong and healthy so that I could maintain my single parent lifestyle in health and happiness.

I know that for some, the mechanisms discussed here and in the previous chapter may seem complex or repetitive in their outcome, but keep in mind that they were revealed to me as a layering process as I was ready to download each step, by having the need and then asking the right questions.

If we look on the inner plane we would see around us the most complex grid structures which are all naturally powered by the violet light, all are constantly operating via a system of bio-feedback looping with the fields of universal intelligence. For most people their natural grid mechanisms have been overwhelmed and drowned out by other projections that come from unconscious living, from lack of holistic education and hence from the choice of toxic thinking, feeling and feeding patterns.

For me consciously knowing that my matrices are there, and that I have carefully re-constructed each grid with set intentions and instructions, allows me to walk through this world with Grace. There is great comfort in knowing that as the universal field of intelligence surrounds us and moves through us, that it responds to very clear instructions that are supported energetically by strong fields. This means that I have a totally different relationship with the universal fields and a totally different set of experiences in this physical world than many others, and hence for me the reality of the type of freedoms discussed in this manual is not difficult when we have utilized inter-dimensional matrix mechanics to open up to such fields.

There are channels of reality like cosmic movies that are just like cable TV and it is as simple in the human mechanism as flicking internal switches to tune us into purer, freer worlds. There are access codes too – like purity of heart, humility, surrender and these codes can be supported by and driven by the type of matrix mechanisms that we have introduced. The point that I wish to make is that when we are feeling stuck in our development and are looking for a solution, then the higher light science can provide solutions for us that we could not even imagine until we ask.

There is much that we will not find in our Beta frequency field world, especially not yet in our scientific or medical field, in fact we will not find these solutions in any field that has not expanded its reaches into the more creative Alpha, Theta and Delta mind waves where all solutions to all problems dwell.

Only when we expand our own consciousness into these fields can we reach into universal mind and download exactly what we need. The key of course to doing this is our lifestyle and how we spend both our clock time and our psychological time.

The 'do it once or do it regularly' game:

This is an interesting reality re the application of matrix mechanisms and I have recently made a shift re this reality. I believe that when we are in certain levels of mastery then we can envisage and create such mechanisms instantly and have them deliver powerful results. However, immediate results may be hindered by

a) cellular dross of memory and emotions i.e. internal sabotage programs
b) the bigger picture blueprint
c) our hidden agendas that may not be universally supported due to b) and
d) simple timing.

As skilled metaphysicians there is much that we can do to retune our selves out of the field influences of a) and c), and we can also tune into and be more aware of b) and d) so that we are more aligned to, and less hindered by, these things. However a person's belief in their own mastery and their own Divine power, is completely personal. It is something based on both faith and more importantly pragmatic experience and the more we witness Grace and the Law of Love in motion as a consequence of consciously aligning ourselves to these things, the easier it is to believe in our mastery and reality creation abilities.

While some things that I think and focus on seem to manifest into being virtually immediately, there are other things that I have been focusing on that have not. However maintaining a clear focus regarding what we as masters require to operate fully empowered in our world, is a basic part of inner plane alchemy.

There is also a vast difference between mental constructs and wishful thinking and cellular reality. Hence I recommend the following once a matrix mechanism has been created, activated and integrated:

- ♥ If you have proof of your own mastery and ability to manifest instantly then do it once, 'it' meaning the matrix creation process and meditation as supplied for the mechanisms in our various manuals.
- ♥ For everyone else do each meditation for the creation of the matrix mechanism that interests you, every day for a minimum of 21 days or until you feel that every cell of your body is familiar with the new grid pathways, commands and your intention in the utilization of this matrix.

For a matrix mechanism to work we have to hold very clear intentions and visual images of what we are wishing to create, plus a clear idea of their outcome so that the model can be directed, and we need to use very specific programming codes that are not ambiguous and that are supported by very particular attitudes, and we need to use energetic systems that have the power to bring to fruition all of the above. Hence the only light system for a grid that I would use is the violet light. The attitude required is that we are totally the master of the system and that as a master of creation we can run any energetic grid system through our current bio-system and set very specific visual images and commands into the system and because of our mastery, we hold a knowing that this can be done, and the outcomes we seek will be delivered.

One of the differences in the teachings of Taoist masters and the matrix mechanism reality is that I like to do things once and have them permanently anchored in the system where they run without further attention and thought. However I realize that most people do not have the ability to 1) create such a mechanism then 2) anchor it permanently and then 3) hold the energy and belief that the mechanism will do as designed for as long as required. For many people unless they repeat the process daily it will stay as a fleeting experience in the body and a passing memory in the mind but does not gain power due to lack of attention. Hence the do it once or do it regularly question.

While I have tried to compensate in my models with programming that says that the model and its programs will grow stronger and stronger every day regardless of our attention to it, it still does not birth things into actualization, for the birthing of a visualization into actualization needs not just the mental construct but also the emotional force of desire behind it. For example we can set up a garden that may have the best pots, soil, seeds and fertilizer, an automatic watering system and the best growing conditions however if we take another garden of the same conditions and add the interaction of the human element, of the tenderness of touch and sound and music and the second garden will grow even more magnificently for it will be fed by that intangible energy called love and attention and care.

Matrix mechanisms are like the first example and yet the system of the ancient teachings of the Tao where we focus our mind in the body, using the ancient tools every day, is like the second example as it adds another layer to the game, the layer of power of love and attention. So the two systems can be combined to get the best results and utilized according to each individual's belief in their own mastery.

Basically the matrix mechanism sets an energetic support structure in motion to improve the chances of a specific outcome particularly when we imbue the matrix with very clear holographic images and intentions.

There are some people who will find a system, a spiritual practice or energy practice, and having applied and enjoyed the benefits of the principles they will focus on this practice for years often teaching it, constantly studying it and looking at the subtle nuances and strictly adhering to the principle to the best of their ability thus keeping the tradition intact and alive.

There are other people who will skim through life stopping here and there to study the different traditions, taking from each tradition what feels right for them and what works for them, and discarding the rest and eventually forming a model that they have made their own and works for them, a model that delivers to them certain outcomes.

The miracle makers create certain models, these models are always based in their own experience and they are also always based on various traditional metaphysical truths, for without this common thread of traditional truths and metaphysical law, the models themselves could not function. Some people take the traditional truths within a model and refine them and combine other tools to make the traditional system either simpler, or work more powerfully or able to deliver a wider range of benefits.

For example, the teaching through most traditions of the need for a heart filled with love and compassion and mercy, in my opinion, needs to then by married with the practice of Ahisma – this is a practice of non-violence, the non-killing of any animal or human life. When we add this practice of Ahisma, the power of love, mercy and compassion that radiates from that individuals field is made so much stronger for they are living the love, living the compassion and living the honoring and respect of all life. That attitude in itself opens the doors for miracles.

Conscious control of our diet is one of the simplest ways to shift the energy flow within us and around us, as is the conscious control over our thinking patterns and feeling patterns and the attitudes that we choose to have as we perceive the world. The fact that some people may find the freedoms we discuss in this book to be as natural a reality to them as breathing is one perception whereas to others' this type of reality belongs to a world that is often alien to their own.

If miracles are the domain of creation, of the Divine, of God, and the result of supernatural forces coming together, then surely they too can be the creation of the human world for it is a metaphysical truth that every human being is made in the image of the Divine and gifted with all the power of the Divine.

As Jesus said, everything I have done you can do and more. It is only when a human being fully embraces their Divine nature, their Divine heart, their Divine spirit, their Divine essence, and aligns with this consciously and manifests it consciously that they can not just be the seekers' of miracles who have found and enjoyed the miracles, but they can become the miracle makers and the makers of models to form miracles.

To me inter-dimensional matrix mechanics is one way of energetically supporting the creation of miracles by utilizing grid structures and software programs that are aligned to universal law.

There are things that I have witnessed in my own life that decades ago I would have classified as miracles and I know that others would relegate them as such as well. The things that I share of such as my meetings with the Holy Ones in my book *Divine Radiance: On the Road with the Masters of Magic*, for me all of this would have once seemed out of reach on one level and totally miraculous and yet as I have delved deeper into the metaphysical mind field seeking insights to its operations and applying the understanding of universal law, I have come to understand, as I have now shared so often, that it is all simply a science.

A science of percentages, of mathematics of time, the science of command over molecular structure, the science of understanding the universal Chi and it's visual aspect of the rainbow spectrum and the violet light, the science of understanding inner alchemy. Perhaps it is a metaphysical science and yet the role of many of the miracle makers in this modern world is to bridge the world of metaphysics back into the quantum field so the experts in the quantum field can mirror this bridge back to us. And yet to me the science is more in the outcome – for example you know that if you do A plus B then you are delivered to C which is a definite outcome. Metaphysics is after all the science of life, of living life to our highest potential in alignment with all the laws that govern all worlds so that all aspects of our being may be enjoyed and not forgotten or ignored.

That we do so in harmony with other life forms is a given in a conscious and compassionate person's world.

THE LAW OF LOVE

INTER-DIMENSIONAL MATRIX MECHANICS

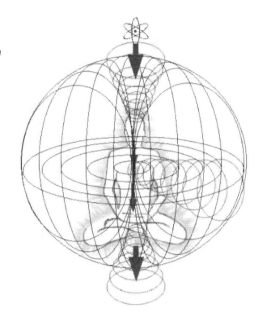

- **TEMPLATES – GRIDS & PROGRAMS & INTENTION**
- **DIVINE ELECTRICITY – VIOLET LIGHT - SOUNDS WAVES – LIGHT RAYS**
- **AGREEMENTS & PRE-ENCODEMENTS for FREEDOM & SERVICE JOURNEY**
- **PERFECT BIO-BODY TEMPLATE – mantras & mind power.**
- **BIO-SHIELDS – PERSONAL, COMMUNITY, GLOBAL – BIO-SHIELD ANGEL team** (as per *Four Body Fitness* manual)
- **SELF-SUSTAINING MECHANISMS – CREATION & MERGING –** inner plane feeding & hydration – GSC FORMULA – Glucosamine, Chi & Cosmic Particles & Saliva
- Do once versus do 21 days
- **FIELD PURPOSE – PLACEMENT – DE-ACTIVATION – REFINEMENT – RE-ACTIVATION & PERFECT FIELD FLOW**

CHI FOLLOWS MIND

Chapter 18

The Immortal Body
& the Tao of the DOW

*Stalk imperfections with great stealth,
Find and connect with inner Self,
Our changeless core, which holds real wealth.*

The first book that I wrote in the Divine Nutrition series I originally titled *Prana and Immortality*, although my publishers around the world re-titled it *Living on Light*. I renamed this book *Pranic Nourishment – Nutrition for the New Millennium* for it is the nourishment that comes from Chi, from the Universal force of the Tao that has the power to bring us into the type of freedoms that we talk about throughout this manual.

After spending three intense weeks in the dark room with the Taoist Master Mantak Chia as if we were a group of students deep inside a Himalayan mountain cave learning ancient secrets, I have tried to piece together the western theosophical understanding with the Taoist teachings, for in the higher practices the Taoist talk a lot of the immortal body, so in this chapter I would like to try to present a correlation between the teachings, and also provide some insights as to the power of the DOW, and how the self sustaining template can work in tandem as a grid mechanism with the Greatest Kan and Li teachings of the Tao.

The Taoists Immortal fetus creation begins with our initial focus on the inner realms of the DOW and the use of tools to encourage this inner being to grow, and the Self Sustaining Template is a fully grown immortal body energy field or matrix that can only be activated when we have aligned more powerfully with our DOW. So from our initial focus we give birth to, or reveal, our DOW and when we are aligned with it, we can experience the benefits of the matrix mechanisms that then self activate. The matrix mechanisms can also be used to aid in this alignment.

I have covered more on the Kan and Li practices in my *Darkroom Diary Download* e-book and more detailed practices are also in Mantak Chia's booklets on this, so I will not digress with the Kan and Li practice further except to say that the Tao Masters call our DOW an immortal fetus as a) it is eternal and immortal and b) it is a fetus within most people simply because it is small like a baby. Although our DOW exists in each cell, it is small for many because it is ignored. As we feed it through our attention and lifestyle it grows and reveals its natural immortal nature.

There are two ways that our immortal consciousness can manifest its being into the physical realms. Firstly it can choose to come in through the normal channels where two people make love, the sperm and the egg come together, a fetus is born and grows and is nourished and eventually enters into our world through the normal process called birth. The second way is to manifest a fully grown body as per the Self Sustaining Template and this occurs depending on the individual's service blueprint.

With the first process of coming in as a new born baby, usually this immortal spirit will go through the channel of forgetfulness – the birth canal – where it will collect enough amnesia so that it can come into the world without the confusion of other memories from other time lines.

Despite this process, there remains something completely aware within us that it still in contact with the unseen worlds and this contact is usually maintained until the child is seven. By this age the child has usually begun to be overloaded with Beta frequencies of the external world and slowly this overpowers the divine impulses and deadens our awareness, creating such heaviness within the system that the DOW appears to go to sleep. Yet it is more that as our DOW is not focused on, it plays instead on other dimensional levels until once more it is called for, invited and given permission to manifest all of its glory in our earth world now.

Once we have become aware of our DOW – our enlightened nature – then we can speed up the process of the manifestation of its gifts on this plane by learning to listen to its guidance and by following its instruction. This means taking time to sit in silence in meditation and listening and feeling its essence. It often guides us to lighten up our diet so that the system can spend less time breaking down and digesting food substances and with lighter foods to deal with, it can divert its energy to develop our paranormal powers and activate our higher senses. It guides us often to do physical exercise like yoga, tai chi, qigong etc where we can develop, through the movements, a strong mind body connection and also a physical sensation feeling of how the prana, the chi, moves through our body to then bring another level of health and flexibility through the temple in which it wishes to manifest more fully.

Also there is the act of surrender where you recognize the potential and the power of this One that breathes us. As I have mentioned so often in other books, when you stop for a moment and surrender every cell, every atom, every molecule to the divine one that is breathing you and invite it to radiate all its glory through you, to guide you, to teach you, to heal you if required, to feed you, to nourish you, to hydrate your system if required, it can provide whatever it is you feel guided to ask for, and all of this will depend on your pre-programmed freedoms. And by the Law of Love – because love is its nature, its essence – by this law so it will be.

When we give the clear chain of command back to the One who created us, back to the One who is breathing us, when we understand that the physical, emotional, mental and spiritual systems are here for one purpose which is to support the manifestation of our divine essence in this plane as it experiences life in the world of form, then the whole power balance shifts just because the nature of our DOW is so loving, and so wise, and so compassionate and so kind, and so in tune with all of the needs of the fabric of creation. Our DOW is what drives the fabric of creation – it is what drives our fellow human beings, it is the common bond with all life, through all planes. Because of what our DOW is, all the universal forces are guided to support this request, this conscious change in the chain of command which comes through the act of surrender, and in doing so our DOW can then deliver its gifts of freedom and immortality.

Because our DOW exists multi-dimensionally, it can take us on journeys throughout the inner realms, journeys that are restricted by our personal keynote which determines our ability to move beyond the veils between all the worlds. The more of this loving presence that we allow to radiate through every level of our system the more realms we can access and the more freedoms we will gain. So in this context the immortal body is a powerful body that we can support into creation.

So let's assume that this is something that we wish to support with a matrix mechanism, a grid system, then we can imagine that the Divine One Within us is the master alchemist of the system and as the master alchemist it can – using violet light – weave the self sustaining template with all its programming and virtues through the bio-systems, to exist as a template, that will lie dormant and be activated when the existing physical system can support its activation, for if our DOW has the power shared then the instantaneous creation of a self sustaining template is not difficult. The choice to take this further and to then overlay this and activate it within our existing systems, this is then up to us.

As mentioned, the second way that consciousness can manifest itself into this plane is in a fully grown body, an immortal body as discussed in the matrix mechanisms chapter. I will not elaborate on the mechanics of creating and using the self sustaining template for we have covered this in great detail previously, suffice to say as a master alchemist once told me: when we focus on being here now, fully present in the now moment, this in itself is a key to open all the dimensional doors, for all are overlaid.

For those who got a 'yes', in the Tao and Tools chapter, if it is part of your encodements to embrace physical immortality in this life, then for you I would like to take this discussion to another level.

Creating a system that is free from the need to age or die to create disease, a system that is in harmony enough to consciously escape the physical death process does not necessarily mean that as an immortal system you are confined to this physical plane, for an immortal system can move in and out of all planes at will. When their work is finished as a divine being on this plane then some people – like the lamas – simply leave the physical system or disintegrate it into the rainbow body and bring it with them to another space and time. This is what the Christ did with his resurrection and transfiguration and ascension to the light. It is not unknown that after this process has occurred that the Being will then re-manifest back in the physical plane to continue with other work that they may see as necessary to aid in the evolution to humanity. There are many options open to the immortalist.

Many of the immortal realms see their body as a temple for the divine one to radiate its love and wisdom through, and many have no attachment to the body, so once their work is complete they often choose to leave it behind and so it appears to go through the death process. Death for an immortalist is quite different to death for one who is unaware.

For the unaware usually death occurs as a breakdown of the physical system which means that the spirit can no longer inhabit the body and so has to leave and later re-enter the cycle of life in a fresh form. An immortalist chooses the time of death and exits once their work is complete – usually through the crown chakra and very often their body has not broken down at all.

Some take it up to the light with them and come and go at will, some spend centuries on different continents continually in service where called, some rest in Shamballa and appear only when called and when necessary. Some shape-shift and change their molecular structure at will. Many remain invisible and unassuming preferring not to draw attention to themself.

In order to embrace physical immortality we need to keep the organs in a self rejuvenating state.

The Tao masters also talk about the spirit in the organs, spirits that are represented by animals that have different virtues and strengths. For example the lungs, here the Tao masters work with a system of glacial white energy, pure cleansing type mountain air and the animal totem of the white tiger as the spirit that brings its virtues into the lungs. When the lungs are overloaded with the toxicity of sadness then the tiger becomes weaker and weaker. The Taoists strengthen and clean the lungs by visualizing a stream of pure fresh mountain air flowing through the lungs and seeing a tiger in each lung growing and becoming stronger and imparting the virtues of courage and righteousness. Connected with planet Venus and the element metal, the lungs are a yin energy organ that respond to the healing sound of "Ssssss".

For the Taoists, the kidneys hold the blue energy of the gentle and timid deer, placid in nature flowing like the gentle waters of life. Yet the deer disappears when we indulge and feed our fears and cannot express its virtues, hence the kidneys cease to function well enough to support immortality. Associated with the planet Mercury, the Taoists often imagine that the 'Yin organ' kidneys are connected on the inner planes to the universal oceans and that blue calm cooling element of water from these oceans constantly flows through the kidneys keeping them hydrated, cleansed and calm so that the deer can express their virtues enough to keep these organs in a state of natural regeneration. For the Taoists, the healing sound used for the kidneys is "Chooo".

In the Tao and Tools chapter we elaborate on using the healing sounds and also the virtues of the organs, and also provide a way to purify these organs, so we will not elaborate again on this here. Suffice to say that the drive for physical immortality can only be successful when the organs are kept in a self rejuvenating state and if the bio-system is driven by one who is pure of heart. If it is done from any other reason, than as a understanding that immortality is a gift from the Divine Presence radiating all its power and glory through our systems, then by the very nature of the Law of Love, it cannot come into being.

Physical immortality requires the human system to be operating by the Law of Love. Without the ingredient of the pure human heart and its virtues of mercy and compassion for self and fellow man and all life, this gift simply can't come into being. Physical immortality comes from an expansion of consciousness where every cell every atom of our being comes to understand and experience the immortal nature of our DOW, where every level of our being has surrendered into its touch and caress, into an experience of DOW love. And in this state of merging and surrender all the freedoms come.

Chapter 19

Coming Into The Light

The essence, the thing to be born,
May be cultivated, like corn,
Many seeds from the cob can spawn.

Coming into the light means also allowing yourself to discover a path of illumination. A way of being in this world that illuminates this world for you, in a way that releases feelings of joy and happiness and peace within you – these are the key emotions in the secret of immortality. The more joy, the more love, the more happiness that we feel, the more all the cells of our body are given the food and the correct nurturing to immortalize themselves into a state that they have the ability to naturally exist in, a state that is based on their divine DNA programs.

I like the title for this chapter "Coming Into the Light" for the whole evolutionary process for human kind at this time, as we work with the Law of Love, is about coming back into the light. Coming back to the light of understanding that we as a species can learn the way of the fields, that we can learn how to control the inner and outer energy flow and how to be the watchers of the fields. Coming into the light means remembering how to work together in love and harmony and realizing that this is part of our next natural step of evolution.

Returning to the light, coming back into the light is also about giving ourselves permission to really allow the light of our DOW to shine through us and to reveal itself to us in all of Its glory. The Law of Love inspires us and lures us back into full remembrance of the very core essence of our being and all of its wisdom and power is waiting to be revealed to us. Whether we discover this aspect of our nature or not, until we truly understand the nature of the one that is breathing us, it is as if we are always running on two cylinders instead of four.

Coming back into the light means understanding the life force contained within the cosmic particles that constantly beam through all fields of life and the properties that they can deliver through the spectrum of the violet light. Coming back into the light means understanding the power of the violet light and the frequencies it carries of divine love and divine wisdom and divine power, and how these are the very driving forces behind all of creation. It is about tapping into the purest source of nourishment that takes away all of our hunger – the realities that we discussed in great detail in the book *The Food of Gods*.

Coming back into the light for some people, particularly after undergoing something like a darkroom retreat, is like having had a chance to sit back and honestly assess everything in their lives and be born again with a new understanding. Having taken the time to assess it all, and found the courage to make the changes that they need to adjust their models of reality, so that they operate in a more stream lined harmonious manner and to live a more desired outcome, rather than continuing to live life habitually without ever questioning if the actions, thoughts and words that they indulge in are bringing them the levels of freedom that they truly desire within their heart.

There are simple questions that a human being must ask themselves before they can progress into the frequency of freedom and the first of these questions are: What sort of freedom do you desire? What does freedom really mean to you? With these questions a new light of understanding can be formed for when we ask we receive.

Coming into the light can be as simple as changing our perception, of asking to perceive the Divine light in all. Coming into the light often comes after we embrace our darkness.

During my time at the darkroom retreat I met one of Osho's devotees who gave me a piece to read from the Vigyan of Bhairav Tantra volume two, chapter eleven titled "Come back to an Existence" delivered by Osho in Bombay India in 1973.

In it Osho concentrates on discussing the benefits of darkness meditation saying that the Essenes were probably the only ancient esoteric school who believed or saw God as absolute darkness and that all of the religious groups tended to see God as light, because of their fear of the unknown that lies in the darkness and because of man's vulnerability when there is darkness. However Jesus was an Essene, and the Essenes also taught how it was important to become one with this darkness, to enter into this darkness and that the darkness is actually the Divine Mother, a source that is infinite and eternal. From the constant source of darkness nothing can rise except the light which tends to come and go.

In this talk Osho sets three exercises. The first one is to meditate for an hour a night in the darkness, just staring into the darkness and feeling your self become one with it. One of the beauties of being in the darkness is that you no longer feel defined, and you no longer feel that you have any boundaries, which is a wonderful gift for you begin to feel formless and free.

Osho said both the Essenes and Shiva offered this technique for people to move beyond their fears so that they could be open and vulnerable and enter into the cosmic realm and allow the cosmic realm to enter into them. This on one level is also about being able to access the cosmic particles for the food that they bring and of course the cosmic particles are a part of the cosmic or the universal ocean from which the higher elements can be absorbed to hydrate our systems if we are choosing to be fluid free.

Osho talks about research being done in Japan where people with various psychosis are left alone for three to six weeks with no light at night, fed and taken care of physically but in total solitude, and how these people cure themselves of their psychosis and madness because they face themselves first in the total darkness and then in the total light.

Osho recommends that we live with darkness for three months, just one hour a day, which will allow us to lose these feelings of individuality and separation and instead of feeling like an island, we feel as if we become the ocean. We feel that we are so vast and so eternal, no longer afraid. In this technique Osho recommends for us to lie down in this darkness and feel as if we are near our Mother, for the darkness is the womb of the Mother so when we lie down and imagine that we are back in the womb of our mother we are also unifying ourselves back into the womb of creation where there is no separation.

The third technique is to carry a patch of this darkness within us – just to carry it, to feel it within us. From my own experience in my three weeks in the darkroom, this is about that feeling of when we are in deep meditation in the darkness, where we feel that we are falling, sinking into that inner universe and that by being one with this universe, we literally are carrying this inner darkness with us, for it is as if we have brought this inner universe right into the surface of our inner being, which allows our body to become so relaxed, so calm and so cool.

Osho says that when you have this darkness within you, this inner cosmos as a conscious part of you, then you can absorb so much more from this world without reacting because it just passes through you into the inner cosmos as if it is moving into a vacuum.

Shiva said that when you practice these three techniques:

a) staring at the darkness with open eyes and allowing the darkness to enter within,
b) feeling the darkness as a mother's womb all around and
c) carrying a patch of darkness where ever we go

then this darkness becomes the light and you will become enlightened. Through this darkness nothing will disturb you and all fears can disappear forever so to truly come into the light, first we must embrace the darkness.

From going through my own intense dark room time I have to agree that it is probably one of the most interesting initiations that I have ever undergone, for while I felt no fear on any level, it has challenged me and expanded me, and bought up to the surface from deep within me things that I was able to transform quite powerfully. My meditations were so deep, my dreams so intense and I feel exactly as Osho said, absolutely expanded and no longer separate from the cosmos in any way.

I was thinking this morning of what I would term a successful conversion to a fluid free diet at least for myself personally. I decided that if I could maintain 30 minutes to one hour of solid weight training plus an hour to two-and-a-half hours of yoga, and of course my more passive meditation time, as well as enjoying my usual daily hour to two walk along the beach, and do all of this while maintaining good energy levels and a stable weight, as well as functioning with a clear head and no block to my creative flow, and do all of this without taking any fluid or food then I would consider that the conversion is physically successful.

Having experienced living for very extremely long periods of time taking water and a little tea each day and maintaining this type of routine with the outcome mentioned, then of course the body should be able to make its adjustments to maintain the same, if it was able to draw enough hydration from the inner universal ocean and cosmic particles, and was then able to come into such a state of inner light that these freedoms would come naturally.

Yet beyond all this, a successful conversion for me is one that occurs harmoniously, not just within the physical system but also within the emotional and mental systems as well. Gliding into it with joy and Grace is also a high priority for me at this time for I know that in the realm of my DOW, Grace and joy are the most natural states of BEing.

Chapter 20

The Pure Land

Heaven has armed with compassion,
The innocent, charged with passion:
Quality's always in fashion.

At one time in China there existed a matrilineal society where people honored the women Shaman who downloaded knowledge of the spirit and nature worlds, knowledge they received with insights and clarity, knowledge that formed the core of Taoism and Chinese Medicine. In 1500-1000 BC references began to be made of a great creator Goddess who reigned alone, complete and without a consort, a compassionate Goddess who the early Taoists called the Empress of the Universe.

Known as Xi Wang Mu (or Hsi Wang Mu) she became the most popular and powerful female deity in China and her realm on Mt Kun Lun in far western China has been described as a place of exalted purity. Said to be the keeper of the medicine and secrets for eternal life, her image has been reduced with the rise of patriarchy and yet as the time of the Goddess reasserts itself, so does her influence as she encourages the merging of the heavenly and earthly realms.

By her Grace the city of the immortals has been born.

Known as Zhang Chu this etheric 'pure land' can be accessed on the inner realms via meditation provided the inner plane traveler is pure of heart.

Purity of heart goes hand in hand with our ability to exist in the higher planes of consciousness that hold the fields of Shamballa and the Immortal City, fields that radiate out visions of the operations of the highest potential of humankind.

I have come to call that state of heart purity that brings the Grace, that state where you feel love and loved and the lover of all; that state of awe and magic; that state of knowing and acceptance and acknowledgment of something so grand – all of this I have come to call a state of BEing in what the Buddha calls the "Pure Land". Pure because to experience all of these things, after being a seeker of miracles, feels so freeing that you enter the purest state of bliss, the purest state of ecstasy, where all of you is consumed by this state.

In this pure state of Divine Emotion or as the Shamans say, pure ecstasy, in this state an all knowing, awareness floods in and a feeling of such fulfillment comes that all our questions disappear. In this state, a pure level of BEingness unfolds and there is nothing that we feel the need to know – it is all complete, all perfect and in that moment of pure awareness there is pure clarity and pure vision. This is the 7th level of consciousness that Deepak talks about, it is an experience of pure Delta frequency.

In that space there is nothing to be sought, nothing to be taught and nothing to be taken. It all just is, yet you see it all through different eyes as if all life is absolute perfection.

Some of the miracle seekers are drawn to the Pure Land for personal and/or global gain. Some seek the perfect formula to tune themselves to its code and some seek to then go one step further and merge into it so that they may be given or be reminded of its gifts.

Like the famed Shamballa, the Pure Land is a state that exists within us, residing in every atom of space and the doorway to it is a compassionate and loving heart. There are a myriad of tools now available for the shape-shifting Shaman to merge into this pure state of Grace. One way is Recipe 2000> which allows us to connect with the Pure Land via a simple lifestyle choice that tunes us to feel its beat, its buzz and its benefits.

It was said by Xi Wang Mu that when we focus on fulfilling our highest, purest, most divine potential that we feed the pure land of Shamballa and the City of the Immortals, allowing these worlds to merge back into our own and that when we focus on materialism and on our denser nature, that these worlds fade. The immortals know that it is our love and attention that feeds their worlds enough to merge with ours so that their powers become our own.

When I began researching for this book I keyed in the words "The Law of Love" to a search engine on the internet and discovered an interesting story told by Joel from the Centre for Sacred Sciences (http://www.centerforsacredsciences.org/teachings/LawOfLove.htm). He writes of an ancient tale that flows like this:

"Once there was a Spiritual Seeker who, after mastering many disciplines and enduring much suffering in the world of delusion, arrived at the Gate of Nirvana (or Heaven as it's sometimes called). Before admission, however, he had to pass an examination by the Gatekeeper. First the Gatekeeper checked the Seeker's life records to verify he had kept all the necessary precepts. Not only had the seeker kept all the necessary precepts, he had observed countless supplementary ones as well.

"Next, the Gatekeeper queried the Seeker about the most esoteric aspects of the highest teachings. But the Seeker was able to answer all the Gatekeeper's questions without hesitation, thereby revealing the profound depths of insight he had attained on the path. Finally, with his clairvoyant vision, the Gate-Keeper scanned the Seeker's heart and mind, looking for any attachments the Seeker might still be harboring for the world of delusion, but he could detect nothing.

"Looks like you've passed all the tests," the Gatekeeper said and was about to admit the Seeker into Nirvana when suddenly he heard a barking sound. Glancing at the Seeker's feet, the Gatekeeper saw a little lame dog jumping up and down excitedly.

"What's this?" The Gatekeeper asked.

"My dog," the Seeker replied.

"But you can't take a dog into Nirvana!"

"You don't understand," the Seeker tried to explain. "This dog has been my faithful companion through all the hardships of the path. I can't leave him behind now."

"Well, you'll just have to. Those are the rules!" the Gatekeeper answered gruffly. Then, noticing a look of hesitation cross the Seeker's face, he adopted a more reasonable tone. "Listen, friend, you've worked very hard to get here. There's only one more step to take and you will be free of delusion forever. All your sufferings will have an end and you will enjoy Eternal Bliss. The only thing you have to do is give up this last little attachment to your dog."

"I don't know," the Seeker said doubtfully, and glanced at his dog.

But even the dog urged him not to forego this golden opportunity. "Listen, O Seeker," he said, "you have already been very kind to me, and I'll always be grateful. Please, don't deny yourself Final Liberation on my account."

Suddenly the seeker made up his mind. "I won't do it," e told the Gatekeeper firmly. "f abandoning my companion is a condition for Liberation then I renounce Liberation." And with that, he scooped the little dog up into his arms. "If you must go on suffering then I'm going to suffer with you. Come on, we'll return to the world of delusion together."

Still cradling the dog, the Seeker started back down the path by which they had come. But hardly had he taken two steps when he found himself once again facing the Gate to Nirvana. He wheeled to the right, then to the left, but no matter in which direction he turned, there was the ubiquitous Gate.

"Is this some sort of trick?" he asked the Gatekeeper angrily.

"Not at all," the Gatekeeper smiled. "You've just passed the final test. In renouncing your desire to attain Liberation for yourself alone, you have overcome the last barrier. Delusion has been destroyed. There is no world of suffering to return to. Welcome to Nirvana."

Joel goes on to say: "Although this story may seem like nothing more than a childish fairy-tale, it illustrates a fact of the utmost importance for the spiritual seeker: There is no Liberation without Love. For while it is true that Gnosis (direct knowledge of Reality) is the key that opens the Gate, no one actually passes through it unless they give everything to Love. This is why Jesus declared that all the laws governing spiritual life are finally subordinate to two Great Laws: "Thou shalt love the Lord thy God with all thy heart, with all thy soul, and with all thy mind. . . . [and] Thou shalt love thy neighbor as thyself."

"Nor is this teaching exclusively Christian. In the *Bhagavad Gita*, Krishna tells Arjuna, "whoever loves me without other desires, and has no ill will toward any creature at all, he comes to me." Likewise, the Buddha instructs his disciples "to do no injury to any living being but to be full of loving kindness," while the great Sufi master Ibn 'Arabi summed up his whole path by saying: "Love is the creed I hold; wherever turn His camels, Love is still my creed and faith."

It's true that when we run our lives by the Law of Love, that its frequency of freedom is revealed, yet liberation comes only when we are in harmony with ourselves and all fields of life, when we know that being in harmony with ourselves and our world is the same thing, for each feeds off the other. In metaphysics we know that what we fear we feed so setting the intention for harmony by applying the Harmony Code is a way of setting our fields to magnetize us to the pure land and so it is a key of entry.

Along with Recipe 2000> and a pure heart, the Harmony Code also allows us to maintain our presence in the Pure Land. Hence I would like to elaborate on this code in its own separate chapter as I feel that on one level if all we maintain is a pure hearted intention to always be in perfect harmony with all life and all energy fields, then this intention used with the code below has the power to draw us into the Pure Land effortlessly.

The harmony code was downloaded to me clearly one day when I realized yet again that to allow ourselves to fear something, or worrying about anything creates disharmony in our fields as it perpetuates separation. As a consequence I was guided to instantly reset all my own fields to be in harmony with all fields of existence for when all is in harmony there can be no separation as all operates knowing it is part of a whole. I did this using the technique below.

MEDITATION 12: *The Harmony Code: How to set our energy fields to be in harmony with all fields:*

- ॐ First center yourself in meditation using the love breath tool or any breath technique that allows you to be aligned and more conscious of your DOW.
- ॐ Next fill your heart with the pink light of Divine Mother love by imagining that your heart chakra is connected on the inner planes to a never ending source of pure love (as in the Love Breath Meditation)
- ॐ Next if you need to come into an emotion of feeling love, think for a few moments of the happiest most loving experience of your life.
- ॐ Imagine your heart chakra now full of love and opening and that you are beginning to beam out beams of pure pink light into the fields around you in a 360 degree motion, just like a lighthouse.
- ॐ Imagine as these beams radiate out from you that you are now connecting via this beam of love into the heart of every living creature, into the heart of every culture and into the very heart of every institution on earth,
- ॐ Just keep pulsing out this love from your heart, beaming throughout the worlds.
- ॐ Imagine that from your heart chakra circles of pure healing green light are now pulsing out like ripples across a pond from where a stone has landed, but that stone, is the center – your heart – a center from where wave after wave of green healing light is rippling out through space and time, washing through all other fields, connecting you in a loving, safe, healing way with all.
- ॐ As you keep this image in your mind, you begin to chant over and over: "Perfect field harmony now. Perfect harmonization with all fields now! Perfect healing and harmonization with all fields now."
- ॐ Ask the intelligent quantum and virtual fields to connect your DOW to the DOW of all life now and state the intention that: "From this moment on I connect DOW to DOW with all life, and flow in perfect harmony through all the fields. Universal waves of harmony and synchronicity constantly flow through me."
- ॐ "So it is! So it is! So it is!"

When a model can be created, duplicated and sustained by delivering very particular outcomes that to some may seem miraculous, then this model perhaps becomes a paradox regarding the very nature of miracles, for miracles as we have shared in our opening chapter are things that are said to operate outside the normal laws of nature, they are things that seem to be gifts from the Divine.

The beauty of the models delivered by the miracle makers is that with every one who applies them, they can add another level, and that is the level of the guidance from their own DOW. Matrix systems can be made simpler, faster and easier to apply as you reach deep within you and add additional tools that you may have utilized over time.

Alchemy is not restricted to the teachings of the Tao, or the teachings of the DOW, alchemy restricts itself to no man or no thing. Alchemy can be found in all the teachings of all the wise ones throughout the world and throughout all time. Alchemy provides ways of transforming, for as Saint Germaine has once said, the best example of Divine Alchemy is a life that is lived impeccably.

Whether that life is lived following the teachings of the Eight Fold path of the Buddhist understanding, or the Commandments of the Christians, or what is suggested in the Purest teachings of the Koran, or any other guidelines that have been offered by the many radiant messengers in our world; to bring miracles, a model must always operate for the good of all which will then support a higher human evolution.

We are after all one species on one planet learning how to co-create a more civilized world, a world where freedom is our birthright, where miracles are a daily occurrence and where the Law of Love is understood by all.

Miracles come into existence because there are those seeking them. They are born from the dreams, and the wishes, and the hopes of the seekers who seek transformation and change, from those who seek to witness a beauty and a 'just rightness' within creation. They come to those whose hearts are open and who have the eyes to see. But more than that, miracles are just science, and in the world of science, the way miracles come into being depends on the matrices supporting them. When the matrix is operating at its maximum potential, driven by the Law of Love and supported by its gift of Grace, events can then unfold within these parameters, that are so synchronistic and magical and awe inspiring, that we tend to term them miracles as if they are things that seem to occur outside the laws of nature. And yet to only consider the laws of nature rather than looking at the laws that govern all worlds is a very limited way of operating. Matrices, as light grids, bridge the two.

One of the gifts of the Law of Love is that it invites us to expand our consciousness and understand the workings of all levels of creation. It invites us to also experience the depths and the magic within each level of creation. The hungrier we are then the more our DOW can reveal our potential and also the mathematics of operating in what the Buddha called the Pure Land.

So again I stress that some of the things shared within this book are not technically miracles for they are simply the result of systems operating as we have described.

If some of us were to encounter the true immortalist, the one who never created disease and never aged and never died, if we were to encounter the one who also was never needing to take food, or fluid, the one who could sit themselves down in meditation and move their consciousness from their body and visit another in need across the other side of the globe and have this person been visited report back their vision; or the one who could dematerialize the body before you and then rematerialize it again in another space and time; to some of us, to witness a fellow human being do these things we may be in awe and convinced that we had just witnessed a miracle, and yet in the space of the Pure Land where the frequencies are just so well tuned, none of it is a miracle, it is just a matter of adjustment of the fields.

It has been most interesting for me, on a personal note, as for the last few years my focus has been coming back fully into this body, grounding myself in this plane to do another level of my work here. No longer do I need to understand the workings of the Cosmos for after seeing all that I have seen, my focus has shifted to be here now, fully in each moment and just allow the river of Grace to bring to my door all that I require, knowing that how strongly this river flows and supports me is determined by my own key-note and how I spend my time.

This is something that I have witnessed over and over again and proven to myself over and over again, that it all comes back to our personal key-note, the beat of our heart, the song that our heart sings throughout the universal fields of space and time.

My journey over the last few decades have allowed me to explore so many realms that I have no desire to be anywhere anymore, but right here, right now enjoying every moment, enjoying the beauty of all creation, knowing that everything that we perceive is just a reflection of our own consciousness and that when we look for divinity, divinity reveals itself in every face, in every tree, in every moment.

It has been a dynamic journey with my DOW, loving its gifts, understanding its essence, appreciating all the things that I have written about, watching it all within and without on all the levels that can be experienced and again always feeling that there is of course so much more in this never-ending journey of darkness filled with light.

Will the elixir Qi Gong prove to be a vital ingredient in the hydration of my body as I continue my journey with freedom from fluid? This is something that time will determine. This elixir of life, this nectar is talked about through all the religions and through all the ancient practices, although of course the versions of its making and utilization all vary.

And yet I know in my heart of hearts that our body as this magnificent 6.3 trillion cell mechanism contains all the ingredients it requires to be completely self sustaining and how to release these ingredients and have them mix in the perfect way is also just a formula of science. To the seasoned metaphysician the perfect field adjustment is often viewed simply as an arrangement of Grace.

Chapter 21

Arrangements of Grace

Life's evolution's driving force,
The universal, binding sauce,
Sanctity of pure thought, the course.

One of the greatest joys of silence and stillness is the ability to witness the flow of the Law of Love in action and its constant delivery of what I term 'arrangements of Grace.'

In July 2003 I was finalizing a Biofield training Retreat near Oslo Norway when I began to sense a strange yet loving energy that seemed to come to me every time I entered the conference room where we had worked all week.

All the meditations and programming had opened up very particular energy channels that had connected our group into C.N.N., the Cosmic Nirvana Network, so it was understandable that this new energy could find and connect with me. Slowly I realized that I was being communicated with by a familiar energy and so I checked with a good friend of mine Erik Berglund who is a wonderful channel and said:

"I keep picking up this energy that is presenting itself as a baby girl. Can you sense her?"

Yes of course he could and we soon realized that this energy was also attached to my eldest daughter so I knew I was soon to be a grand mother and shortly after returning home from my tour, my daughter announced that she was pregnant. To me the timing of it all was perfect as I was due to begin my sabbatical after consciously unhooking from a tremendously creative and busy life, and so I would be able to be home with my family and enjoy my grand daughter for nearly a year.

In line with the 'BE here now' reality, I had already long decided to create a field in my life where everything just comes to me, where my personal time is spent on thinking, feeling and being and thus beaming myself into particular channels of energy and maintaining that. In my field telepathy is normal, as are the use of all our higher intuitive capabilities, hence connecting on those summer days in Norway with the incoming soul of my 'grand daughter to be', was welcomed and enjoyed. Also as I was soon to read Michael Newton's *Destiny of Souls* book, all of it was even more fascinating as I know that our family was about to be joined by a soul we had all loved before.

There was also another interesting factor for me regarding reality creation and arrangements of Grace for as I shared in my book *Divine Radiance*, a few years before my desire for solitude began, I had been given the key to the door to leave this plane and I had nearly allowed myself to be totally seduced by the Law of Love and literally leave my physical body and disappear.

The Law of Love when it is fully operating at maximum capacity within us, dissolves us, merging us back into a consciousness where everything but Itself disappears. In that moment we are the beloved and the belover of all.

The seductive merging stopped when my husband, who was seated beside me and had sensed something was happening, began to squeeze my hand which brought me back into a mind state. After a few moments of internal discussion and with full awareness of what was being offered to me, I decided to stay on this plane. This was a decision that meant that a part of me would remain separate from this zone of pure love, for as I said, to merge with It means we disappear into the Oneness that It is.

For some this process of seduction happens to us naturally when we have completed what we agreed to do here, as with the completion, an energy band of such love finds us, overshadows us and absorbs us back into Itself. One of the reasons I gave myself for not allowing the completion of the seduction was that I wanted to be here for my grand children. Of course there were other considerations as well.

And so I have stayed individualized enough to function and remain on this plane and yet still be carried and maintained by a wave of Grace that has me mesmerized. My current fascination is with what I call 'arrangements of Grace'. How Grace arranges Itself in our life is so evident to us when we become the watcher and the one who is silent and still.

The co-creation that occurred, from attracting the soul that is my grand daughter, to the fun of her conception, to the nine months plus period of gestation, to the expulsion from her mother's womb and the child's passage into our world; all of this requires the most elaborate arrangement of Grace – an arrangement that delivered a very particular outcome.

For me that outcome was instant love.

I never believed in love at first sight but now I am beginning to understand it and also just how the Law of Love can also deliver instant love.

When everything in the fields around us and within us is fully conscious of the Law of Love, it is flooded by It and we enter the pure land and the experience of this frequency, when It floods us, all of this is completely freeing. To choose to stay individualized, when we know that this channel of pure love and Grace exists, is a very strange experience. It's like graduating from high school and then rather than attending the most amazing graduation party and the most incredible university, we choose to go back to kindergarten.

For me this kindergarten was to be a field of silence and solitude, an ashram of virtually celibate living where I could focus on the Law of Love and Its principles as I waited to welcome and enjoy my grandchild. Little did I realize that this experience would be the purest demonstration of the Law of Love in action that I may ever enjoy and witness.

And so I watched my daughter blossom and bloat as her body fed and cocooned another being. Finally after a four day labor, when the stars had shifted themselves into Taurus, my grandchild chose to be born and my daughter's body co-operated enough to deliver her into a room full of love.

Joyous expectation, tears of appreciation, warm embraces and big smiles all fused themselves as her head crowned and she popped pure and perfect into our world.

And so I fell in love. Instantly.

I asked myself why it felt different to delivering a child of my own and I realized that there was no 'shock of the reality of labor' for my physical body to deal with and so emotions of appreciation and awe could flow purely through my field. I was obviously in a much less painful state than my daughter who had valiantly meditated for nearly 100 hours using the most intense focus and breath control that I have ever witnessed. To me she became an Amazon and was instantly welcomed into the club called "Women who have given birth". This is a club of people fired by unconditional love as they discover the selfless and sometimes martyring role of mother. A club way beyond intellectualism, a club of tough women who have to dig deep from within to deliver each day in life into an arrangement that works for both herself and those she loves.

Sometimes this, like creating the perfect life, can be a huge challenge.

Unless when we can maneuver ourselves into the channel of Grace.

In this channel everything is delivered to our door and we begin to interact with everything around us in a much more conscious way as the power of the now charms us.

Baby bonding is like that and it is easy to spend hours lost in the pure land of baby bliss. At three weeks old my grand daughter gets absorbed looking at the field that surrounds me, her eyes aware and darting all around me as if she sees my invisible friends and perhaps she does. Now and then she fixes her gaze upon me and her mouth muscles rearrange themselves into what I choose to see as a smile.

At three months old she does it more often but now with a surety and Grace.

On another level I know that we have spent time before, that we have had other bodies and another history and that now we regather via one of the most miraculous arrangements of Grace that I can recall, only to fall instantly in love, with a love based on both history and a new beginning.

Our whole lives are an arrangement of Grace and we have the opportunity to fall in love in every moment. Because I have tested and applied the tools in our previous manuals, somehow my energy fields have been set to a pattern where Grace has delivered the most amazing life to my door. To have the freedom of time and be in a position where I can love and create with this new being is a miracle. To begin it all with a bond of unconditional love is even better and to recognize and appreciate the way that Grace can arrange things, and to encourage and allow It to do so, is a way of paying homage to human potential and the master DOW.

Transferring this feeling across the board to humanity and to every relationship we have is freeing. It means accepting the perfection of everything that has been and now is, accepting that it has been our co-creation. It means deciding to be more aware and more conscious about how and what and why we create and then perhaps finding the courage to do things a little differently so that Grace can arrange Itself more powerfully through our life. We do this firstly by being a more awake being and secondly by treating others as we ourselves wish to be treated. Next comes the act of surrender where we sincerely invite our higher eternally pure land dwelling Self to merge us into the stream of Its love, and then finally to allow Grace to rearrange Itself throughout our life until all we feel is:

Appreciation and love.

The lover and the loved.
The blesser and the blessed.
The watcher and the creator.
The sage and the servant.
The smiling one who's pure of heart.
The one who breathes Itself out from the pure land enough to radiate throughout all time and space and to be the All That Is.

When we stop and be still and be silent we move from being the seeker of miracles to the one who has found because in the stillness, when we are silent we can step back and recognize the miracle of life and the Law of Love in action and finally see that love like life is already all around us for it is not a state to gain but rather a state to just be.

THE LAW OF LOVE
How to influence an 'Arrangement of Grace':

■ **Step 1:** Begin to, or continue to, explore all 7 levels of your consciousness. Live with kindness and compassion.

■ **Step 2:** Sincerely surrender to your DOW.

■ **Step 3:** Via your lifestyle choice, tune yourself to maximize your experience and awareness of your DOW until there is no separation and you live constantly in the field of its Grace.

■ **Step 4:** Commit to harmoniously fulfill your part in the current paradise agenda on earth.

■ **Step 5:** Consciously open up inner plane channels of communication to the higher realms by activating your pituitary and pineal glands.

■ **Step 6:** Apply the Harmony Code.

■ **Step 7:** Witness, allow, then appreciate and enjoy the Grace as it flows. Seek to see the good in all and the God in all.

■ **Step 8:** Give Gratitude.

Chapter 22

Journey Through the Field of Love

Changing your view from I to we,
Flowering from consistency,
Becoming fruit of harmony.

While many people seek the type of freedoms that we cover in this manual, to me the greatest gift of the Law of Love when it is fully operational and acknowledged in our life is not these freedoms at all.

The greatest gift is Grace.

I suppose for me it is easy to say this as I no longer hunger for these things but it is more than that. Because I have experienced these freedoms and also the joy, the Shamanic ecstasy that comes with that continual flow of Grace, I know now which I value more. To me there is nothing as magical as being bathed in the pure land zone of Grace and the more we love the more we are magnetized to Its field.

Arrangements of Grace surround us and all of them are driven by the power of love for it is the loving that attracts Grace to our door.

Does it matter if we eat or sleep or drink or age or die?

No, not in the greater scheme of things where all that counts is the depth of love that emanates from our heart.

Is it possible to be free from the limitations these things bring?

If it is our deepest desire then we can free ourselves from anything.

Dreams and desires, faith and feeling, words and actions, all of it brings an arrangement of Grace, an arrangement that can be strong or weak, fulfilling or freeing, or frustrating when it seems just out of reach.

And yet Grace is the current of every river destined to reach the sea and Grace is carried on the river of love whose flow feeds our destiny. Grace is manna in motion, it moves the creative fire of chi, it brings power to prana and the evidence for us to see, for Its existence is confirmed by the way It magically arranges Itself through our life.

Can miracle making be guaranteed?

Again it depends on what we call a miracle yet to me miracles are just arrangements of Grace. While we have shared that Grace cannot be captured, nor can we capture compassion, and yet a heart filled with compassion is one of the most powerful field transformers.

The Law of Love & Its Fabulous Frequency of Freedom
with Jasmuheen

If we were to say that we are offering ourselves as co-creators of paradise or even co-creators of peace to our world, then what dynamics would we need to follow through to bring this state of peace and paradise into being?

We know that how we spend our clock time determines our levels of freedom just as we know our intention sets choices in motion to deliver certain outcomes. We also know enough about the power of field sensitivity, the why's and the how's and the benefits we gain when we explore our more sensitive nature. Many of us even have reason and motivation and common vision and wisdom and a thirst to be aligned to the field of love that gives us life. We know from personal experience that Grace finds and surrounds the pure of heart and those whose fields emanate compassion.

This is a lot to know.

Yet to know something and to live it can sometimes be at odds.

It was interesting to find myself living beachside surrounded by family after many years of sporadic visits. Although I had enjoyed a close involvement with my girls while they created as young women in the world, with the death of the family patriarch, and the matriarch long gone, the family field dynamics shifted. For the first time in a long time I consciously placed myself in a stable community situation surrounded by both family and new friends which has given me the opportunity to more powerfully apply the Law of Love.

It's so easy to feel wave after wave of pure love emanate from my heart as I hold my grand daughter in my arms. Her smell and warmth and awareness, her innocence and openness all add to the pull as we envelope ourselves in love's field but transferring this love across the wave of humanity is another ability again, yet love cannot be coerced, for like the Tao, it can only flow.

The Taoist say that if your want to understand the teachings of the Tao you just need to understand cooking and sex and while this is simplistic it is of course quite right, for in the Taoist sexual practices we learn to make love with our cells, to work with the energies of procreation and our opposite sex gland – the pineal gland and its release of pinealian – and to mix it all together with a good dose of love, of heart virtues.

It is this mixing of this perfect mix that is the cooking process within, for true alchemical changes to be manifested using all these energies, and yet it begins with the desire to make love with our cells, to really love ourselves, to combine our higher attributes and hormones and when these ingredients come together in the perfect mix, yes our key-note changes – the key-note of our whole physical system and of every cell.

The more we allow our DOW to dominate our inner resonance, the more freedom and magic we magnetize in life for the more our keynote changes the easier it is to see the good and the God in all, particularly as the flow of the Chi field strengthens. I know that the more that I immerse myself in the Chi field of love, the more that I lose my desire to be fed in any other way.

I must admit that I admire people like Zinaida who can just move straight into this system, riding on a wave of faith, never appearing to question or to struggle with their baser desires. It did not help the fact that I had positioned myself within a family structure of people who love to cook and eat thus representing the absolute antithesis of everything that I am doing and thus creating an energy field that I have had to weave myself around quite delicately in order to honor other people's lifestyle choices. Now that I have chosen to live alone again in my beach ashram with its sacred space there is no food in the fridge which is a welcome change.

I feel at times a little like an athlete for an athlete must involve themselves in intense physical training every day if they are to attain Olympic gold medal status. Their eye is constantly on this and hence they pay the price of the program to deliver their goal.

It is the same for myself through the conversion for a food and fluid free diet. I know the goal, I have experienced the benefits of the goal and hence I need to apply a daily training program that encompasses all levels of my being to bring myself into a state of physical, emotional, mental and spiritual harmony so that the goal can not just be attained, as I have in the past, but maintained regardless of circumstance around me.

For those able to sequester themselves into more of a continual ashram/sanctuary type environment without the constant exposure to high levels of physical and emotional pollution that I have encountered this last decade, then perhaps for them the journey will be quicker and easier to maintain. But it was not my path to make a conversion with this and stay with it, it was my path to learn how to switch the system back and forth and to constantly experiment and report on this – all of the things we have shared about in our previous manuals.

I find now that my body is leading me further in its desire to go on and it is overriding – through physical actions and responses – impulses in my emotional body which seem to becoming weaker and this is a wonderful thing to witness. To be able to go this past decade for such long periods without any food at all is a wonderful achievement especially when full health and vitality levels have been maintained.

Imagine what would happen to our world's resources if everyone could healthily exist on perhaps just one flavorsome cup of something per day, just for the fun of it and not for the need? Even to bring the diet down to such minimalist requirements similar to the lama diet of one type of food ingested once a day – all of this would have a huge impact on how our physical system functions, particularly if we have all learnt how to draw our vitamin and mineral requirement from the pranic energy sources and its field of love.

Also too, imagine the impact on a global level regarding resource sustainability, waste disposal and the whole economics of the food, pharmaceutical and medical industries as hand in hand along with the prana diet goes the freedom from the need to create dis-ease and so both our global economy and social structures will change. Imagine the freedom of time this will bring and how much effort goes into the production and distribution of food and fluid to take care of 6 billion people?

We still have a way to go in our personal journeys with this – researching, experimenting, applying the tools, refining, fine-tuning and modifying it all as we learn to listen to the body and our DOW and while I know that still so much needs attending to until we can all reach the final freedoms discussed in this manual, nonetheless so much has been achieved.

They say that pride cometh before a fall and yet I feel to acknowledge our accomplishments so far for while the journey has been arduous on some levels it has also been fruitful and rewarding. It's nice to stop for awhile and smile and look back with gratitude to all the forces that have supported what we have done and to acknowledge the courage that we have all had to walk the path that has led us to this point.

So to my own inner being and to all the thousands of people who are now consciously walking this path with me, I simply say thank you. What we have done already has created a shift in the morphonogenic field that has created a space for another shift in human evolution, a shift that has been recorded in history. Although perhaps not yet a science or not a historical event that has been totally understood in its significance, or given the due support or respect from our physical plane systems, it is nonetheless forever etched in time and from this point can only grow as more recognize that DOW devotion is the key to embracing a brighter future and a brighter now.

Yes I acknowledge that the sort of freedoms discussed in this manual may seem intangible or even of little interest to many, I also acknowledge that for me personally, this learning to be in complete harmony with my molecular system, is a pre-cursor of greater things to come, things that tantalize me for their practicality and the freedom that they bring. And yet beyond it all as I have often shared, the greatest lure is the love that comes when you have positioned yourself to witness and feel the beauty and joy that comes with the flow of pure Grace.

I spent a year fine-tuning my system with Lucinda and completed it all with a L.I.S.T.E.N. diagnosis that declared me in excellent health. Through working with Lucinda my body has confirmed an acceptable weight that it will settle at with a food and fluid free existence and for this I am grateful. Nonetheless there comes a point when we must take the next step alone, having prepared ourselves well, then the freedom journey is ours to walk surrounded only by a loving field that calls us home.

It has been ten months since I walked down the Place de Gracia in Barcelona and received my freedom assignment, ten months of being free from travel, ten months focusing on family and witnessing the Grace of the Law of Love. While I have not yet achieved my freedom from my interest in the flavor of fluid, what I have gained is a pure appreciation of the Law of Love and the consequent doubling of my personal happiness levels.

And so I return to the same conclusion as I did when I completed the book *The Food of Gods* that it is really love that feeds us and love that frees us. There is no model for love and there is no miracle regarding our capacity to love.

Love expresses itself in so many ways through all dimensions, first beating a path of sound waves as the divinely loving heart of the mother of creation, pulsing through the fabric of all existence and then streamlining itself into its various expressions of unconditional love, romantic love, paternal love, sibling love, maternal love and all the other loves that we can sample through the journey of life.

Can a model be made of this?

Perhaps in a future world where there is acceptance of the higher light science whose practice is based on understanding the Law of Love and the benefits of bathing in love's field. But this is not a science that has yet been given its rightful place in our human world and yet it is the very nature of the Law of Love that all must return back to the Source from which it has come. And so we witness not so much a time of human evolution but more a time of involution as the inward journey leads us to a place where we are free from all the limitations that we have ever known.

As I complete the final edits for this book, I think about how misleading the title "The Law of Love" may be and yet the subtitle is the key. There have been countless books written about love and while many contain wonderful insights few touch on the field of loves greatest gift which is its fabulous frequency of freedom. I have been blessed to know great love in my life and so my journey could move quickly through love's field into the deeper levels of its freedoms particularly from self imposed human limitation.

A natural consequence of being born into a field of love, and nurtured by family and early life situations, is that we gain an early appreciation of the Law of Love plus the interest to explore more of loves freedoms, for when one has a natural knowledge of love's field, then it is easier to embrace the fields gifts, for the field of love is in itself a field that is so enticing.

If I was to just look at my memories of this life then I could state how nourishing it is to be loved purely on the maternal and paternal levels, to bask in a mothers embrace, a mother who is always there for you, always loving and supporting, to have a family that is nurturing and stimulating as it pushes you outside of your comfort zones, just as a mother would push a baby bird from its nest so that it could learn to fly.

I have known the purity of adolescent love, of that willing exploration of the bonds that come between the male and female and the blossoming of intimacy and sexuality. I have lain in the field of the love of then being the mother, to give birth to souls who would become incredible friends and support systems as the decades have passed. I've lain in love's field with a lover of the Tao whose commitment to Tantra matched my own and I still walk in love's field with this one.

I have bathed in the fields of instant and unconditional love with the coming of my grandchild, feeling a bond that only a grand mother can know, like secret women's business.

I've known the love of the Holy Ones, of beings who reside in the purest bands of consciousness, who as I have surfed through love's fields in that awakened and sometimes hungry state in meditation, whose company I have found walking beside me, unexpected but appreciated and enjoyed.

The field of love is endless in its depth and range of experience.

We can know love when we surround ourselves in nature and feel the beauty of creation or when we sit under a star filled sky sensing the both the enormity of it all and glimpsing where we fit in with the greater field of creation. In this state we feel the pulse of an endless stream of love that first births everything and then draws everything back into Itself when its time is done.

I have known of the love of friends who regardless of how often you meet them, love you unconditionally, forever supportive and true, seeing the deepest part of you beyond the changing patterns and fields that may mesmerize you from time to time.

I have known of the love of animals – of birds, and rats, and dogs, and cats, and all creatures great and small that we can bond with and appreciate and be amused by and amuse. I have known of the love of the dolphins and the whales whose intuitive capability and awareness of exactly who we are is outstanding, for they are creatures who we cannot veil ourselves from but who long to share and play.

There is so much joy to be known when we dive into love's field and seek the nourishment there as we open to the feel of love's field, yet all of these are feelings that are indescribable until the field is accessed and the loving is done.

Through my inner plane journeys I have seen the mathematics of life and the codes that drive creation and I have seen and felt the force that then breathes life into the equation. And all of this adds depth to our journey through love's field and beckons us on until we dive deep enough to eventually find its fabulous frequency of freedom, for the seekers always find.

As I walk along my sunlit beach aware of the cloudless blue sky, warm waves caress my feet as a jade green ocean gently calls me to swim. Instead I walk and sing songs of praise for this life and the field of love that I now see constantly flowing through it.

And my DOW begins to smile.

The more I appreciate love's field, the deeper and wider my DOW smiles and I realize that DOW smiles have become the best barometer for knowing when the Law of Love is most present in my life.

And my journey into freedom?

It lures me with love to just enjoy each moment for freedom, like happiness and enlightenment, is not a destination but instead a state of Grace.

Personal Calibration and Testing methods for safely fulfilling the freedom agenda:
Post-script with Jasmuheen – January 2005

In 2002 a book called *Power vs. Force* was released and read with great interest. In it the author David Hawkins, a psychiatrist and spiritual teacher, shared his research findings on a simple method to calibrate levels of human consciousness and the various spiritual paths that many of us undertake plus much more. An in-depth twenty-year study using the applied science of behavioral kinesiology, I highly recommend this book.

Excited by the possibilities that his calibration system offered as far as a way of checking our freedom models, I began to apply it during my October/November 2004 tour. Quickly recognizing that we can use this system as a base to move into levels perhaps unexplored by David Hawkins, during this tour I took advantage of testing and confirming my findings with hundreds of special test subjects from four different countries – France, Italy, Germany and Switzerland.

In order to understand what I'm about to share in this post-script, it is important for you to read and understand what David Hawkins is talking about in his *Power vs. Force* book, nonetheless I will provide a brief synopsis here so that its relevance to our own findings is a little easier to understand.

Hawkins sees the potential of kinesiology as "the 'wormhole' between two universes – the physical, and the mind and spirit – an interface between dimensions … a tool to recover that lost connection with the higher reality and demonstrate it for all to see."

Founded by Dr George Goodheart and given wider application by Dr John Diamond, Behavioral Kinesiology is the well established science of muscle testing the body where a positive stimulus provokes a strong muscle response while a negative stimulus provokes a weak response.

Using Diamond's system, Hawkins developed "a calibrated scale of consciousness, in which the log of whole numbers from 1 to 1,000 determines the degree of power of all possible levels of human awareness." In this model 200 represents emotions of positive stimulus where muscle response remains strong and below 200 is where muscle response weakens as emotions anger, fear, guilt or shame, begin to influence the body.

200 is the energy of truth and integrity, 310 is the calibration for hope and optimism, 400 is the energy of reason and wisdom, 500 is the energy of love, 540 of joy, 600 is perfect peace and bliss and 700 to 1000 represents even higher levels of enlightenment.

Hawkins shares: "The individual human mind is like a computer terminal connected to a giant database. The database is human consciousness itself, of which our own cognizance is merely an individual expression, but with its roots in the common consciousness of all mankind. This database is the realm of genius; because to be human is to participate in the database, everyone, by virtue of his birth, has access to genius. The unlimited information contained in the database has now been shown to be readily available to anyone in a few seconds, at any time in any place. This is indeed an astonishing discovery, bearing the power to change lives, both individually and collectively, to a degree never yet anticipated.

"The database transcends time, space, and all limitations of individual consciousness. This distinguishes it as a unique tool for future research, and opens as yet undreamed-of areas for possible investigation." He is of course talking about accessing the universal field of intelligence which is within and around us all.

Applying the Kinesiology principle and test results re the freedom agenda:
When I start to download a book from universal mind, information that is needed to be incorporated is always given to me, particularly when the research is beneficial to my findings. Consequently I experienced great joy when I read David Hawkins's work as I realized that I was finally able to provide a safety check for the freedom model, particularly for someone who tests yes as per the questions asked meditation 4 in Chapter 16.

For example, among the hundreds of people that we tested in the countries mentioned:
- ♥ 80% tested yes that it is part of their blueprint to create a disease free life.
- ♥ 70% tested yes that it was part of their blueprint to learn how to be free from taking nutrition through food and access it through feeding from the divine nourishment flow within.
- ♥ 18% tested yes for setting up the reality of being free from the need for fluid, this lifetime, by again allowing that divinely nutritional source of prana within them to hydrate their body quite perfectly without the need for external fluids.
- ♥ 40% tested yes that it was part of their pre-agreed service blueprint to demonstrate physical immortality;
- ♥ 15% tested yes for pre-agreeing to learn, and demonstrate, the art of dematerialization and rematerialization and
- ♥ 70% tested yes for developing the ability to stop the ageing process.

As you can see from these figures the type of people that are attracted to the freedom agenda and the workshops that I do are a very particular group of a very specific calibration. Hence having a model that can ascertain our calibration level before we enter into the release of these types of limitation adds a very beneficial layer.

What I would like to offer therefore is the use of David Hawkins's work as one layer, in a three layer testing system, some of which we have already touched on previously in the sacred support systems chapter.

A THREE LEVEL CONFIRMATION SYSTEM
This three layer testing system is outlined as followed:
1) DOW – Divine One Within – our inner voice. This must always be our first method of testing in that it is the only reliable source of confirmation that is completely incorruptible. This requires us to establish a clear line of communication between ourselves and our divine nature – whether we call this our DOW, Monad or Atman or whatever. This level of communication comes via our sixth and seventh senses of intuition and knowing and needs to be, in my opinion, our first barometer of guidance in everything that we do in life; particularly in accessing and manifesting our pre-agreements. Our DOW is the

only thing that all humanity has in common, It is pure, It gives us life, It breathes us, loves us and guides us to evolve into our perfection. Learning to listen to It and trust Its guidance is a basic part of self mastery and self knowledge.

2) The second level of testing is to use the art of kinesiology to gain information confirmation using muscle responses in the body. Kinesiology, as many trained in this field know, has its limitations because it depends on how it is used and how strongly people's muscles test. It also depends on the calibration purity of the one being tested, the one doing the testing and the questions being asked. Reading David's book on this subject will provide a deeper understanding. I also recommend that when we use kinesiology that we ask the Divine One Within to confirm data, using the muscle testing system through the body, rather than asking the body's consciousness itself.

3) The third level of testing that is a wonderful support system for us as we journey through the freedom agenda, is to ask to receive clear confirmation from the universal field of intelligence which is all around us. This goes back to the story of people who, looking for answers, walk into a book shop, find that a book falls off the top shelf and hits them on the head, then spirals around and falls at their feet, open, the right way up and when they pick this book up, there is the answer to the very question that they had been thinking about. This is one way that the universal field of intelligence responds to our telepathic thought patterns when we have a strong desire for further knowledge, particularly when the knowledge that we are seeking is supporting our own evolutionary path in a positive way and is also beneficial for the world.

So these three levels of testing 1) accessing and listening to the divine voice within then 2) confirming its guidance or your query through muscle testing with kinesiology and c) asking for further confirmation from the universal field; these are three wonderful ways to provide a very clear system of guidance and a safety mechanism for human beings who are ready, willing, able and who are preprogrammed to display 'freedom from human limitation' to the degrees that we have discussed in this book.

When people go through the testing program in Chapter 16 to ascertain their pre-agreements, and if they receive a clear yes, then they will find that the universe will provide them with all the support that they need to fulfill this. There are many different ways to move into this agenda and setting the intention that we fill our preagreed agendas with joy and ease and Grace, allows the universal field to deliver whatever information and tools that we need to do this. Also as time goes by and the calibration of the mass morphonogenic field changes, then the way to attain and demonstrate these freedoms will become easier.

We have often had people receive an answer of 'no' during the meditation even though their own inner feeling was that these freedoms were something that they would like to embrace. Receiving a 'no' from the testing mechanism simply means that it is not part of your 'preprogrammed' blueprint, however as a being of free-will you may choose to exhibit these freedoms anyway as a side issue along with your main service agenda.

We also had people test the following using the David Hawkins *Power vs. Force* system, and I recommend that you may like to look at these yourself in more detail. These are:
- a) The testing of your birth calibration.
- b) The testing of your current calibration.
- c) The testing of your home field calibration – which will allow you to see how supportive your home field environment is for you to move into these agendas.
- d) The testing of your work field calibration.
- e) The testing of your current biological age plus
- f) the testing of the biological age your body is happy to support you into demonstrating.

From these tests we also found some interesting things. Firstly it is imperative that if someone tests 'yes' for a fluid free agenda then we can only recommend that they let go of fluid when the bio-systems calibration can support this in health and safety.

By first checking if it is in your blueprint and then checking, after intensive preparation using the methods discussed in *The Food of Gods* and *The Law of Love* books, when/if the bio-system is ready and able to sustain this, we then have a safe system to advise us. To attempt to do this without the support of the right calibration is only asking for potential physical trouble.

Other points to note regarding testing calibration levels:

Calibration limits: While David Hawkins shared in his book that most people in general society rarely move more than 5 calibration points per lifetime, this is not true for the spiritual student who lives a lifestyle that allows them to download and radiate more of their Divine essence or their DOW power; for this essence is able to create instant change provided that our bio-system can handle it.

Another anomaly with David Hawkins's system is a process that I call weaving.

Field Weaving: This relates to a discovery I made when I wanted to test my youngest daughter's calibration. The first thing I did was to check with her own divine force if it was okay for me to be given this data to which I quickly received a 'yes'. However when testing her calibration using muscle testing on my body I kept getting some very strange readings which intuitively I felt could not be right. Switching to Erik's body, who was testing with me, we realized that because I had an emotional attachment to her, sometimes the readings can be incorrect, but more than that we also realized that because I have been consciously weaving my energy through her energy fields to support her these last few years, by the conscious weaving of my field with hers, then her calibration was changing, because of how I calibrate, and so we had to look at the question differently. Using Erik's body to check, we procured a truer reading which we then confirmed using additional methodology.

Interestingly enough the calibration was still quite high even though at this time she does no meditation or yoga or the practices that I recommend in *The Food of Gods* book, however what this particular being does have is an incredibly open, loving, caring and compassionate heart. She is someone who has a huge network of friends and is always there for others. This in itself will bring a human being into wonderful calibration levels and can sometimes compensate for a lifestyle that maybe not as supportive of the physical bio-system as it could be.

The process of weaving is also very interesting because it can allow conscious access to other beings of great light and great love. For example, when we connect strongly through the doorways of love and devotion, to Mother Mary or to any of the other Holy Ones, that opens up an energetic path through our will and intention, for us to connect to their energy field, which then can weave back through into ours as we are all one and connected.

The recognition of this type of connection and possibility allows the weaving to begin and also is a way of fine tuning our calibration and strengthening it quite quickly. For people who do play with these realities, who are not living the sort of metaphysical lifestyle that we recommend in our previous manuals, then David Hawkins sharing that most people will only move 5 points in their calibration per lifetime is truth.

Personal Calibration Requirements for the Law of Love Freedom Agenda:
When originally tested, via two test subjects using kinesiology and David Hawkins's system, and confirming this via an additional two sources using the pendulum and inner plane Divine One Within confirmation, thus using a triple blind test with metaphysical tools – we originally found the following regarding the freedom models. These calibrations were then confirmed by approximately 500 test subjects and this is what we have noted:

- ♥ In order to establish a disease free existence where there is no physical, emotional, mental and spiritual disease a human bio-system needs a personal calibration of 635.
- ♥ The creation of an ageing free system where the ageing process is literally stopped a human bio-system needs a minimum calibration of 637, which is interesting as this is very close to the calibration of a disease free existence.
- ♥ In order to safely exist on purely a pranic flow for nourishment and no longer need to take physical food a human bio-system needs to calibrate at 668.
- ♥ In order to safely exist with the fluid free existence a human bio-system needs to calibrate at 777.
- ♥ The calibration for physical immortality for a human bio-system is 909
- ♥ and the calibration for successful dematerialization and rematerialization is 1367.
- ♥ I then asked for the calibration of classic miracles; to really witness the flow of Grace in such a powerful way, that the majority of people would deem it a miracle, the field around it needs to calibrate at around 1450.

For the last two calibrations, which are over Hawkins's 0-1000 scale, these are possible due to field weaving and coming into the consciousness of pure Oneness.

I do recognize in these results that we have been given, that as the general morphonogenic field of the mass of humanity changes, then the hundredth monkey system kicks in to change these calibration levels. According to Hawkins, while 78% of people calibrate at less than 200, mass consciousness as a whole registers at 207 due the process of entrainment where 22% of people of higher calibration are dominating the field enough to shift it into the level of truth and integrity en mass.

Another thing that we asked the bio-systems of the groups was to ask the body consciousness at what weight, in kilograms, that their body would stabilize at, once they entered in the food free and then later the fluid free existence. I felt that by asking the body consciousness this question this is another wonderful way to affirm our readiness. For example, a few years ago when I checked where my body weight would stabilize at with a fluid free existence I was told 45kgs. For me intellectually and emotionally I rejected this simply because I felt that it was not good for me to look so skeletal, and perhaps the health that I was seeking would not be maintainable, and so I held off on my decision to go onto a fluid free existence. When testing this same question this year, I was told that my body can now sustain a fluid free existence at 51kgs because my calibration has changed over the last few years. This is a lot more acceptable for me and therefore makes the movement into this level of freedom far more attractive.

Hence if you get a confirmation from your body of a weight that you feel is unacceptable to you then the advice is to wait and increase your personal calibration levels before going into this additional level of freedom.

The quickest way, as we all know, to increase calibration levels is simply to love a lot in life, for love is one of the most powerful feeding mechanisms that we have to match our calibration levels with our DOW because the divine essence is a being of pure and limitless love.

As we mentioned in earlier chapters, setting the home field calibration and refining it, is something that is easily done through the art of Feng Shui, and also through how life is conducted within the home field. It is important to have a field calibration in your home of a minimum of 200 which is, as David Hawkins has shared, the beginning levels of operating in truth and integrity. The higher the home field calibration then obviously the more supportive the environment is for you to move into and maintain these levels of the freedom agenda.

When Hawkins's book was first published in 1995, his research shared that only 4% of the world's population calibrated at over 500, while in 2004 it is now 6%; and in 1995 only 1 in 10 million calibrated at over 600. Nonetheless a person calibrating at 300 has the enough DOW power radiation to energetically influence 90,000 people; at a calibration of 700 we can counterbalance the energy of 700 million. These figures confirm that if all we do is refine our personal calibration levels to radiate maximum DOW power, this in itself is a valuable service, for not only does it deliver us naturally into the freedom agenda but it will also allow our presence here to positively influence the world.

♥ Namaste – Jasmuheen

The Law of Love

Epilogue & Update June 2007

It is incredible to find that when we are prepared to let everything go that we actually loose nothing at all and instead gain much more. I also tend to forget how much I reveal about myself, in the capturing of my research, for sometimes many years have passed since the writing of a book and its publication. Those who have read each book from *In Resonance*, to *Pranic Nourishment (Living on Light)* through to *The Law of Love* are now quite intimately connected with my personal journey with The Prana Program.

Often when I am on tour, as I am now in Russia, they stop to ask me for an update on various things in my personal life and I naively think, 'How does this stranger know this?' but while they may appear to me to be a stranger, due to my writings to them I am no stranger at all. It is of course all revealed as we write, for many of the greatest insights that we have always come in the day to day living of our lives.

Some people reveal so little of themselves in their writings, whether they be fictional or non-fictional works, whereas other authors expose themselves quite openly as I have done. Personally I have found that teachings given that are based on personal experience tend to have more impact, rather than teachings that are given from a book that the writer has not personally experienced or lived and deeply understood. As we all know there is a huge difference between something lived, that is anchored in our cells as true, and something we like the idea of and know only as part of a good intellectual model.

It took me until the end of 2006 to attain the freedoms I set out to achieve at the beginning of this book. To really understand the path of the true breatharian and know – via powerful personal experiences – that my body can receive not just its nourishment but also its hydration from an internal inter-dimensional Source. Having achieved this pragmatic experiential knowledge now I stand at a cross roads with no real impetus to drive myself on, for what came with this final revelation was an experience I could never have imagined; an experience that leaves a seeker with nothing to seek anymore.

As I talk about this in detail in my book *The Bliss of Brazil & The Second Coming* I will not elaborate on it all here suffice to say that when we really seek to experience the Law of Love and joyously surf through its multidimensional field, we discover the Source of such power, such nourishment, that the seeker can be the seeker no more and the miracle maker sits back to watch and enjoy the miracles that abound around us all of their own accord.

My husband and I are now well settled in our separate ashrams and thoroughly enjoy each moment we share. It is a lifestyle choice that has brought us the benefit of time spent in stillness and silence, and of more poignant times, when we come together and share. This may not suit other married people, who have differing agendas to ours, but it suits us both so well. It is wonderful to have people in our lives who know the source of pure love, and so can love unconditionally in return, which is one of the greatest gifts that I have learnt.

To be free enough with our loved ones to be able to stay true to the voice of our own heart's song while giving and receiving unconditional love is such a blessing, particularly in a marriage. Nonetheless when both parties are committed to Divine Marriage, where they realize that with the merging of their higher and lower selves comes all that we seek, and then to share with each other as complete beings – well this makes it all easier still.

And yet there is more.

The deeper we dive into the field of the infinite web of love that pulses through us, the more subtle and yet profound it all becomes. In this web I have found the deepest levels of a seemingly permanent contentment and peace, in this web I have found that champagne like feeling that bubbles away in a layer that I call the field of love's pure joy.

And still there is more.

Our physical system can only handle what it can handle regarding the voltage of this Divine Matrix as it flows through us firing up our chakras, light-body and meridian system; yet we can always adjust ourselves to handle more. Sometimes we pause awhile, no longer seeking, feeling full as if our cells are saying: "No way, there can't be more, I am full, have been overflowing in fact with love and light and joy and now I am content and full of peace - this is perfection itself…" and so maybe we rest awhile just to enjoy this feeling; and in the resting somehow we get used to this level of flow and expand in this journey through love's field and find that yes, there is even more.

At times in my work I feel like the yogi who walks through life in that state of ecstatic bliss, so locked into Samadhi that there is nothing to say, nothing to explain, nothing to do. A tiny part of me sometimes would just like to touch a crowd with one small finger and let them feel this peace, this joy, so that they will know that their journeying is worth it, that there is a pot of the purest gold at the end of the rainbow, even though at times it may not look like there is.

Sometimes when we begin our journey of self exploration, of self mastery, it seems as if we encounter challenge after challenge as we struggle to understand the bigger picture behind life and our role within it. And yes peace pools, and joy fields, and love's truest gifts come to the hungry of heart like unexpected blasts from the past that catch us unawares. While how we spend our time can place us in the vicinity of these fields, or in its denser layers, the keys to accessing its deeper aspects lie in the realm of the virtues we gain as we live our life and all of this is something that no books can teach.

Virtues are attained through the living of life, through interacting and learning in a hands on way, so that our cells are imprinted with something real and true that goes beyond mental plane understanding. Some of the wisest people I know have very little metaphysical knowledge, and nor are they well read, yet their heart space is pure and true and so they appear to magnetize a steady flow of Grace and magic in their lives.

This is the alchemy of the Law of Love, and this is that virtues gained release a frequency through us, that will magnetically align us into the deeper levels of love's pure field, and it is here that a human system can really begin to thrive and know life's truest food.

Empty yourself of everything.
Let the mind rest at peace.
Ten thousand things rise and fall while the Self watches their return.
They grow and flourish and then return to the source.
Returning to the source of stillness, which is the way of nature.
The way of nature is unchanging.
Knowing constancy, the mind is open.
With an open mind, you will be open hearted.
Being open hearted, you will act royally.
Being royal, you will attain the divine.
Being divine, you will be at one with the Tao.
Being at one with the Tao is eternal.
And though the body dies, the Tao will never pass away.
From the Tao Te Ching

And when we understand the Law of Love, nothing ever dies.

Further Information

Details of where to find the meditations mentioned in the Inter-Dimensional Matrix Mechanics chapter:

- ♥ *1. Love Breath Meditation* – Cosmic Cable Hook-In to the channel of Divine Love, Divine Wisdom & Divine Power using specific breathing rhythm. Learning to alter our external & internal energy fields using the Divine Love Breath. This works similarly to the 11 strand healing system. Ch 6. *The Food of Gods*.

- ♥ *2. Divine Electricity of Love Meditation* – Body Love Tool, violet light flooding & data downloads, pituitary & pineal gland activation. Ch 6 *The Food of Gods*.

- ♥ *3. Bio-shield creation*: Books containing the details of this: *Four Body Fitness: Biofields & Bliss* plus an extended version in Ch. 11 of *The Food of Gods*. The audio guided meditation of this can also be downloaded as an MP3 file from:
  http://www.selfempowermentacademy.com.au/htm/cia-education.asp#audio
  It is found as Meditation 1 in the Portuguese language section and as it is in English with Portuguese translation, it is suitable for all. There is also a version in German.

- ♥ *4. Digestive Grid* – Book containing the details of this: Chapter 11 of *The Food of Gods*. No audio guided meditation at present.

- ♥ *5. Self Sustaining Template* – Books containing the details of this: *Four Body Fitness: Biofields & Bliss* plus an extended version Chapter 11 of *The Food of Gods*. No audio guided meditation at present.

- ♥ *6. 11 Strand Healing system* – The audio guided meditation of this can be downloaded as an MP3 file from:
  http://www.selfempowermentacademy.com.au/htm/cia-education.asp#audio
  It is file no. 11. Self-Healing Meditation and is a meditation utilizing creative visualization and light to activate the light body and retune and revitalize the skeletal system, the nervous system, the bloodstream, the organs and increase the energy flow through the meridians. Also meditations 1 & 2 above.

- ♥ *7. Akashic records* – Details on the Akashic Records can be found in the manual *In Resonance*.
  The audio guided meditation of this can be downloaded as an MP3 file from:
  http://www.selfempowermentacademy.com.au/htm/cia-education.asp#audio
  Akashic Records Meditation – Activating the Inner Pyramid & Accessing the Akashic Records: Activating the crown & brow chakras, the medulla oblongata, the pituitary & pineal glands to form the inner pyramid for active telepathy and higher communications. Then using energy grids for linking into the Akashic Records to gain information for our life purpose and blueprint.

***Other Tools that are detailed in the book:* The Food of Gods**
LEVEL 2 & 3 Nourishment & Sensitivity Development Tools

Chapter 6
    Technique no. 1: Love Breath
    Technique no. 2: Holy Vedic Breath
    Technique no. 3: Inner Smile
    Technique no. 4: Body Love
    Technique no. 5: Lifestyle Recipe

Technique no. 6: Minimization Tool
Technique no. 7: Conversion Tool
Technique no. 8: Solar Food Access
Technique no. 9: Healings Sounds
Technique no. 10: Programming Codes
Technique no. 11: Sacred Sex Food
Technique no. 12: Violet Light Flooding
Technique no. 13: Divine Amrita Channel
Technique no. 14: Pineal & Pituitary Food
Technique no. 15: Downloading Goddess energy

LEVEL 2 & 3 Nourishment & Sensitivity Development Tools
Chapter 7   Technique no. 16: Cosmic Cable Hook-In
Chapter 8   Technique no. 17: Nurturing Home
Chapter 9   Technique no. 18: Yoga Teacher Tool
               Techniques no. 19a, b, c, d, e: Silence Training, Darkness Training
                   Field Non-Displacement Training,
                   Ambidextrous and Weather Training

LEVEL 3 Nourishment & Sensitivity Development Tools
Chapter 11
            Technique no. 20: Discover your Encodements
            Technique no. 21: De-Tox Program
            Technique no. 22: DOW Surrender
            Technique no. 23: Cellular Pulsing & Forgiveness
            Technique no. 24 & 25: Alternate Breathing & Tratak
            Technique no. 26: Digestive Bio-Shield
            Technique no. 27: Basic Bio-Shield
            Technique no. 28: Bio-Shield Maintenance
            Technique no. 29: Self-Sustaining Template
            Technique no. 30: Chi Machine
            Technique no. 31: Maltese Cross Meditation
            Technique no. 32: Field Weaving Personal Tuning
            Technique no. 33: Field Weaving Global Tuning
            Technique no. 34: Field Cocooning & Extensions
            Technique no. 35 & 36: Field Resetting

BENEFICIAL READING

Recommended Reading to understand more of the Law of Love:
In Resonance, Divine Radiance : On the Road with the Masters of Magic, The Divine Nutrition Series of Living on Light, *Ambassadors of Light & The Food of Gods*; The Biofields & Bliss Trilogy of Four Body Fitness, *Co-Creating Paradise & the Madonna Frequency Planetary Peace Program*; plus *Streams of Consciousness*.

The above e-books can be purchased & downloaded at:
http://www.selfempowermentacademy.com.au/htm/cia-education.asp

Links to The Divine Nutrition Series:
http://www.selfempowermentacademy.com.au/htm/cia-education.asp#divine

& the Biofields & Bliss Series:
http://www.selfempowermentacademy.com.au/htm/cia-education.asp#biofield

BIBLIOGRAPHY

1. Mantak Chia, *Cosmic Smile* & other relevant manuals

2. Deepak Chopra M.D, *Synchrodestiny: Harnessing the infinite power of coincidence to create miracles,* Rider & Co, July 2005, ISBN: 1844132196 & any of his books

3. David R. Hawkins M.D, PhD, *Power vs. Force: The Hidden Determinants of Human Behavior,* Hay House, April 2002, ISBN: 1561709336

4. Doc Childre & Howard Martin, *The HeartMath Solution,* Harper San Francisco, August 2000, ISBN: 006251606X

5. Michael Newton PhD, *Journey of Souls: Case Studies of Life Between Lives,* Llewellyn Publications, September 2002, ISBN: 1567184855 & *Destiny of Souls: New Case Studies of Life Between Lives,* Llewellyn Publications; 2nd edition, May 2000, ISBN: 1567184995

6. John Perkins, *Shapeshifting: Techniques for Global and Personal Transformation,* Destiny Books, September 1997, ISBN: 0892816635

7. Don Miguel Ruiz, *The Mastery of Love: A Practical Guide to the Art of Relationship,* Amber-Allen Publishing, May 1999, ISBN: 1878424424

8. Eckhart Tolle, *The Power of Now: A Guide to Spiritual Enlightenment,* New World Library, September 2004, ISBN: 1577314808

9. Jasmuheen, relevant books as mentioned above.

Plus any other book that you are guided to read to tune you further to the Law of Love.

JASMUHEEN'S BACKGROUND

- ♥ Author of 24 books;
- ♥ international lecturer,
- ♥ leading researcher on pranic nourishment;
- ♥ founder of the Self Empowerment Academy ;
- ♥ co-facilitator of the C.I.A. – the Cosmic Internet Academy; publisher and
- ♥ editor of the on-line M.A.P.S. Ambassadry Newsletter – *The ELRAANIS Voice (TEV)*.

❖ 1957 – Born in Australia to Norwegian immigrants
❖ 1959 – Began focus on vegetarianism
❖ 1964 – Began to study Chi
❖ 1971 – Discovered the Languages of Light
❖ 1974 – Initiated into Ancient Vedic Meditation and eastern philosophy
❖ 1974 – Began periodic fasting
❖ 1974 – Discovered telepathic abilities
❖ 1975 - 1992 – Raised children, studied and applied metaphysics, had various careers
❖ 1992 – Retired from corporate world to pursue metaphysical life
❖ 1992 – Met the Masters of Alchemy
❖ 1993 – Underwent Prana Initiation and began to live on light
❖ 1994 – Began 7 year research project on Divine Nutrition and pranic nourishment
❖ 1994 – Began global service agenda with the Ascended Masters
❖ 1994 – Received the first of 5 volumes of channeled messages from the Ascended Masters
❖ 1994 – Wrote *In Resonance*
❖ 1994 – Founded the Self Empowerment Academy in Australia
❖ 1994 – Began to hold classes in metaphysics and Self Mastery
❖ 1994 – Began *The Art of Resonance* newsletter renamed later as *The ELRAANIS Voice*
❖ 1995 – Traveled extensively around Australia, Asia and New Zealand sharing Self-Mastery research
❖ 1995 – Wrote *Pranic Nourishment (Living on Light) – Nutrition for the New Millennium*
❖ 1996 – Invited to present the Pranic Nourishment research to the Global stage
❖ 1996 – Began re-education program with the Global Media
❖ 1996 – Set up the International M.A.P.S. Ambassadry – Established in 33 countries
❖ 1996 – Created the C.I.A. – the Cosmic Internet Academy – a free website to download data for positive personal and planetary progression. Web address: www.selfempowermentacademy.com.au
❖ 1996 - 2001 – Traveled extensively to Europe, the U.K., the U.S.A. and Brazil with the 'Back to Paradise' agenda
❖ 1996 - 2004 – Talked about Divine Power and Divine Nutrition to > 900 million via the global media
❖ 1997 – Began to set up scientific research project for *Living on Light*
❖ 1997 – Began the Our Camelot Trilogy, wrote *The Game of Divine Alchemy*
❖ 1997 – Formed the M.A.P.S. Ambassadry Alliance – people committed to global harmony and peace
❖ 1998 – International tour to share the Impeccable Mastery Agenda
❖ 1998 – Wrote *Our Progeny – the X-Re-Generation*
❖ 1999 – Wrote the *Wizard's Tool Box* which later became the Biofields and Bliss Series.
❖ 1999 – Wrote *Dancing with my DOW : Media Mania, Mastery and Mirth*
❖ 1998 – 1999 Wrote and published *Ambassadors of Light – World Health World Hunger Project*
❖ 1999 – Began contacting World Governments regarding Hunger and Health Solutions

- 1999 – International tour to share the Blueprint for Paradise
- 1999 - 2001 – Began M.A.P.S. Ambassadors International Training Retreats
- 2000 – International tour 'Dancing with the Divine' to facilitate the election of an Etheric Government in 28 key cities and also shared the Luscious Lifestyles Program – L.L.P.
- 2000 - 2001 – Wrote *Cruising Into Paradise* an esoteric coffee table book
- 1999 - 2001 – Wrote *Divine Radiance – On the Road with the Masters of Magic* and
- 2001 – Wrote *Four Body Fitness : Biofields and Bliss Book 1*
- 2000 - 2001 – Launched the OPHOP agenda One People in Harmony on One Planet
- 2001 – Wrote the book *Co-Creating Paradise : Biofields and Bliss Book 2*
- 2001 – Launched Recipe 2000> as a tool to co-create global health and happiness; peace and prosperity for all on Earth
- 2002 – Launched www.jasmuheen.com with its Perfect Alignment Perfect Action Holistic Education Programs; and its I.R.S. focus to Instigate, Record and Summarize humanity's co-creation of paradise.
- 2002 – Did the 'Divine Radiance FOUR BODY FITNESS – Unity 2002' World Tour
- 2002 – Received, wrote and launched *The Madonna Frequency Planetary Peace Program* as the free e-book, *Biofields and Bliss Book 3*.
- 2002 - 2003 – Wrote *The Food of Gods*.
- 2003 – World Tour 'Divine Nutrition and The Madonna Frequency Planetary Peace Project'.
- 2004 – Wrote *The Law of Love* then toured with 'The Law of Love and Its Fabulous Frequency of Freedom' agenda.
- 2005 – Wrote *Harmonious Healing and The Immortals Way*, then toured with the 'Harmonious Healing' agenda.
- 2005 – Began work on *The Freedom of the Immortals Way* plus continued with writing *The Enchanted Kingdom Trilogy & The Prana Program* for Third World Countries.
- 2005 – Presented THE PRANA PROGRAM to the Society for Conscious Living at the United Nations Building in Vienna – Nov. 2005
- 2006 – International tour with THE PRANA PROGRAM

Jasmuheen's books are now published in 17 languages.

EDUCATIONAL E-BOOKS
http://www.selfempowermentacademy.com.au/htm/cia-education.asp

Education eliminates ignorance which eliminates fear which leaves more room for love ...

The following e-books are just a few of the 20 books Jasmuheen has provided the Self Empowerment Academy and its online representative the C.I.A. All provide many wonderful tools and insights for the co-creation of personal and planetary paradise.

"THE PRANA PROGRAM": Can we eliminate all health & hunger challenges on our planet? Is there a way of satiating everyone's physical, emotional, mental and spiritual hungers and do it in a way that creates peace and harmony in our world?
After over a decade of experiential research in the field of alternate nourishment utilizing chi or prana – also known as cosmic particles – Jasmuheen as leading researcher in this field, now puts forth a program to do just that. Specializing in Third World countries, THE PRANA PROGRAM e-book is an encyclopedia type compendium of 'everything you always wanted to know about prana and more'. This book covers alternate methods of nourishing and even hydrating the body using an inner energy source already produced in the body thus freeing us from our dependence on world's food resources and changing the economic status of our world. Add this e-book to shopping cart. http://payloadz.com/go?id=163985

"IN RESONANCE": This book can be likened to a 'motor mechanic' manual except it is for tuning and aligning the four body system – physical, emotional, mental and spiritual – for a blissful life! The book covers 20 years of well-researched information on the Ancient Wisdom, plus many practical techniques to create positive change from breath and light work to bi-location, universal law, and telepathic communication! (No 2 with Esotera Magazine Best-seller – August 98 Germany) Add this e-book to shopping cart. http://payloadz.com/go?id=59295

THE DIVINE NUTRITION SERIES
BOOK 1 of the Living on Light – Divine Nutrition Series: "PRANIC NOURISHMENT – Nutrition for the New Millennium": Jasmuheen's fourth book which details her journey and experiences plus a detailed process, that allowed her to be physically sustained by the chi of life. This book also covers immortality and tools to stop the aging process. Living on Light is available in 15 languages – go to http://www.jasmuheen.com/who.asp#author for a list of publishers in other languages. Add this e-book to shopping cart http://payloadz.com/go?id=59292
BOOK 2 of the Living on Light – Divine Nutrition Series: "AMBASSADORS OF LIGHT – Living on Light – World Health, World Hunger Project" is Jasmuheen's tenth book and the follow on to her best seller *Pranic Nourishment – Nutrition for the New Millennium:* In this book Jasmuheen offers practical solutions to world health and world hunger related challenges. This entails an in-depth look at global disarmament, the dissolution of prohibition, the forgiveness of Third World debt, holistic re-education programs for long-term resource sustainability, and the elimination of all dis-ease. This book is a collation of research, recipes and recommendations that if adopted, will radically alter the path of humankind! Imagine a world without war or hunger or fear? Imagine a world that is dis-ease free and unified where all life is honored? These are the dreams of the Ambassadors of Light. Add this e-book to shopping cart http://payloadz.com/go?id=59293

BOOK 3 of the Living on Light – Divine Nutrition Series: "THE FOOD OF GODS": Powerful solutions, and meditations and tools on how to nourish all our hungers and eliminate our physical, emotional, mental and spiritual anorexia so that we can all be healthy and happy and peaceful and prosperous. Perfect nourishment utilizing Divine power. Jasmuheen's 18th book. Add this e-book to shopping cart http://payloadz.com/go?id=59294

THE BIOFIELDS & BLISS TRILOGY:
BOOK 1: "FOUR BODY FITNESS": Written as a simple education manual for schools, in this book Jasmuheen shares details of Biofield Science which includes programming codes plus a lifestyle recipe that will create inner and outer peace; harmonize all people, and inspire great change. Bridging the ancient Wisdom with Futuristic Science, Biofields and Bliss also introduces the Higher Light Science of advanced bioenergetics and its pragmatic application for personal and global refinement. This book covers Recipe 2000> in great detail and offers many practical tools for successful living. Add this e-book to shopping cart http://payloadz.com/go?id=59243
BOOK 2: "CO-CREATING PARADISE": Covering the Dimensional Biofield Science of fine-tuning our Social and Global Biofields to create paradise on Earth, this book offers simple and powerful tools for positive personal & global transformation. It also provides a synopsis of religions, the ancient wisdom and quantum principles plus self-empowerment and peace tools. Add this e-book to shopping cart http://payloadz.com/go?id=59291
BOOK 3: "THE MADONNA FREQUENCY PLANETARY PEACE PROJECT": This free e-book carries the slogan "Change our Focus & Change our Future" and provides 9 practical projects and action plans and agreements and tuning tools that will create deep and lasting planetary peace by eliminating the root reasons and causes of war and terrorism. This manual is a timely, PERFECT ACTION solution for the chaos of this current millennium. Available ONLY as a free e-book. Also in **ENGLISH** – **DEUTSCH** – **ESPANOLE** – **FRANCAIS** – **ITALIANO** – **DUTCH** – **ROMANIAN** – **PORTUGUES** – **CZECHOSLOVAKIAN** – **CROATIAN**.
http://www.selfempowermentacademy.com.au/htm/peace.asp

"DIVINE RADIANCE: ON THE ROAD WITH THE MASTERS OF MAGIC": A detailed account of the life of the messengers of the Masters of Magic. A 'heart' book filled with transformational tools and stories of Jasmuheen's interaction and experience with the ones she calls the Masters of Alchemy plus tips for improving our Divine Communication, Divine Revelations and more. Add this e-book to shopping cart http://payloadz.com/go?id=59297

"STREAMS OF CONSCIOUSNESS UNIFIED": A collection of recorded live channeling taken from the previous 5 volumes of the "Inspirations" trilogy and Vol. 1 and 2 of "Streams of Consciousness". As a volume of communications received by Jasmuheen from C.N.N., the Cosmic Nirvana Network, during the 1990's; these divinely inspired messages cover attitudes and life skills and as such will never date. Add this e-book to shopping cart http://payloadz.com/go?id=59301

"DARKROOM DIARY DOWNLOADS": This book was written during February 2004 at the Tao gardens in Chiang Mai Thailand as I underwent an experience of spending 21 days in the dark to receive training in the practice of Lesser, Greater and Greatest Kan & Li with Master Mantak Chia. What is recorded here are simply my experiences during this retreat and how they relate to my own journey in learning more of the freedoms of the Law of Love as detailed in the book "The Law of Love". My focus at this retreat was to learn tools to effectively rehydrate the human body and free it from the need of not just food – but also from the need to take fluid. To read more of Jasmuheen's journey in the dark, as a **FREE** e-book http://www.selfempowermentacademy.com.au/htm/files/e-books-free/Darkroom-Downloads.pdf

EDUCATIONAL AUDIO & BENEFICIAL TUNING TOOLS
MP3 AUDIO FILES – GUIDED MEDITATIONS

1. **Love Breath Meditation** – 30 mins with Jasmuheen – Cosmic Cable Hook-In to the channel of Divine Love, Divine Wisdom & Divine Power using specific breathing rhythm. Learning to alter our external & internal energy fields using the Divine Love Breath. USD $5.55. Add this MP3 to shopping cart http://payloadz.com/go?id=62278

2. **Divine Electricity of Love Meditation** – approx. 48 mins with Jasmuheen, music by Erik Berglund. Body Love Tool, violet light flooding & data downloads, pituitary & pineal gland activation. USD $5.55. Add this MP3 to shopping cart http://payloadz.com/go?id=622789

3. **Divine Marriage** – merging our masculine & feminine selves, yin/yang blend, Divine Self connection – approx. 17 mins with Jasmuheen. Music by Erik Berglund. USD $5.55. Add this MP3 to shopping cart http://payloadz.com/go?id=62280

4. **Tuning to your Guardian Angels** – downloading data re your gift to the world & your life purpose, spinning chakra & violet light feeding meditation & general self nurturing. 24 mins with Jasmuheen. USD $5.55. Add this MP3 to shopping cart http://payloadz.com/go?id=62281

5. **Celestial Sounds & Galactic Civilization tune-in** – 31 mins with Jasmuheen. Meeting your future self & bridging inner and outer worlds and timelines. Music with Brain Vale. USD $5.55. Add this MP3 to shopping cart http://payloadz.com/go?id=62282

6. **The Breath of Life** – Breath and light techniques for deep relaxation and to connect consciously with and experience the universal life force within (22 minutes each one – with a discourse then a guided meditation. USD $5.55 Add this MP3 to shopping cart http://payloadz.com/go?id=59303

7. **The Inner Sanctuary** – Creating the inner sanctuary for inner peace. Again using breath and light techniques and guided visualization for deep relaxation (22 minutes) USD $5.55 Add this MP3 to shopping cart http://payloadz.com/go?id=59304

8. **Emotional Realignment** – Dealing effortlessly and effectively with negative emotions and releasing past emotional 'baggage'. Realigning the energy field of the emotional body to higher frequencies of light using visualization with breath and light for an inner 'spring clean' (33 minutes). USD $5.55 Add this MP3 to shopping cart http://payloadz.com/go?id=59305

9. **Empowerment Meditation** – Working with Ascended Master Lady Kwan Yin and the three-fold and violet flame. Connecting with and being empowered by the God/Goddess within (44 minutes) USD $5.55 Add this MP3 to shopping cart http://payloadz.com/go?id=59306

10. **Ascension Acceleration** Meditation – Powerful affirmations, mantras, breath and light techniques to increase our light quotient and harmonize our energy fields. Combines the work of Jasmuheen and Dr J.D. Stone (44 mins). USD $5.55 Add this MP3 to shopping cart http://payloadz.com/go?id=59307

11. **Self-Healing** Meditation – Meditation utilizing creative visualization and light to activate the light body and retune and revitalize the skeletal system, the nervous system, the bloodstream, the organs and increase the energy flow through the meridians. A gentle daily healing meditation to strengthen the physical body set to relaxing classical music. USD $5.55 Add this MP3 to shopping cart http://payloadz.com/go?id=59308

12. **Akashic Records Meditation** – Activating the Inner Pyramid & Accessing the Akashic Records: Activating the crown & brow chakras, the medulla oblongata, the pituitary & pineal glands to form the inner pyramid for active telepathy and higher communications. Then using energy grids for linking into the Akashic Records to gain information for our life purpose and blueprint. USD $5.55 Add this MP3 to shopping cart http://payloadz.com/go?id=59310

NOW AVAILABLE: audio and also videos that are now available
free from the C.I.A. website at the URL addresses of:
http://www.selfempowermentacademy.com.au/htm/visual-welcome.asp#video
http://www.selfempowermentacademy.com.au/htm/auditory-welcome.asp
http://www.selfempowermentacademy.com.au/htm/peace.asp#LANGUAGES

Stay up to date with Jasmuheen's activities
via the Cosmic Internet Academy's Contact Updates List:
http://visitor.constantcontact.com/email.jsp?m=1011160294062
For those of you who choose to register with our C.I.A. CONTACT LIST,
you will receive general monthly or quarterly updates
or whenever we at the Self Empowerment Academy
and the C.I.A. feel there is something of value to share with you.

Please note that your details are kept confidential at our C.I.A. and are not passed on.

For more copies of this e-book go to:
http://www.selfempowermentacademy.com.au/htm/cia-education.asp

For copies of this book as a hard-cover:
http://stores.lulu.com/jas-1

THE LAW OF LOVE
& Its Fabulous Frequency of Freedom

As I travel this world sharing of our research in the Divine Nutrition fields I continually find people who have the desire to be free. Some desire Freedom from the need to age or die, or Freedom from the need to create disease or even to eat or drink or sleep. Others desire Freedom to control the molecules of our bodies so that the universe supports us in a limitless river of synchronicity and joy and Grace. To witness these freedoms come into being, is often called a miracle.

I wrote in *The Food of Gods* that this type of Freedom is what I have come to call Level 3 in the Divine Nutrition Program, a level where we know how to release enough Love through our systems so that everything comes into a miraculous state of perfect balance and harmony.

The dance of Freedom is a complex one until we understand not just the science of the fields but also how the universe is preprogrammed to recognize and respond to us all. When we understand this, doors of limitless possibility reveal themselves to us and beckon us to enter and explore.

This journal thus becomes my journey through these doors, a journey to what the Buddha calls the Pure Land, to what others call Shamballa. Some people may feel inspired to join me on this journey for as you read through these pages something within you may respond in excitement, for perhaps this is part of your journey too. If that is so then please note that some aspects of this journey should not be attempted until you have understood and applied the principles and meditations in our other manuals*.

Some people may see this level of Freedom as a restrictive lifestyle choice, because there are certain lifestyle actions we need to implement and maintain in order to manifest these Freedoms; yet to others this level of Freedom opens within them hitherto unimagined doors that when accessed bring their own sublime rewards. I call these ones the seekers of miracles.

As this journey unfolded, I found myself downloading a constant stream of data from Universal Mind. Once I accepted the title of "The Law of Love" and the idea of Its freedoms, it was as if a gate opened and my dreams and meditations were suddenly flooded with data – data on destiny, data on how we can find it, embrace it, fulfill it or sideline ourselves, data and tools on how to achieve real freedom, data and visions on shape-shifting Shaman, data on how to create miracles and how to apply these to our world and even data on prophecy and the cross road of choice. I was also guided to summarize all of the freedom tools that we have provided in our various manuals at the Academy over the years and to offer these in Part 2, along with tools that were downloaded during a month long retreat that I attended with the Taoists in Thailand.

And so once again, this book, like all books that I download, has developed a life and a flavor unique unto itself. All I can do upon its release is trust that it will find its place of relevance within our constantly shape-shifting world.

ISBN: 978-1-84799-846-0

Made in the USA
Lexington, KY
03 November 2014